CRUISING GUIDE TO
FLORIDA'S BIG BEND

Apalachicola River Beach

CRUISING GUIDE TO
FLORIDA'S BIG BEND

By Captain Rick Rhodes

PELICAN PUBLISHING COMPANY
GRETNA 2003

Drawings by Pat Champagne
Photographs by author, Cecile Sangiamo, and Kent Wiley

Library of Congress Cataloging-in-Publication Data

Rhodes, Rick.
  Cruising guide to Florida's Big Bend / by Rick Rhodes.
      p. cm.
Includes bibliographical references (p.) and index.
  ISBN 1-58980-072-9
  1. Boats and boating—Florida—Big Bend Region—Guidebooks. 2.
Intracoastal waterways—Florida—Big Bend Region—Guidebooks. 3. Inland
navigation—Florida—Big Bend Region—Guidebooks. 4. Big Bend Region
(Fla.)—Guidebooks. I. Title.
  GV776.F6 B547 2003
  796.1'09759—dc21
                                                              2002015615

Information in this guidebook is based on authoritative data available at the time of printing. Prices and hours of operation of businesses listed are subject to change without notice. Readers area asked to take this into account when conulting this guide. Drawings and NOAA chart extracts are not for use in navigation.

The publisher and the author make no guarantee as to the accuracy or reliablity of the information contained within this guidebook and will not accept any liablity for injuries or damages caused to the reader by following this data.

Printed in the United States of America

Published by Pelican Publishing Company, Inc.
1000 Burmaster Street, Gretna, Louisiana 70053

Contents

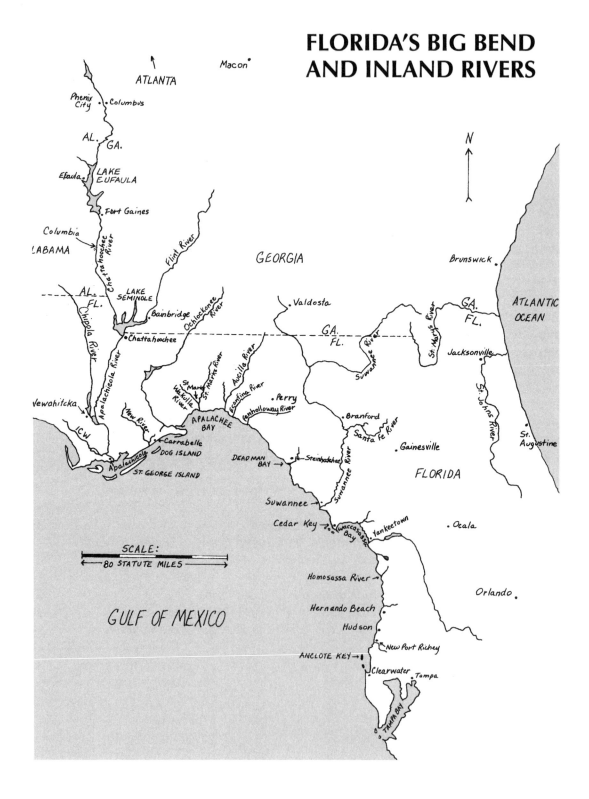

FLORIDA'S BIG BEND AND INLAND RIVERS

Introduction

guide covers the west coast of Florida from Apalachicola to Anclote Key (i.e., near Port Richey) on the Gulf of Mexico. This coast, or parts of it, have been known or are known as the "Nature Coast" (from Wakulla to Pasco counties), the "Forgotten Coast" (centered around Apalachicola and Carrabelle), and the "Hidden Coast" (a section around the middle of the Big Bend) or the "Big Bend." In this book, we'll just call the coastal area—from Apalachicola to Port Richey—the "Big Bend of Florida," even though we'll be covering a slightly expanded area from what is traditionally thought of as the Big Bend. Florida's Big Bend can also be viewed as that uncongested coastal link connecting the urban sprawl associated with the Tampa area to the strip of modern coastal developments stretching westward from Panama City, Florida. This swath of coastline is nearly 300 miles long and is a sizable chunk of Florida's entire coastline. And this region consists of about forty percent of Florida's entire Gulf Coast.

West of Apalachicola, the coast has a protected Intracoastal Waterway (ICW). This Gulf Coast intracoastal waterway extends westward through the panhandle of Florida, Alabama, Mississippi, and Louisiana, all the way to south Padre Island, Texas (or for more than 1,000 miles west and south of Apalachicola). At the other end of the Big Bend, the Florida coast south of Anclote Key also has an ICW extending about 150 miles south to Fort Myers, Florida. At Fort Myers, there is an adjoining waterway connecting the Gulf of Mexico to the Atlantic Ocean

through Lake Okeechobee. On Florida's east coast, at Stuart, this "Okeechobee Waterway" connects to the Atlantic ICW. The Atlantic ICW provides protected waters for about 1,100 miles between Miami and Norfolk, Virginia. South of Miami and Fort Myers, and throughout much of the Florida Keys, there are many long stretches of ICW-like protected waters. But on this part of Florida's coast—the Big Bend coast—there is NO protected waterway. For this section, cruisers will have to plunge into the moody Gulf of Mexico. This coastal section between Carrabelle and Anclote Key is the longest "unprotected" portion of "open water" between Newport, Rhode Island, and Port Isabel, Texas, in a coastal stretch of about 3,000 miles.

While on previous boating research, through the heartland of America (from Chicago, Illinois, to Mobile, Alabama), I heard much apprehension among fellow boaters about this forthcoming unprotected long jaunt into the looming Gulf of Mexico. Down on my luck—hurting after a fifth knee operation and recently unemployed—I aimed to turn things around with another "long, low-budget boat trip." In early October 2001, I trailered my live-aboard 25-foot Nimble Nomad to Apalachicola, Florida. The plan was to explore along the Gulf Coast southward toward Anclote Key and to go into as many of the Gulf Coast channels and rivers that I possibly could. While researching along the Gulf, small-craft advisories (with winds forecasted over 18 knots or 20 miles per hour) were posted every single day that I was out in this big fickle body of water. Nevertheless, no day was ever lost due to the adverse weather. (On a few of those days, the seas grew as big as five feet high on the Gulf.) It was sometimes uncomfortable, but along the way and upon learning more and more about this part of the Gulf of Mexico, my apprehension and fear ebbed. And there was another enchanting element to this research: the nearly two dozen calm and charming rivers on this part of Florida's coast.

Like the Mississippi, the Ohio, and other major inland rivers, the Apalachicola-Chattahoochee-Flint River System is maintained by the U.S. Army Corps of Engineers. Given overhead-clearance considerations, commercial barges and many sea-going vessels can travel over 250 miles from the Gulf of Mexico up the Apalachicola and Chattahoochee rivers to Columbus, Georgia—and within about 100 miles of Atlanta. From Lake Seminole, and near where the states of Florida, Alabama, and Georgia meet, the Flint River takes a navigable route about 30 miles to lovely Bainbridge, Georgia. The Suwannee River, like the Apalachicola-Chattahoochee-Flint River System, extends far inland, away from the Gulf. Less than a mere century ago, steamboats plied over 100 miles up the bucolic Suwannee River. Today, the river is no longer maintained as an official navigable waterway. Nevertheless, many sea-going vessels, given overhead-clearance constraints, can reach neighborly Branford, Florida, about 80 miles from the Gulf of Mexico. These four major Gulf-flowing rivers—the Suwannee, Apalachicola, Chattahoochee, and Flint—have their own devoted chapters in this guide.

Besides these four, there are another 17 rivers that were explored inland from the Gulf of Mexico to varying degrees—the Carrabelle, New, Crooked, Ochlockonee, Sopchoppy, St. Marks, Wakulla, Aucilla, Econfina, Fenholloway, Steinhatchee, Waccasassa, Withlacoochee, Crystal, Homosassa, Weeki Wachee, and Pithlachascotee. We also explored and noted observations on Apalachicola Bay, St. George Sound, Dog Island, Alligator Harbor, Apalachee Bay, Ochlockonee Bay, Spring Creek, Shell Point, Kings Bay, and Gulf Harbors.

Along the Gulf of Mexico, we spent time in, and will present highlights of the towns of, Apalachicola, Carrabelle, Panacea, St. Marks, Keaton Beach, Steinhatchee, Horseshoe Beach, Cedar Key, Yankeetown, Crystal River, Homosassa, Hernando Beach, Hudson, Port Richey, and New Port Richey.

While on the haunting Apalachicola River, we visited Fort Gadsden, Blountstown, and Chattahoochee. We went as far as attractive Bainbridge, Georgia, on the Flint River. Upon circuiting the Chattahoochee River, we visited Eufaula, Alabama, and Florence and Columbus in Georgia. We spent time on Lake Seminole and Lake Eufaula. From our tour on the Suwannee River, we can tell you about Suwannee, Manatee Springs, Fanning Springs, Old Town, Branford, and the Santa Fe River. The map in the introduction depicts some of the important rivers and highlights in this region.

In the past, many cruising boats have looked at the Big Bend of Florida on their charts and then "waited for the weather" (and sometimes waited and waited) to make "that crossing in the Gulf of Mexico." Instead of waiting, and then rushing across the Big Bend, why not slow down, "smell the tupelo blossoms" in this part of Florida, and poke your bow into some great Florida rivers? At the very worse, and depending on your timing, you may have to wait for a short time for that low tide to rise before entering a few of the more shallow rivers. Here is just one of many possible southbound itineraries for requiring either five and a half or three and a half feet of draft at mean low water (MLW) beneath the keel. And generally, there are no overhead obstacles along this itinerary. Actually, in many of these channels, we discovered significantly more water depth, even factoring at lower water than what NOAA or the *U.S. Coast Pilot* has stated. We have noted some of these disparities. If you are heading north from Clearwater, reverse this table and read from the bottom up. And transient rates between Carrabelle and the Suwannee River are often most reasonable (usually anywhere between four dollars for the entire boat to 50 cents per foot, per night).

Book Organization

The first four chapters of this book are catch-the-flavor and how-to chapters designed to give you an appreciation of the area and offer you some helpful and region-specific boating suggestions. The next eight chapters cover the coast along the Gulf of Mexico and up the smaller Gulf Coastal rivers. These eight chapters are organized from points northwest to points southeast. If you are traveling in the reverse direction (from the Tampa Bay area to the northwest), these eight regional chapters are short and easy to follow. The last chapters (chapters 13-17) cover the four major boating rivers flowing into the Gulf of Mexico from the Big Bend area. The Apalachicola-Chattahoochee-Flint River System is covered in chapters 13-16. Lastly, but by far from the least, we end with a trip up the idyllic Suwannee River in chapter 17.

Mileage throughout this guide is stated two ways. Along the coast and in the Gulf of Mexico, we use nautical miles. Once inside the coastal rivers, we switch to river or statute miles. Eight statute miles is equivalent to about seven nautical miles. Once in a river (and sometimes even in a channel), the location of a facility is described using the common river convention of LDB or RDB. The LDB is the LEFT descending bank and RDB is the RIGHT descending bank.

GPS way points are often used along the coast in the Gulf of Mexico. Often, but not always, if you plug in one of our GPS way points, you would have about a 180-degree "safe-semicircle of approach" from the seaward direction before arriving at that way point. Nonetheless, when approaching one of our GPS way points, do not neglect other common-sense cues (shoally areas, obstructions in the water, and other waterborne traffic).

Barbara Edler, one of our book reviewers, suggested highlighting or flagging the more dangerous navigational nuances. I thought this was a great idea, but I didn't want to overdo it or make it too complicated. So, when warning readers of potential overhead-clearance obstacles, or cautioning them that they've arrived at the lowest obstacle in a series of overhead clearances, the word HAZARD was used; so take note. The same goes for instances where readers are being forewarned of potentially dangerous situations beneath or on the surface of the water. And just because we may note the hazard by use of small caps in a certain section does not mean that there couldn't still be dangers lurking nearby. This notation is meant to be a supplement—a red flag—to better assist you in safe navigation.

Cautionary Note

In researching this guide, we expended great effort to ensure accuracy and provide you with

Day	FROM	TO	Naut. Miles	Control Depth in Chn-Rvr	Marina Facilities	Restau-rants	Comments
	(At Start of Day)	(At End of Day)	(Along Coast)	(MLW)	(At end of day)	(At end of day)	(At end of day)
—	Gulf ICW	Apalachicola	—	12 feet	four	eight	Soon leaving the ICW
1	Apalachicola	Carrabelle	28	12 feet	five	four	A real boater's town
2	Carrabelle	St. Marks	36[a]	6 feet	three	four	Loaded with Florida history and local color
3	St. Marks	Steinhatchee	46	5½ feet	three	three	Great fishing, scalloping
4	Steinhatchee	Cedar Key	46[b]	6+ feet	none[c]	dozen+	The night at anchor
5	Cedar Key	Withlacoochee River	28	5½ feet[d]	three	one	A unique mix of Old and New Florida
6a	Withlacoochee	Crystal River[e]	30	5½ feet[fg]	two	three	The clearest spring-fed water around
OR							
6b	Withlacoochee River	Homosassa River[e]	46	3½ feet[gh]	five	six	The last bastion of Old Florida before Tampa
7	Crystal or	Port Richey	39 or 23	5½ + feet[i]	two	four	Try to visit New Port Richey—upriver
8	Port Richey	Clearwater	22	9 feet	many	many	Back on the ICW

Note: On day six, there are overhead powerlines over the Homosassa River and over a possible spur route on the Crystal River.

[a]This does not include about seven to eight miles from Carrabelle to the Gulf of Mexico and another estimated eight miles up the St. Marks River channel and the St. Marks River before reaching the town of St. Marks.

[b]**McGriff Pass Channel**, leading to the town of Suwannee and the Suwannee River, starts about 20 nautical miles north of the Cedar Key Channel. In 2001, the McGriff Pass Channel was only three to four feet deep, MLW. However, by the fall of 2002, work should have begun on dredging this channel to six feet deep, MLW, making Suwannee another enticing stopover for deeper-draft vessels.

[c]There are no real marinas for transients in Cedar Key. There is a nice semiprotected anchorage off Atsena Otie Key and a protected dinghy dock close to dozens of restaurants, all of Cedar Key. Willis Marina (inaccessible to traveling boats) can run fuel out to the city docks for transient boats.

[d] Despite only a five-and-a-half-foot stated depth, we encountered much deeper controlling depths at about ten to thirteen feet, MLW.

[e] We think there are two quite different, and equally good, options at the end of day six. Crystal River is a shorter run from the north (by about 16 miles) and has a slightly deeper channel. Crystal River is New Florida—with all its conveniences and trappings—and a good "auto destination."

On the other hand, the Homosassa River is quite different. More varied and economical haunts can be found along the Homosassa. We got the impression that the Homosassa River was a bit more boater friendly and more accommodating than the "car touristy" Crystal River area. There may also be more bargains for boaters on the Homosassa. Both rivers are well known for manatees. Maybe the best thing to do is visit both rivers.

[f] The NOAA controlling depth is stated at five and a half feet, MLW. We thought there was more water, but the *U.S. Coast Pilot* indicated that there was even less water.

[g] One branch of the Crystal River (leading to one of the marinas) has an overhead power line. The Homosassa River also has an overhead power line. There are anomalies with both of these power lines. The 47-foot line over the Crystal River spur was knocked down and replaced with a "temporarily lower" line in early 2002. The *U.S. Coast Pilot* and NOAA can't agree on the height clearance of that Homosassa River power line—55 feet versus 45 feet. Before negotiating beneath either of these lines, if you're not comfortable, use your VHF radio and ask for some local knowledge.

[h] As it is on the Crystal River, you must navigate a long channel on the Homosassa River—more than 10 miles long—before reaching an area of a half-dozen marinas and a few restaurants. Although reasonably deep through most of its length, there is a shallow spot in the Homosassa Channel, near the entrance to the river, that is about four feet deep, MLW, and about a foot shallower than the Crystal River Channel at MLW.

[i] The controlling depth is stated at five and a half feet. We found it deeper, at six to ten feet, MLW.

---

the most up-to-date information. However, it is not possible to guarantee total accuracy. Nothing ever remains the same. Marinas, restaurants, other shoreside facilities, and the level of accommodation at marinas and restaurants change. On-the-water navigational information—such as shoals, the location of a river channel, aids to navigation, and water depths—is also subject to change.

For navigating in the Gulf of Mexico, NOAA charts are the present standard. For navigating on the Apalachicola-Chattahoochee-Flint River System, the U.S. Army Corps of Engineers' aerial photograph book is the best resource. The Mobile, Alabama, Corps of Engineers District publishes this aerial photograph book. There is no official public information for navigating on the Suwannee River.

This guidebook is intended to be a supplement to official U.S. government publications. Failure to follow the current navigation realities, even when it differs from the situation presented in this guide, could result in an accident. We have worked hard to help minimize your risks and offer you options, but there are many potential hazards in any boating situation. Safe boating is ultimately in the hands of the captain and crew. The author disclaims liability for loss or damage to persons or property that may occur as a result of interpreting information in this guidebook.

CRUISING GUIDE TO
FLORIDA'S BIG BEND

Our boat at anchor on the Apalachicola River

CHAPTER 1

History

Native Americans have been living in Alabama, Georgia, and Florida for at least 12,000 years. Other Native Americans from as far away as present-day Michigan, Illinois, and Indiana began visiting the Big Bend about 6,000 years ago during the cold winter months—the first Florida tourists. Many centuries before the Spanish came, the Apalachee Indians were dominant around the Big Bend. The Apalachee may have had a population of 100,000 when the Spanish arrived. Apalachee braves were warlike and skilled at guerrilla fighting. Primarily due to the explorers' diseases, the Apalachee population (as well as other Native American populations) was decimated to one quarter of its size in only 80 years. And 100 years later, by the early 1700s, the Apalachee were all but extinct. Today we have one large untamed bay—Apalachee Bay, right in the heart of the Big Bend, between Alligator Harbor and the Fenholloway River—to remind us of the rich Apalachees' past.

At the time of the arrival of the Spanish, other parts of Florida were inhabited by the Calusa and Timucan Indians. The Timucans were primarily in the northern and eastern parts of the state. The Calusa Indians lived along Florida's Gulf Coast, south of the Apalachee region, possibly from about the Homosassa River all the way down to and in the Florida Keys. In Charlotte Harbor, it was a Calusa Indian arrow that mortally wounded Ponce de León. The Ochese Creek Indians (the named was later shortened to "Creek") lived peaceably in many areas of present-day Georgia and Alabama during and before the 1500s. The Creeks were primarily farmers and had a stronger bond with the land. During the Trail of Tears roundup, when the Creeks were forcibly removed in 1836, one very classy Creek chief near Eufaula, Alabama, sincerely stated, "I see the Indian fires will soon be cold as I leave the graves of my fathers," and he continued to bid "the great people of Alabama" a touching good-bye as he and his people were shipped west.

There is sound speculation that, between 1502 and 1507, no less than four Europeans visited Florida before Ponce de León. But in 1513, it was Ponce de León who was officially recognized as the "discoverer" of Florida. In any event, Florida was visited by Europeans more than a hundred years before the English Pilgrims ever landed at Plymouth Rock. De León arrived somewhere between Cape Canaveral and St. Augustine during Easter week and named this "new" land La Florida for the feast of flowers. He was looking for gold, not that romantic fountain of youth.

De León first arrived in the New World even earlier than 1513. He was aboard the second Christopher Columbus expedition in 1493 when Puerto Rico was "discovered." Later, on a subsequent voyage to Florida's west coast in 1521, more than half of de León's troops were killed or wounded in an encounter with the fierce Calusa Indians in Charlotte Harbor. In this battle, de León was mortally wounded by an arrow that severed his femoral artery. In the early 1500s, the first contacts between the Spaniards and the Native Americans were generally friendly on the part of the natives. But subsequent contacts were much more hostile. On good reports, it has been stated that, during those first contacts, the "civilized" Spaniards conducted themselves in such ways as to offend native cultures (demanding food and women and carrying off many Indians to be "specimens" or slaves). Furthermore, some Caribbean slaves who had escaped to Florida years earlier had forewarned the Calusas, Timucans, and possibly even the Apalachee of the Spanish treachery.

Within seven years after de León first landed, a handful of Spaniards sailed into the Gulf of Mexico, but they seldom disembarked far from their vessels. The most noteworthy may have been Alvarez de Pineda. In 1519, Pineda was tasked to find a route to the Pacific Ocean and

became the first European to circumnavigate the Gulf of Mexico. He was also the first to correctly determine that Florida was a peninsula. (Previously, Florida was thought to be a large island—even by "discoverer" Ponce de León.) During his nine-month voyage, Pineda discovered the mouth of the Mississippi River, the Yucatán Peninsula, and he also discovered that there was NO water route to the Pacific Ocean. Most of these early Florida expeditions were launched from Spanish Cuba.

In 1528 the one-eyed and red-bearded Pánfilo de Narváez landed near Tampa. The first overland expedition searching for gold in the direction of New Spain (present-day Mexico) had begun. By the time Narváez's 300 men reached present-day St. Marks, illnesses and nearly impassable swamps thwarted them.

Salt marshes near the St. Marks River

Narváez and his men sustained themselves by eating their horses. In St. Marks, the Spaniards built five rafts, most likely the first ships built by Europeans in the New World. Narváez's men had changed their plans and hoped to travel the rest of the way to New Spain by sea and aboard their newly constructed vessels. But this expedition ended in disaster. All but two men were either swept out into the Gulf of Mexico and drowned or taken captive and killed by Native Americans along the shore.

Conquistador Hernando De Soto explored Florida's Gulf Coast in 1539. But prior to this trip, De Soto spent four years with deceitful and extremely murderous Francisco Pizarro, looting the Inca civilization in what is now Ecuador and Peru. With his ill-gotten fame and wealth, stolen from the Incas, De Soto was able to position himself to command another expedition to the New World. The Spanish crown chartered De Soto to conquer and govern La Florida. De Soto landed in Tampa Bay with an army of about 600 and marched north. It took his men four months to reach the Aucilla River, and they were constantly harried by the fierce Apalachee warriors. De Soto built a winter encampment near present-day downtown Tallahassee and celebrated the first Christmas Mass in this new land.

De Soto also was an exceptionally cruel conquistador. While in Tallahassee, he supposedly cut off the noses of 50 Indians before executing the newly disfigured. He would typically burn Indians alive at the stake, trying to extract information. After five months in Tallahassee, De Soto and his force departed the Apalachee territory and headed northwest to present-day Bainbridge, Georgia. By 1540, his army was soon commencing northeast, searching for gold in the present-day Carolinas. After the Carolinas, the inland expedition turned west and crossed the Mississippi River. Instead of heading down the Mississippi River, the army tried heading overland southwest, toward New Spain. This force reached well into present-day Texas but was beginning to starve because there were very few native crops to sustain them along this arid route. In 1542, they retreated back to the Mississippi River where De Soto died of a fever. The remainder of the expedition built boats and rowed down the mighty Mississippi. In 1543, and more than four years after they arrived in Tampa Bay, only 311 survivors of the De Soto expedition (about one-half of the original force) reached safe haven on the Gulf of Mexico near present-day Tampico, Mexico. In early Florida, most, if not all, of the Spanish conquistadors met the same fate before Florida was wrested from the Native Americans.

Finally in 1565, on Florida's east coast, Pedro Menéndez de Avilés established a permanent European settlement at St. Augustine. By 1639, waterborne commercial traffic aboard a Spanish frigate connected St. Augustine to the Port of Apalachee (later to be known as St. Marks). In 1680, the first fort on the Gulf of Mexico was constructed at St. Marks. A series of Franciscan missions, about 20 miles apart, also helped Spain maintain loose-knit control along the Gulf Coast. Spain ruled Florida as two provinces, with the seat of government for East Florida in St. Augustine and the seat of government for West Florida in Pensacola. The boundary between these two provinces was the Apalachicola River. St. Marks was the only major Spanish fortification between these two seats. The Spanish influence lasted for about two centuries. But from the west and the Louisiana Territory, the French also had their fingers on the Gulf Coast, with settlements in Mobile, Biloxi, and later Pensacola,

St. Marks Lighthouse, the sentinel of Apalachee Bay

which they took from the Spanish in 1719. This coastal area changed hands between the French and the Spanish several times. And there were convoluted Indian alliances on all sides.

In the meantime, the British were also gradually forcing the Creek Indians, who lived in Georgia and Alabama, to move farther and farther south. The Seminole Indians were an offshoot—and a rebellious, nomadic branch—of the more principled Creek. The word *seminole* means "runaway or broken off." The Seminoles were relative newcomers to Florida but they too were being gradually forced to move farther south. By the 1700s, and about two centuries after the Apalachee Indians, the Seminoles were inhabiting many areas of Florida's Big Bend. Runaway African slaves also entered and blended into Seminole culture. Three wars took place between the Seminole people and the United States.

By the mid-1700s, Great Britain was gradually wresting control of Florida from Spain and France. The British often had Native American help against the Spanish, because of the previous record of Spanish depredation against the Indians. By 1763, when Spain was defeated in the Seven Years' War, Britain gained control of East and West Florida. But the British occupation was short-lived and all but gone by 1769. In 1783, after the American Revolution and the Treaty of Paris, Florida was handed back to Spain. But soon, the Creek and Seminole Indians were harassing the Spanish in Florida, with encouragement from the leftover British. For about a month in 1800, the Indians actually took the fort at St. Marks from the Spanish.

After the War of 1812, there was mayhem and disarray in south Georgia and north Florida. Meanwhile white American settlers were pouring into Native American lands. The weakened Spanish were mired in one revolution after another in Central and South America. Closer to home, Spanish colonists, runaway slaves, and more Seminole Indians were finding their way to this no-man's land of north Florida. New alliances were being formed between the Spanish and the Seminoles. The Seminoles needed guns, blankets, and other manufactured goods, while the Spanish required a military force.

Tasked to champion the white American newcomers streaming into north Florida, U.S. general Andrew Jackson waged war against the Indians. In 1817, the first Seminole war was underway. Jackson, though of American heritage, was much like earlier Spanish conquistadors in his ruthless defeat of the Indians. Jackson didn't mind stepping all over the British and Spanish, too. Along with the needless killings of many Indians, Jackson summarily executed two British citizens suspected of trading goods with the Indians. This incident almost started a third war with Britain.

In 1819, Spain ceded Florida to the United States. About two years later, Florida became a U.S. territory, and the heavy-handed Andrew Jackson became the first territorial governor. Later, in 1830, with President Jackson's tyrannical and strong pressure, the shameful Trail of Tears removal plan was legislated. Many of the Native Americans who were subject to this ignominious blotch on our history had adopted some very civilized mores (especially the Cherokee). The Native Americans did have a handful of supporters in Washington—congressman and former president John Quincy Adams, Daniel Webster, Henry Clay, Sam Houston, and Davy Crockett. But the supporters lost, and the relocation proponents, spearheaded by Pres. Andrew Jackson—the man whose countenance now graces our twenty dollar bill—won the decade of

Old Cotton Warehouse in Apalachicola

the 1830s. All the Native Americans east of the Mississippi River were to be forcibly shipped west to the Oklahoma Territory. A horrific number of Native Americans died during this march. There are even allegations that the Native Americans were provided with small-pox-tainted blankets during their commanded relocation.

One Seminole chief, Osceola, was enraged. Prior to the 1830s many Seminoles had been living in "the green swamp" east of Florida's Withlacoochee River. The second Seminole war was soon underway. For a time, 3,000 to 5,000 Seminole warriors, using guerrilla tactics, stood off many more thousands of American troops and several unsuccessful generals.

Gens. Winfield Scott, Edmund Gaines, Duncan Clinch, Richard Call, and Thomas Jesup each drove the war against Osceola and the Seminoles. In 1837, the deceptive Jesup captured Osceola under a truce flag and threw the brave warrior into prison. Osceola soon died there and was posthumously beheaded. But the spirit of the Seminoles was not so easily subdued, and other generals followed Jesup, including another president-to-be, Zachary Taylor. More Seminole chiefs were hood-winked and captured under truce flags. Eventually much, but not all, of the Seminole contingent was shipped west to Oklahoma. In 1842, a nominal end to hostilities arrived, but the Seminoles never signed a peace treaty with the Americans, and a few Seminoles still remained in Florida.

Thirteen years later, in 1855, the third Seminole war broke out. Once again, newcomer white settlers were pressuring the remaining Seminoles off "their" land. Under the leadership of Chief Billy Bowlegs, the Seminoles fought back. Eventually Bowlegs had to retreat deep into the Florida Everglades. He and his Seminoles never surrendered, although their numbers in Florida were as small as 200 by 1858. Thankfully, a few Seminoles are still in Florida to this day. Although the Seminoles arrived in Florida relatively late (about two centuries after the Spanish conquistadors), their heritage remains indelible.

Today's Seminoles are much associated with Florida. Interestingly, many of those strange-sounding names in or near the Big Bend region are of Seminole origin (e.g., Chattahoochee, Econfina, Fenholloway, Tallahassee, Chassahowitzka, Weeki Wachee, and others). Most place names ending in *sassa* and *hatchee* are of Seminole origin.

Forewarning: This book contains more unpronounceable names and tongue twisters than you can shake a stick at (e.g., Pithlachascotee, Wewahitchka, Waccasassa, Withlacoochee, Homosassa, Hatcheehubee, Ochlockonee, Eufaula, Chewalla, and many others). We recommend—and it will read much faster—you try not to read this book aloud.

Shrimp fleet on the Withlacoochee River

CHAPTER 2

Wildlife, Flora, Recreation, and Industry

This region of northern Florida and southern Georgia and Alabama abounds with wildlife. Manatees, alligators, black bears, river otters, wild hogs, bald eagles, wild turkeys, egrets, and several types of herons can be encountered, with a varying degree of frequency, in just about all of the coastal regions. Be watchful when you decide to take a dip (especially with small children). There are alligators inhabiting all of these waters, even as far north as Columbus, Georgia, on the Chattahoochee River. Black bears exist everywhere on Florida's Big Bend, but they are most common along the coast from Apalachicola to St. Marks and again around the Chassahowitzka Bay area. We saw wild hogs not far from urban Crystal River. Bald eagles are occasionally spotted flying over the coastal rivers.

The endangered Gulf of Mexico sturgeon can be found in many of the rivers and bays in the Big Bend. The range of the sturgeon's habitat is from Louisiana to Tampa Bay. In Florida's Big Bend, sightings of this great fish are most common on the Suwannee and Apalachicola Rivers. The Apalachicola River is Florida's largest river in terms of volume, and the river basin supports the greatest diversity of amphibians and reptiles found anywhere in the entire United States.

Of course, commercial fishing, oystering, shrimping, and crabbing are common everywhere on the Big Bend—from Apalachicola to Port Richey. Apalachicola Bay, one of the nation's most productive estuaries, produces 90 percent of Florida's, and 10 percent of the nation's, oyster harvest. You'll see large shrimp fleets parked in Apalachicola, Hernando Beach, and Carrabelle. Smaller shrimp fleets will be seen in every single port on Florida's Big Bend, including tiny Horseshoe Beach and the urban settings of Hudson and Port Richey. Many books have been written about sportfishing in this area. It very well may be the best in Florida. But did you know that spearfishing and diving for scallops are also popular in this area during the summertime? Sponging and turtling were once popular also.

Manatees are just about everywhere in the Big Bend, especially in the Crystal, Homosassa, and Wakulla Rivers. Many old timers—and folks who know and love the Gulf Coast of Florida—from St. Marks to Fort Myers have told me that there are now more manatees than ever before. I recently read an article in a prominent Florida newspaper stating something like, "Manatee deaths are on the rise . . . and there should be even more done to protect them."

Frankly, I am often bemused at the bias of and lack of scientific data in this and other similar newspaper articles on manatees. If the population is growing, mother nature will see to it that there will be more (natural) deaths (along with the many more births, too). Behind any "Save the Manatee" program, there ought to be good data collection and good science instead of an emotional environmental movement. And besides, an 800- to 3,000-pound herbivore needs to eat up to 100 pounds of beneficial sea grasses every single day. Sea grasses are actually "flowering

Shrimper on the Gulf of Mexico

plants" and are very vital to the overall health of the aquatic ecosystem.

I guess, once again, I'm politically incorrect for not wrapping myself in a "Save the Manatee" banner. I have nothing against manatees, but I do have some concerns about people who put this rallying cry ahead of good statistics and good science. There is little doubt that a large "Save the Manatee" industry has been created and I suspect that many have gotten quite rich with this latest chic topic. In Crystal River alone, manatees have been parlayed into a multimillion-dollar industry. Granted, many large integrated operations are good in that they make manatees more accessible to more tourists, but there are likely some downsides (e.g., the pushing out of smaller operations, increased tourist usage of once quasi-remote areas, etc.). I have encountered

folks who have been hurt by this overindulgence in "Save the Manatees." When an entire long river channel was declared a No Wake Zone, boaters went elsewhere, and a small boating-facility owner took a financial bath.

Manatees are often scarred, injured, and sometimes fatally wounded by boat propellers. Any responsible boat captain passing through a known manatee area should definitely slow down to minimize the inadvertent likelihood of injuring one of these docile creatures. But let's support good monitoring, good statistics, and good science. And let those variables drive an objective and reasonable "Save the Manatee" policy.

Besides the newly developed manatee industry, other industries have come and gone along the Big Bend. Harvesting live oak trees was once a major industry and a significant

Railroad and old ironworks in Columbus, Georgia

source of lumber in the northern part of this region. Florida live oaks were shipped to New England for ship building. Unfortunately, most of the commercial live oak was irresponsibly harvested before Florida became a state in 1845.

Cedar trees were once plentiful, especially around Cedar Key. The cedars were harvested for pencil slats. By the early 1900s, this natural resource was also irresponsibly depleted.

Today slash and longleaf pine forests are very common in the upper parts of the Big Bend. By and large, these forests and plantations are now managed sustainedly with an eye on the future.

Large, efficient pulp and paper mills are important to the economy of northern Florida, as well as to the entire southeastern United States. If you travel up the Chattahoochee River, you'll see two paper mills.

Tupelo honey is a much smaller and also a sustainable industry. This just may be the healthiest honey known to man. Tupelo honey is collected in a small area along the banks of the Apalachicola and Chipola Rivers.

There is more salt-marsh acreage between Apalachicola and Cedar Key than there is in any other coastal section of Florida. Salt marshes, or tidal marshes, occur between the boundaries of high and low tides and only in coastal sections where the pounding wave

Paperboard mill on the Chattahoochee River

action is minimal. Salt-tolerant tidal-marsh plants—such as grasses, rushes, and sedges— provide a safe haven to many small and immature species of fish, crabs, and shellfish. Larger predator fish cannot physically reach the small or juvenile fish when they're hidden in the salt marshes. And there is plenty of food in the marshes for the smaller fish to eat. Scientists estimate that about 90 percent of all landings by commercial and sportfisherman are species that grew up in the salt marshes. Salt marshes also make a great environmental buffer strip. The marshes can trap and absorb many pollutants and sediments flowing down the tidal creeks. Though these salt marshes appear colorless and lifeless, they are a dynamic ecosystem. There is little doubt that the abundance of healthy salt marshes is one major reason why the near off-shore fishing in the Gulf of Mexico remains so good in this part of Florida.

West of Apalachicola, there are several large bays providing a slightly different coastal ecosystem. And south of Cedar Key, the salt-marsh environment thins in favor of mangroves. The mangrove thickets are another vital element of the shoreline ecosystem. Like salt marshes, mangroves provide protected nurseries for juvenile fish, crustaceans, and shellfish. Mangrove branches are often the nesting zones for many coastal birds. Unlike salt marshes, mangroves cannot tolerate freezing weather, and that is why mangroves are only found south of Cedar Key. Of the three species of mangrove found in Florida (red, white, and black), the red mangrove is the most common. Red mangrove is distinguishable by its many reddish prop roots buttressing the plant. Mangroves have the unique ability to obtain the fresh water needed for photosynthesis from the salt water. They either secrete the salt through their leaves or block the absorption of salt at their roots.

There are seven astonishing national wildlife refuges in our area of Big Bend research—St. Vincent, St. Marks, Lower Suwannee, Cedar Key, Crystal River, Chassahowitzka, and Eufaula in Alabama and Georgia, off the Chattahoochee River. The National Wildlife Refuge System is an extensive network of lands and waters that are managed for specific or general wildlife habitats. Refuges are administered by the U.S. Fish and Wildlife Service.

The St. Vincent National Wildlife Refuge sits on an island in the western end of Apalachicola Bay. The island is about nine miles long and four miles wide at its widest point and has a few freshwater lakes. Bald eagles, loggerhead turtles, gopher tortoises, red wolves, and coyotes live on this island. Peregrine falcons and wood storks are migrational visitors. The St. Vincent Wildlife Refuge has a most informative visitor center in Apalachicola, near the commercial-shrimp dock basin.

The St. Marks National Wildlife Refuge sits on the Gulf Coast between the Sopchoppy and Aucilla Rivers. This refuge was established in 1931 and is one of the oldest in the National Wildlife Refuge System. The St. Marks refuge serves as wintering grounds for many migratory birds. Throughout the course of a year, over 270 species of birds inhabit the refuge. Seven rivers, including the St. Marks, Wakulla, and Aucilla, are within the boundaries of this refuge. In late October and early November, fascinating monarch butterflies arrive at the St. Marks refuge. St. Marks is their last landfall before a long migratory flight across the Gulf to Mexico. Deer, armadillo, and wild boars can be found in St. Marks. There is also a great variety of fish found in its waters. Scalloping in the shallow waters is a pleasant summertime pastime in this area. The relatively dry environs of the refuge favor growth of yucca and prickly pear cactus. But you can also find Sabal palms, wax myrtle, willow, and red cedar growing in this region.

The Lower Suwannee National Wildlife Refuge, with twenty-six miles of Gulf of Mexico frontage, was established in 1979. Most of this refuge stretches along the coast on both sides of the Suwannee River. Another arm of the refuge reaches up the Suwannee River for 23 miles. This may be one of the largest undeveloped river-delta systems in the United States. Beyond the coastal tidal marshes, the large cypress, live oak, and pine trees dominate. Some of the wildlife includes alligator, black bear, otter, and over 250 species of birds, including the colorful wood duck.

Cedar Keys National Wildlife Refuge was established by Pres. Herbert Hoover in 1929 by naming three of the islands as breeding grounds for birds. This area might harbor the largest wading-bird rookeries in the nation. Thirteen islands comprise the Cedar Key Wildlife Refuge.

Crystal River National Wildlife Refuge consists of barely 40 acres on nine small islands in Kings Bay. Numerous springs in Kings Bay produce daily 600 million gallons of sweet, fresh water. The relatively warm 72 degree year-around water temperature attracts manatees, especially in the colder water months (between November and March). It is estimated that about 15 to 20 percent of all Florida manatees visit Crystal River. This wildlife refuge, especially developed to protect manatees and the Florida panther, is only accessible by boat.

Chassahowitzka National Wildlife Refuge was established in 1941 to benefit migrating wintering waterfowl, especially coots and ducks. The refuge is home to about 250 species of birds. This 30,000-acre refuge is only accessible by shallow-draft boat. Chassahowitzka was in the Florida news in the fall of 2001. An ultralight aircraft had shepherded six endangered whooping cranes from Wisconsin to Chassahowitzka National Wildlife Refuge in the hope of imprinting a successful annual migration pattern on these rare birds. Whooping cranes learn how to migrate from other whooping cranes. But since there are only about 400 cranes in North America, and no migratory cranes in the East, an ultralight had to be used to "teach" these birds this 48-day wintering journey to Chassahowitzka. If successful (e.g., if these cranes can learn on their own to make this an annual migratory trip), another ultralight-led squadron, with a new flock of migrating cranes, might take place to Chassahowitzka each fall and for many years to come. However, within weeks after their arrival at Chassahowitzka, one of the cranes fell victim to natural predation. The crane was found dead and partially eaten by

Petroleum terminals in St. Marks

the hungry local bobcat. A second crane also fell victim to the bobcat before a now-smaller flock successfully migrated back to Wisconsin the following April.

The Eufaula National Wildlife Refuge was established in 1964 to provide a habitat for migratory birds and other wintering waterfowl. Thousands of these winter-migrating birds come down the Atlantic coast and Mississippi River flyways. This refuge is in the upper reaches of Lake Eufaula on the Chattahoochee River.

The Apalachicola National Forest covers almost 900 square miles and is the largest national forest in Florida. The Apalachicola, New, Ochlockonee, and Sopchoppy Rivers flow through this forest. After the turpentine and logging industries claimed much of the present forest, and the Apalachicola Northern Railroad ceased operations, most folks had already left the area. This was all during the Great Depression, and the federal government was able to acquire most of this land.

On or near Florida's Big Bend, there are three state historic sites. Fort San Marcos de Apalachee, (850) 922-6007, and the Natural Bridge Battlefield, (850) 922-6007, are near St. Marks. Yulee Sugar Mill Ruins, (352) 795-3817, is in Homosassa.

Four Florida state parks are also on or near the coast: St. George Island, (850) 927-2111, Ochlockonee River, (850) 962-2771, Wakulla Springs, (850) 224-5950, and Econfina River, (850) 922-6007. Two other Florida state parks are on the inland rivers: Manatee Springs State Park, (352) 493-6072, is on the Suwannee River, and Torreya State Park, (850) 643-2674, is off the Apalachicola River.

There are also two state museums and an archaeological site on this coast. The John Gorrie State Museum, (850) 653-9347, is in Apalachicola, and there is another state museum in Cedar Key, (352) 543-5350. There is a state archaeological site in Crystal River, (352) 795-3817. A great little aquarium—the Gulf Specimen Marine Lab Aquarium, (850) 984-5297—is situated in Panacea. There is also a most informative historical museum in Cedar Key.

This just may be the only part of Florida where the sometimes brutally invasive hand of modern man has been kept in check—sometimes by mother nature herself. In all of our Big Bend area, with the possible exception of chapter 12 (the southernmost chapter in this guide), the pace of life on the Gulf and along the rivers is more tranquil than many other, and even nearby, on-the-coast localities. We think this will make your trip through this unique area unforgettable. Many people call this area "Old Florida." Other folks prefer to call this region "Real Florida." Maybe they are both correct. During our research, we've met more than a few hardworking locals in boatyards relaying that there is nowhere else in the entire world that they'd rather be than right here, working, hunting, fishing, and living on Florida's Big Bend!

Dredge working the Horseshoe Beach Channel

CHAPTER 3

Navigating along the Gulf of Mexico

Water Depths

While boating in the Gulf of Mexico, or any-where else, it is always a most prudent idea to be cognizant of where the "deeper" water is—that is, in which direction you may need to quickly turn if suddenly shallow-water depths surprise you. Generally (but not always) this direction is "out" to sea. In between St. Marks and about Horseshoe Beach, turning more seaward is usually the correct choice. But in other areas of the Big Bend, it's not so simple. Many areas have shallow reefs farther out, and you wouldn't want to inadvertently turn into one. If you carefully study the NOAA charts BEFORE you arrive at your position, you should be able to avoid reefs and shal-lows. Should you encounter a shallow sur-prise in these waters, by knowing your general position, you should be able to make an informed decision—and turn in the correct direction—in order to get out of any potential shallow danger.

There is an old-time Gulf adage concerning water depths: The Gulf deepens by one foot for each mile out from shore. This is probably a good average. But more often than not, you will not be floating over an average spot. It very well could be deeper than three feet, three miles out. And, on the other hand, it could be shallower than five feet, five miles out. An average is just that, an average—not a bad index but a long way from being the gospel in any given spot on the water. The NOAA charts, albeit far from perfect, are a better tool than this average.

There are reefs in the Big Bend, but these are not the coral reefs like those found farther south in the Florida Keys. Many of the reefs in this area are oyster bars. Like a living coral reef, living oysters grow atop the shells of their ancestors and eventually form hard, underwa-ter obstructions that can become impassable to boaters. There are also a few solid rock reefs in this area. A boat traveling at a signifi-cant speed encountering a submerged rock will likely be severely damaged.

When sailing in the ocean, I'm far from an advocate of sailing within sight of land. Many times it's much safer to be farther out than nearer to the land. Nevertheless, it is possible to safely make this Big Bend passage and never lose sight of the shore. Some boaters may find this reassuring.

Until recently, there was about a 200 nau-tical mile "near-shore passage" along the Big Bend marked by about 18 navigation aids. This route had sometimes been referred to as the "Big Bend Buoyage System." These navi-gation aids were usually anywhere from four to sixteen miles apart and were numbered from G1 off Anclote Key to R26 or R28 off either Carrabelle or Apalachicola. These old aid positions are still depicted on our most recent NOAA charts. However, some, if not all, of these aids have been extracted and have not been replaced. Local boating interest groups in the entire Big Bend region are very unhappy about this latest government move. No one could provide me with a rationale for the government's latest action. In any event, without these "near-shore" navigation buoys, a near-coastal long-distance Gulf passage has just become more difficult. Instead of having three options—(1) a rhumb line in the Gulf of Mexico from St. George Island to Clearwater, (2) following this well-buoyed and near-coastal 200-mile route, or (3) gunk-holing along the Big Bend's coast—shortly, we will only have two good options (options 1 or 3).

Anchoring in the Gulf

Anchoring in the Gulf of Mexico might be miserable, but it can be done with enough heavy ground tackle in normal sea conditions. And sometimes, anchoring out for the night may be the more prudent course of action. Leaving the Waccasassa River late one afternoon, I wasn't quite able to make it to the Withlacoochee Channel and the calm Withlacoochee River before nightfall. Instead of trying to pick my way through that rock-strewn Withlacoochee Channel after dark, I decided to anchor in seven feet of water depth with a miserable three-plus foot chop all night long, even though I could clearly see the many lighted buoys of the Withlacoochee Channel less than two miles away. That night, unable to sleep on an uncomfortably bouncing boat, I often second-guessed my decision to stop short. However, the following morning, when I saw in daylight just how rock-strewn that Withlacoochee Channel was, I immediately knew that I had made the proper decision.

Any anchoring system is only as good as its weakest link (e.g., the anchor's ability to hold, the strength of the anchor rode, the shackle connections in that rode, the boat's cleat, or the cleat's backing plate). Cleat-backing plates on a few stock-production vessels are some-times substandard (e.g., nothing more than small metal flat washers). The last eight feet or more of your anchor rode should be chain. This chain will weigh down the stock of your anchor, thereby reducing the pull from being a three-dimensional space to a two-dimensional plane. The chain also provides an abrasion-resistant section on the bottom. Who knows what may be below—oyster shells, rocks, or something else sharp. More length of anchor rode (i.e., nylon line plus chain) is better. Conventional wisdom usually recommends about a 7:1 (i.e., horizontal distance to vertical depth) anchor scope. In the Gulf waters, we'd recommend no less than a 10:1 scope. If you get stuck in the Gulf, like I did that one night, you usually don't have to worry about swinging into other boats on even 20:1 scope. The only drawback is retrieving all of that anchor line in the morning. If the water is warm enough and the daylight permits, I like to put on a dive mask and swim down to my anchor and inspect "the holding."

Many sections of the Big Bend reminded me of the Florida Bay side of the Florida Keys. There are many shallow areas, floating patches of sea grass, low-lying islands in the distance, and in some places, the water is gin clear—clear all of the way to the bottom.

Tides

You might already know that the range between high and low tides is slightly greater during the times of a new and a full moon. This makes sense, because when the moon is full or new, three bodies—the sun, earth, and moon—are pretty well in a celestial line. With the moon and the sun being on this same "line" as the earth, the gravitational

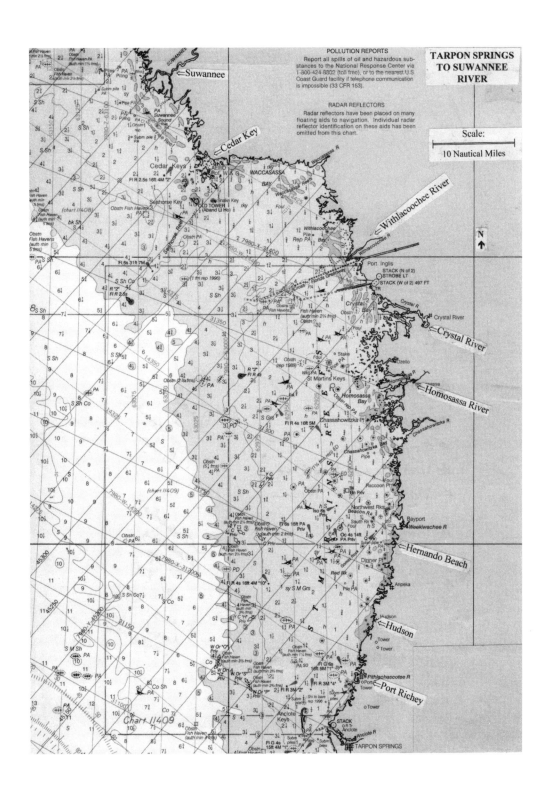

**TARPON SPRINGS
TO SUWANNEE
RIVER**

Scale:

10 Nautical Miles

←Suwannee

←Cedar Key

←Withlacoochee River

N

Crystal River

←Homosassa River

←Hernando Beach

←Hudson

←Port Richey

Chart 11409

TARPON SPRINGS

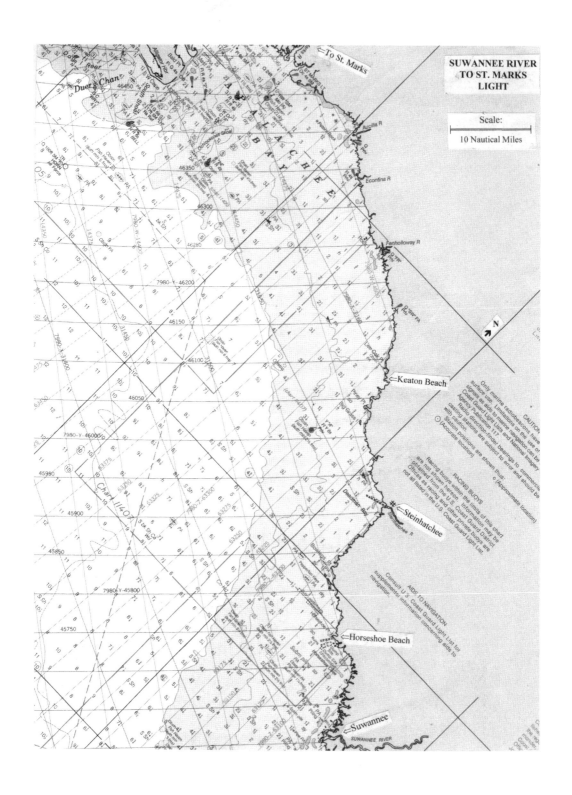

SUWANNEE RIVER TO ST. MARKS LIGHT

Scale:

10 Nautical Miles

To St. Marks

Duer Chan

Aucilla R

Econfina R

Fenholloway R

N

Keaton Beach

Steinhatchee

Horseshoe Beach

Suwannee

SUWANNEE RIVER

Chart 11407

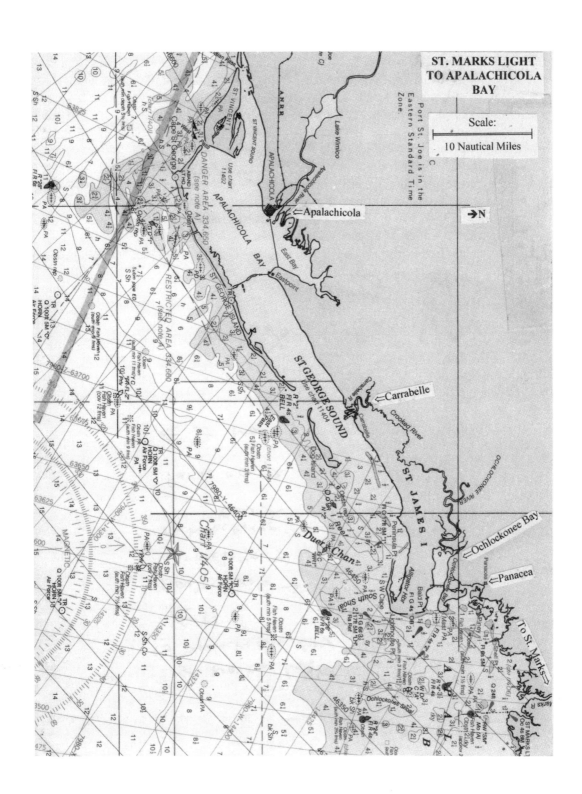

ST. MARKS LIGHT TO APALACHICOLA BAY

Scale:

10 Nautical Miles

Port St. Joe is in the Eastern Standard Time Zone.

→N

Apalachicola

Carrabelle

Ochlockonee Bay

Panacea

To St. Marks→

effects of these two celestial bodies upon our globe are additive—thus the greater tide ranges.

The level of the high-tide "peak" and low-tide "low" are seldom the same from one high tide to the next, or from one low tide to the next. In a month of tidal observations, we noted that the range in the "highest" predicted high tide was about one and one-quarter feet greater than the "lowest" predicted high tide. Generally, the high tides are about one and a quarter feet higher during the new-moon and full-moon phases than the are on the quarter-moon phases. But more interestingly, we noted that the range in the "lowest" low tide was over two feet lower than the "highest" low tide during a typical month. Even more consequential, the difference between one low tide and the NEXT semidiurnal low tide was sometimes as great as one and a half feet, with very common differences of over one foot between one low tide and the very next low tide. And this phenomenon twice got me in trouble. I had made it "in" a river on one dead low tide, so I figured that I'd surely have no problems getting out on the next low tide—about 13 hours later. This proved not to be the case. Twice I had to wait about two hours after that second (and

much lower) low tide. We weren't able to pin this difference-in-subsequent-low-tide-level phenomena to any particular phase of the moon, even after studying several months of observations. It is probably a function of where the moon is located in the sky and interacting with the normal tidal water on the earth's surface. On the other hand, the difference between one high tide and the next semidiurnal high tide was never much more than two-thirds of a foot, with most subsequent high-tide fluctuations being slight and in between one-tenth and one-fifth of a foot.

Even though there is no such thing as a "typical tidal week," the following is a "fabricated graph" in which I attempt to illustrate some of the tidal phenomenon found on the Big Bend. The 0 on the vertical, or *y*, axis is the mean low-water level. The *x* axis is the HOUR of the week (e.g., 24 hours x 7 days = 168 hours). And for certain places on the Big Bend, this fabricated tidal week is even less apropos. Nevertheless, we hope it helps.

Capt. Bill Roberts of Cedar Key also edified me on another related nuance. During the two quarter-moon phases, the shift from high to low tide, or vice versa, takes longer. Looking at more than a month's worth of observations, we noted that it took about 11½

An Example of Hypothetical Tides for One Week on the Big Bend

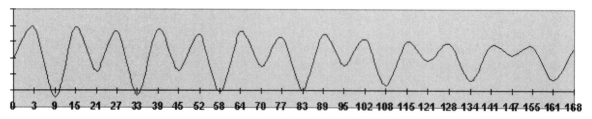

HOUR of the Week

to 12½ hours to go from one high tide to the next (or from one low tide to the next) near the full- and new-moon phases. But near the two quarter-moon phases, the time from one high tide to the next high tide increased to about 14 to 16 hours. Near the quarter-moon phases, the time difference between succeeding low tides was slightly less dramatic and usually never greater than 14 hours.

Generally, the tides in the Big Bend are semidiurnal (i.e., two low tides and two highs within about a 25½±-hour tidal period) but not always. After studying several months of tidal observations, we noticed that there were some days when there was only one low tide and one high tide during the typical tidal day (the 25½+-hour tide cycle day). These unusual single-tide days may not occur every month. They seem to occur in certain months and for a duration of one to four consecutive days. We didn't observe a strong enough pattern to correlate these single-tide days to any particular lunar phase. But we did observe that these one-tide days occurred with more frequency farther south in our region. These peculiar single-tide days are more apt to be observed near Anclote Key and much less frequently observed near St. Marks. After completing our boat research, we interestingly discovered that in the Sarasota area (not far south of the

Floating nun buoy near St. Marks Lighthouse

Big Bend), and also in the Pensacola area (not far west of the Big Bend), there was usually only one high tide and one low tide during each of the 25½+-hour tidal cycle day.

Tidal currents need to be considered. They are strongest for the two hours about halfway in between the slack low tide and the slack high tide. Tidal currents can be significant in some of the bays and rivers with a large tidal-flushing area. And they can be even stronger in some of the cuts and channels in the barrier islands. Government Cut, west of St. George Island, and East Pass, west of Dog Island, are two areas where you don't want to be negotiating an adverse tidal current in an under-powered displacement-hull vessel.

At peak high tide and dead low tide, there is virtually no tidal current. This is known as either slack high or slack low tide. As already mentioned, the maximum tidal current occurs halfway in between slack high and slack low tide. If the tide is rising, we call it a flooding current. If the tide is dropping, it's called an ebbing tidal current. Knowing your times of high and low tide for a typical diurnal tide, you can do some rough calculations with respect to the predicted tidal level and the tidal current in x hours. This is called the rule of twelfths. For simplicity, let's assume that there are six hours between slack high and slack low tide, or vice versa. During the first hour after slack tide, $\frac{1}{12}$ of the expected tidal range takes place. Between the first and second hour, another $\frac{2}{12}$ take place. Between the second and third hour another $\frac{3}{12}$ of the tidal range are consumed. Adding the cumulative effect of these three hours ($\frac{1}{12} + \frac{2}{12} + \frac{3}{12} = \frac{6}{12}$), we see that we have dropped (or risen) half of our tidal range by that middle hour. And this is just what we'd expect. But this also tells us that

the greatest water movement, level- and currentwise, is occurring around those middle hours between high and low tide. And that first hour around high or low tide has minimal tidal movement (around $\frac{1}{12}$ of the entire tidal range). If we continue our rule of twelfths for the next three hours, we get $\frac{3}{12}$ of the movement for the fourth hour, $\frac{2}{12}$ for the fifth hour, and $\frac{1}{12}$ for the sixth hour. All of the six hourly numerators (1+2+3+3+2+1) equal 12—or our total tidal range. This rule of twelfths is a helpful rule of thumb, but it is possible that there may be other things happening that may offset some of this pattern (e.g., strong winds holding up or blowing in the tide).

In the temperamental Gulf of Mexico, mean low water (MLW) may not always be "low" water. There are many times when the water level is less than MLW. In the winter half of the year, north and northeast winds predominate. These winds from the land side can often blow the water out of bays and river mouths, making the water level even shallower than MLW. One should be especially mindful of this phenomenon near the mouths of rivers and bays. We have also been told that winter tides are quite different from summer tides. Although the tidal range between high and low may be the same (i.e., between a three-and-a-half- and a four-foot range) in both winter and summer, the high and low water levels may be as much as a foot lower during the winter months (i.e., from about December to February). Thus, wintertime navigation may be even trickier. In the Carrabelle area, we were told there is a three-foot tidal range in the winter but less during the summer. Also in the northern Big Bend area, the winds in the fall and winter months ranged more in a swath from the northwest to the east. This could also affect the water level.

The stated daily times of a high or a low tide creep north up the Gulf Coast from near Anclote Key to St. Marks and then west to Apalachicola. It was a puzzle trying to find a tidal time pattern. This "pattern" was very irregular and varied from week to week. Generally, and on a rough average, the time of tide at St. Marks occurs about one hour and 20 minutes after the time of that same tide off Anclote Key. Hernando Beach's tide is about 30 minutes behind the Anclote River's. Both the Crystal River and Cedar Key have tides occurring about the same time, approximately another 20 minutes after the Hernando Beach tide. But the Withlacoochee River and Waccasassa Bay, being situated in an indentation on the Gulf, have slightly later tides than those of both Crystal River and Cedar Key. The tides in Steinhatchee are about 20 minutes later than those in Cedar Key. And the tides in St. Marks occur another 10 minutes later than in Steinhatchee. But in Apalachicola, the tide occurs almost two hours later than the tide in St. Marks.

When we made our water-depth observations, we copiously noted (1) the water depth at a specific location, (2) the date, and (3) the time. Afterward, and with a reconstructed tide table in hand, we backed into the mean low-water depth for any particular spot. Sometimes we were able to further confirm a nearby tidal time with the daily tidal predictions over the VHF weather channel. Unless it already happened to be the time of low tide, we reduced our observed depth readings even more. Thus, we attempted to adjust our depth observations

Twin cooling towers of the Crystal River Power Plant

for mean low water. For example, when we state we observed the mean low-water depth to be x feet, we actually measured $x + y$ feet of water depth. Afterward, noting the day, the time of low tide, and the tidal range for that day, we determined the y variable (i.e., the water level above low tide at the time of our observation). Then we took our observed depth (i.e., $x + y$) and subtracted out the y to arrive at the MLW depth (i.e., x) for any particular spot. This tedious interpolation was not an exact science, and other variables could have thrown our MLW adjustments off slightly. These variables are not limited to, but could have been (1) wind blowing the surface water in or out of a particular area; (2) an extended duration period of wind from one particular direction holding back the normal ebb or flow of the tide; (3) the lack of a good precise "nearby" time of low or high tide; or (4) we may have luckily just missed a shallow spot or a submerged obstruction that you may unluckily encounter. We hope not, but this is not outside the realm of possibilities. Please use prudence and other common sense cues when "integrating" our hopefully helpful (but not gospel) "adjusted MLW observations" in your overall plan for safe channel navigation. Nevertheless, we tried to err on the conservative side (i.e., possibly stating shallower MLW depths)

We did much of our traveling on the Gulf of Mexico when there were very fresh northeast winds. This could have had an effect of blowing more water than usual out of the many channels between St. Marks and the Pithlachascotee River. Thus our interpolated calculation of the mean low water might be even lower than the "usual." Our water-depth observations were made reading an LCD transom-mounted depth finder from a displacement-hull (i.e., slow-mov-ing) boat and recording the significant deviations beneath our keel.

We all could probably steal a page or two out of the playbook of the local Gulf Coast shrimpers. There are many shrimpers with fairly deep-draft vessels (e.g., three and half to four and a half feet and sometimes even more draft) parked behind several channels that may hold as little as two or three feet of water at MLW. What gives? The shrimpers give—they know how and when to live by the rhythm of the tides, departing and returning on one of those twice-daily high tides.

If you are willing to work with the tides—or better yet, let the tides work you—you can gain access to many more harbors than just those where your boat meets the MLW requirement. But this will require a bit of schedule adjusting. There were a few times when I got up earlier than I wanted in order to make it out of a channel before a predicted low tide restricted me. And there were times when I had to wait around and kill time for a sufficiently higher tide. But, by knowing the tide schedule, you can plan for these things. And with a little Big Bend planning, you should be able to be see and visit a significant part of coastal "Old Florida."

Weather Broadcasts

At any location along our Big Bend swath, or in the inland rivers, we were able to receive a VHF weather broadcast from at least one station (i.e., VHF weather channel 1, 2, 4, 5, 6, or 7). We received VHF weather channel 6 west of Shell Point and especially well in St. George Sound. Channel 6 broadcasts weather conditions from the Suwannee River to Apalachicola. We started catching weather broadcasts on VHF weather channel 4 south of St. Marks and along the east coast of Apalachee Bay. East and south of Shell Point, VHF weather channel 2 was also received intermittently. VHF channel 2 started coming in regularly well south of Cedar Key. VHF 2 broadcasts out of Ruskin, Florida (i.e., in Tampa Bay). We started picking up VHF channel 1, which is broadcast out of St. Petersburg, south of Hernando Beach. About 30 or 40 miles up the Suwannee River, VHF 5, out of Live Oak, Florida, came in well. Near the Crystal River area, we were also able to pick up VHF channel 7, out of Ocala, Florida.

The "Local Notices to Mariners" are issued by the Seventh Coast Guard District in Miami or the Eighth Coast Guard District in New Orleans. These notices provide important information affecting navigational nuances of a temporary nature (e.g., a certain lighted navigation aid being extinguished, dredging operations in Horseshoe Beach, the navy test-firing missiles in a certain section of the Gulf of Mexico, etc.). The "Weekly Notices to Mariners" are issued by NIMA (National Imagery and Mapping Agency—the old defense mapping agency) and are of a more permanent nature (e.g., the replacement of certain navigation aids, the dredging of a new channel, etc.).

Diamond Channel marker near Shell Point

WIND ROSES
ON THE NORTHEAST GULF OF MEXICO

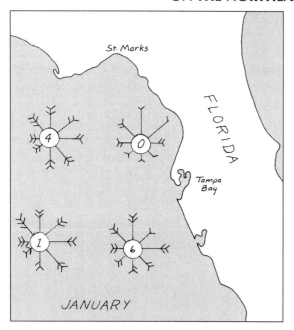

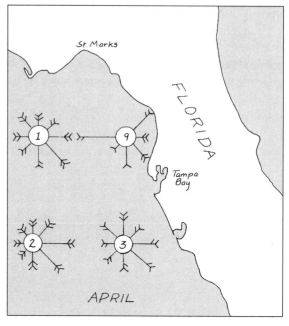

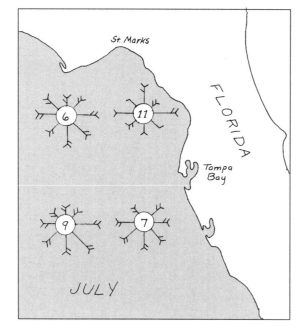

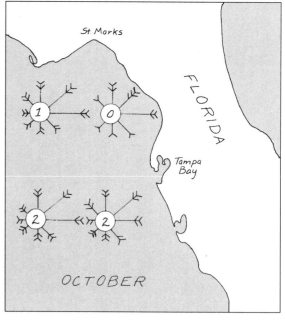

Winds, Waves, and the Wave Interval

Pilot charts of the Caribbean and Gulf of Mexico present climatic information—such as prevailing currents, average sea-level pressure, the distribution of wind directions, and the average force of the wind—on a monthly basis. This wind information (i.e., the average direction and the average force) is presented as a wind rose on these pilot charts. The specific wind roses in the Gulf of Mexico sit atop an area of more than 10,000 square nautical miles (i.e., an area of more than 100 nautical miles by 100 nautical miles). A wind rose may have as many as eight arrow shafts pointing toward the center. The shafts represent the cardinal and intercardinal compass points (i.e., N, NE, E, SE, S, SW, W, and NW). The longer the shaft, the greater percentage of historically observed winds that came out of that direction flying toward the center of the circle for that particular month. The number in the circle at the center is the percentage calms for that month. There are also feathers on each shaft (i.e., from one to five feathers on our particular sector of the northeast Gulf of Mexico). The number of feathers depicts the average force of the wind on the Beaufort scale (e.g., two feathers represents winds between four and six knots, whereas five feathers represents winds between 17 and 21 knots). We will present four sets of wind roses on the northeastern Gulf of Mexico for four different months—January, April, July, and October—to give you a sense of the prevailing wind directions and wind strength patterns that you may expect during these months.

Studying our wind roses, we observe that in January winds from the northeast and north are most common, but they are relatively light. But the strongest winds come out of the west and northwest, and these westerly and northwesterly winds are stronger farther out into the Gulf of Mexico. No doubt, this is related to the normal passage of those regular winter cold fronts sweeping down from the Great Plains.

In April southeast winds, many at Beaufort scale four (i.e., winds between 11 and 16 knots), become prevalent. In the northeastern-most corner of the Gulf of Mexico, nine percent of the time, the winds were calm in April.

In July, there seems to be no real discernible wind-direction pattern. However, the percentage of calms increased on all four of our July wind roses.

By October, relatively stronger (i.e., at Beaufort scale four and five) winds from the northeast and east dominate, and there are fewer days of calms.

Because of the generally shallow waters, especially most of the area south-southeast of Dog Island, the waves near the Big Bend can't get too terribly tall (in contrast to those 10 or 20 miles farther out in the Gulf). But the wave interval is another story. The wave interval is the distance between one wave crest and the next wave crest. This interval is measured in seconds. The generally shallow water depths also create a very short and uncomfortable wave interval. In the open ocean, much larger waves (spaced with a much longer wave interval) offer a smoother ride than choppy short-interval waves. On any boat, three-foot seas with a six-second interval are much more comfortable than two-and-a-half-foot seas with a two-second wave interval.

But two-and-a-half-foot seas with a two-second interval are often the norm along the Big Bend. This is rather uncomfortable for a small boat. Every single day that we were in the Gulf of Mexico, there were small-craft advisories (i.e., predicted sustained winds lasting more than two hours and ranging between 18 and 33 knots). These winds invariably produce wave heights between two and a half feet to four and a half feet tall. But again the worst part of that ride is the short wave interval. Later, after our trip through the Big Bend was over, I counted 19 nonconsecutive days of these uncomfortable choppy experiences. But even in my small 25-foot boat, on the Gulf of Mexico, a day was never "lost" due to staying put in port.

GPS Methodology

To help you navigate this area, we captured 66 GPS way points—48 on the Big Bend and another 18 on the large Lake Eufaula. You should never rely solely on GPS way points for navigation. If you just plug in a GPS way point and don't weigh other surrounding variables, bad things are likely to happen (like encountering other waterborne traffic or shallow spots). GPS usage in navigation is great, but it should be used in conjunction with other common-sense cues (e.g., your eyeballs scanning the area, looking at the compass or the depth finder, etc.). In the Gulf and Lake Eufaula, our GPS way points are on-the-water target spots to aim for from somewhere out in the deeper water. Once you arrive at our way point, other, mostly visual, cues should take over (e.g., sighting the sea buoys at the beginning of a particular channel).

Often, *but not always,* our GPS way points have a 180° safe semicircle approach from the deeper-water semicircle. There are more than a few places on the Big Bend where there was NOT a 180° safe semicircle approach (e.g., the Withlacoochee, Crystal, Weeki Wachee river entrances, Hernando Beach, Alligator Harbor, and a few others). Our GPS way points are points that I would want if I were coming from seaward and looking for the beginning of a channel (or possibly a safe place to intercept a channel). Ours are basically a point of change—the transition from a rough heading to reach that way point to the point where a marked channel can be followed after the way point. The GPS way points we collected in wide Lake Eufaula are usually takeoff points from just outside the Chattahoochee River Channel (i.e., either off the red buoy line or the green buoy line) and toward some particular creek.

At sea, distances are usually measured in nautical miles. On land, in rivers, and on ICWs, distances are measured in statute miles. I debated whether to convert the nautical miles—measured on the Gulf of Mexico, along the coast, and on the NOAA charts (and likely what's programmed in many GPS units)—to statute miles for consistency OR convert the river statute miles—measured on river navigation-supporting materials—to nautical miles. In the end, I did neither. If we're talking about miles in the Gulf of Mexico, on NOAA charts, or along the Gulf Coast, we're speaking in nautical miles. If we're talking about miles up a river, on an ICW, or from one point to another on a river, we're speaking in statute miles. The difference between one nautical and one statute mile is not all that great. The slightly shorter statute mile is about $7/8$ of one nautical mile. But be mindful of this slight difference. And please note the context of the mile referenced (e.g., in a river or out on the Gulf).

A GPS unit may be calibrated either to degrees/minutes/and *hundredths* of a minute or to degrees/minutes/*seconds*. A second is a sixtieth of a minute. Beware, the difference between 29°08'59" N in seconds and 29°08'59" N in hundredths is nearly 800 yards or four-tenths of a nautical mile. Our GPS unit was calibrated to hundredths of a minute. We carried out our "hundredths" observation to three digits for way points along the Gulf of Mexico but only to two digits for way points on Lake Eufaula.

The Boat's Magnetic Deviation

After the outside or "seaward" approach to a river or channel is reached via a GPS way point, we'll often provide you with an initial magnetic heading in a channel. Near those "way pointed" sea buoys, it may sometimes be difficult finding the next, or very often next series of, daymark(s) or buoy(s), especially if the distance between this outside aid to navigation and the next one is substantial. So we'll try to help out with our initial magnetic headings.

There are some caveats to using magnetic headings. The magnetic heading that I see on my boat's compass is not likely the same one that you see on your boat's compass on the exact same course. And, very likely, neither yours nor mine is lining up correctly to the real magnetic north pole. This is called magnetic deviation, and it varies from one boat's compass to the next boat's compass, and from one boat to the next boat. Usually there is nothing wrong with either the compass or the boat. The compass is being affected by nearby metal "furnishings" aboard any individual boat (e.g., the engine block, metal steering components, or even an electric current passing through nearby wiring).

Bicolor junction daymark on Apalachicola Bay

This boat-specific deviation is usually a sine curve. At two points (i.e., headings), this deviation crosses the zero axis (i.e., where both the boat's compass and the magnetic heading are the same). Elsewhere, the observations are above or below the "zero difference" axis. On my boat, *Free State,* at the 45-degree heading, and again at the 170-degree heading, both my compass's heading and the magnetic heading were in sync. Hence, if my compass is pointing 170degrees (or 45 degrees), I am heading 170 degrees (or 45 degrees) relative to the magnetic north pole. At the worse point, and when my compass was pointing 340 degrees, I was heading 355 degrees magnetic. Many skilled skippers make a quick and easy-reference magnetic-deviation table for their vessels. Below is that information, presented on a sine-curve format, for my vessel. Oh, and, you ask, how did we figure out this boat-specific deviation? I give the ingenuity and the credit to Capt. Kent Wiley. Observing our GPS, we ran short straight courses at 10-degree increments and noted the difference between our compass course and our GPS course. If you have a GPS, you too can try this exercise.

When we provide you with the initial headings for channels, we have already adjusted or "zeroed out" my compass and boat's magnetic deviation. Nevertheless, it is very likely that your boat will have some different internal magnetic deviation that may be considerably different than the actual magnetic heading.

Aside from the magnetic heading, there is true north. At any stationary position on earth, our relationship with the true North Pole is unchanging. True north does not change, but that magnetic north pole "floats" around nearby. Even if we are stationary for many years, our relationship with the magnetic north pole will change slightly from year to year. The magnetic north pole shown on our compasses, even if we remain stationary for years, will point to a very slow-moving target. The difference between that moving magnetic north pole and our stationary position on earth is known as the annual magnetic variation, which usually changes from year to year. In 1998, the latest NOAA charts indicated the magnetic variation in the Big Bend region ranged from 2 degrees 15 minutes west (near Carrabelle) to 3 degrees 30 minutes west (near New Port Richey). So, in 1998, the "average variation" in our Big Bend region is about 3 degrees to the west. But in 1998, this variation was increasing, or creeping, westward by an estimated 8 minutes per year (i.e., about 1/7 of a degree per year). So in 2002, let's

Magnetic Deviation for MV Free State

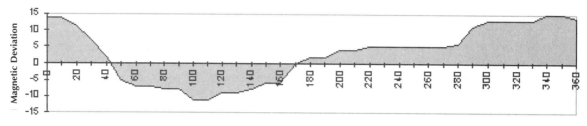

Compass Heading

Rocky channel edge near Hernando Beach

assume that the average variation throughout the Big Bend was about 3½ degrees west. If we are on one of those rare headings where our boat's internal deviation and the magnetic heading are one and the same, true north will still be about another 3½ degrees to our west.

This sounds more byzantine than it really is. Nevertheless, the compass is still one of the most practical and useful devices aboard any boat. Furthermore, anybody who can steer a boat within two compass degrees is either really special or pulling your leg. And often, we round our "corrected magnetic heading" to the nearest five degrees.

Entering Channels

The *U.S. Coast Pilot, Number 5,* is the official word on controlling depths at mean low water (MLW), as well as controlling overhead clearance at mean high water (MHW). But it seems that our observations, factoring in the time and tidal range, were sometimes quite different from what we read in the *U.S. Coast Pilot.* This gave me a headache. Should I throw out our own observations and fall back on the U.S. government's *Coast Pilot,* with its usually much more shallow and conservative water-depth observations? That would be the easiest and least confrontational thing to do. But this tack very well might close options for a boat captain that need not necessarily be closed. Hence, whenever possible, we presented both the *U.S. Coast Pilot'*s information and our own low-tide observations. If it's low tide and your boat's draft ranges in that gray area between the *U.S. Coast Pilot'*s information and our low-tide observations, please get on your VHF radio and obtain a third opinion from another reliable source or from a local boater in the area.

We obviously had no means to measure especially high overhead clearances. More so, we had to rely on information presented on the NOAA chart and/or in the *U.S. Coast Pilot*. Nevertheless, we found a few low bridges that might be slightly lower at mean high water (MHW) than stated in the *U.S. Coast Pilot*. When we encountered these discrepancies, we listed all "observations" (i.e., our own estimates plus those found in the government publications). Remember, a prudent mariner will not rely solely on one source of information.

There are many dangerous submerged and partially submerged rocks at the edges of many Big Bend Gulf channels. This uncomfortable phenomenon is more prevalent from about Horseshoe Beach to nearly all of the channels to the south. Many of these channels are dicey, at best, for nighttime navigation. Some of the larger channels to the north are likely much less dangerous for a first-time and/or nighttime approach (e.g., Steinhatchee, St. Marks, Carrabelle, and Apalachicola).

When we describe a specific navigation aid in this book, we put that aid in quotes (e.g., "R2"). The *R* or the *G* mean red or green, respectively, and the number within the quotes is that number associated with the navigation aid. If two navigation aids are paired near one location in a channel, we often state both aids within the same set of quotes (e.g., "G3 and R4"). We usually don't mention all of the buoys or daymarks in a particular channel. But we try to mention those navigation aids where there is either a depth change or a significant turn in the channel. We attempt to note lighted navigation aids, but since we negotiated nearly all of these channels before sunset, we couldn't confirm if the lighted aids were functional or extinguished. At many navigation aids, or in stretches between navigation aids, the channel depths are noted. Before arriving in a river proper, we usually describe the path and turns that the channel will take (e.g., straight, a dogleg to starboard, a 90-degree turn to port, or a hairpin). A dogleg is a turn in a channel somewhere less than 90 degrees, most commonly between 20 and 45 degrees. Typically, many Gulf channels have several dogleg turns. As you look for successive channel-navigation aids, don't wait until you arrive at an aid before prowling the horizon for the next aid. Always try to look ahead and have at least the next two navigation aids spied as you are entering (or departing) a channel.

Patriotic daymark on the Homosassa Channel

Lighted green and red daymarks near Keaton Beach

Quadrapod and bird roost on the Gulf of Mexico

Often while I was near the outside of a channel, a small friendly pod of porpoises, or a sole porpoise, would show up and then "guide" me in the channel. This occurred in the Gulf over a half-dozen times while I was in Florida's Big Bend. Sure, I think I could have found the route in without them. Nevertheless, I still thought that it was a very nice gesture on the part of so many neighborly porpoises. Sometimes I could hear their playful language, and their wake would oftentimes splash me. Were they playing with me? Toying with me? Or really trying to help me out? Are these creatures so smart that they can even read a human mind when it's looking for a channel or a river entrance from out on the Gulf of Mexico?

Fog

Fog poses a special threat to boaters who navigate close to shore and in the rivers. During our time on these waters, in the mid- and late-fall months, we experienced morning fog a couple of times—60 miles up the Suwannee River and a few times on the Apalachicola and Chattahoochee rivers. Fog occurs when warm air—laden with moisture—cools down. Warmer air is capable of holding more water vapor than cooler air. When the warmer air cools, the once-invisible water vapor condenses from a gas to a liquid state. The liquid is still suspended in the air and these small, suspended liquid droplets create the fog that obstructs visibility. The air's capacity to produce morning fog becomes greater as the early-morning temperature becomes colder. Radiant heat from the sun will sometimes "burn off" early-morning fog, but it does not always do so. We have observed instances in the wintertime when the coastal fog never burned off over Gulf waters. But two miles inland, even along a coastal river, this fog was almost nonexistent. The fog only seemed to hang over large bodies of water, and sometimes it hung around all day.

The most prudent course in a fog is to wait it out. In foggy conditions, a boat could easily collide with something dangerous, like another boat. Visibility in fog is much worse than nighttime visibility. At night, when it's not foggy, lights can usually be seen at a distance away. In fog, this isn't true. If you must travel during fog, or other impaired visibility conditions, your chance of successfully negotiating through the area is improved by slowing down, listening intently to the VHF radio for other nearby boat traffic, using a radar, and utilizing sound-producing devices.

CHAPTER 4

Navigating up the Coastal Rivers

As mentioned earlier, every single doggone day that my 25-footer and I were out in the Gulf of Mexico, we were experiencing small-craft advisories. It was uncomfortably rough on my small boat. But there was always something to look forward to near the end of each windy day: poking my bow into another enchanting and calm Big Bend river and anchoring or tying up for the night. Previously sailing in the blustery northwestern Caribbean, my young and always-up-for-another-adventure crew used to call me "Captain Calm Water," because I often went to great lengths to try to get our 33-foot sailboat out of rough and blustery conditions. This sometimes meant traveling out of the way to find a calm harbor for the night. But that will be no problem on Florida's Big Bend. You can find that calm harbor, out of the Gulf of Mexico, every single night! Please revisit the table at the end of the introduction of this book. I don't think that there are many other places in the world where you can do this type of boating for several days in a row. For the better part of each day, you can stare down the challenges that the moody Gulf of Mexico throws your way, and then, before sunset, you can bid that moody Gulf adieu as you retreat into another delightful Big Bend river.

Upon entering a typical Big Bend river, generally the first few miles are nothing more than uninteresting salt marshes and savannas. This often belies the beauty found farther up the river. After entering a Gulf river, unless you are into salt marshes, you need to go well past the "marsh line" to appreciate and savor the

flare of any of these rivers. This boundary between the two ecosystems is reasonably well portrayed on NOAA charts. The salt-marsh area is shown in green and the "harder ground" (i.e., where palms, cypress, tupelo, sweet gum, live oak, and pines can grow) is depicted in a tan color on NOAA charts. This coloration scheme seems backward to me but you will not be able to make a judgment as to the aesthetic nature of any river until you have traveled into the tan-colored area on any NOAA chart.

Other coastal/inland river delineation features include the tide and the salinity. The Suwannee River has a tidal effect farther up than any other coastal river. The effect on the Suwannee goes about 25 miles up to about Manatee Springs. Beyond Manatee Springs there is no backward or flooding tidal flow. For other rivers, the tidal effect doesn't extend as far inland. The salinity of a river loosely correlates to the tidal range. On the Suwannee River, the salinity drops (i.e., the river becomes almost all fresh water) well below Manatee Springs. Usually, and especially on the longer rivers, the salt content in the water diminishes well before the tidal effect fades out.

Man-made canal development is very prevalent from Hernando Beach south (e.g., in Hernando Beach, Hudson, and Gulf Harbors). To a much lesser extent, there are man-made canals dug in Crystal River, Suwannee, Weeki Wachee, Keaton Beach, and the Homosassa River regions. Usually a

Red navigation aid on tree on the Apalachicola River

channel will be dredged in the Gulf of Mexico and connect to a major canal or series of canals. We've invariably observed that a canal will be no shallower than its Gulf of Mexico channel. Depthwise, if you can make it through that man-made channel in the Gulf, generally you'll have enough water depth for any "man-made" major connecting canal. Typically, the canal will be a foot or two deeper because the Gulf channel has a higher propensity to fill or "silt in" than the still-water canals farther removed from the turbulence of the Gulf.

Aids to Navigation and Finding Deep Water

Except for the Apalachicola, Flint, and Chattahoochee rivers, the Gulf Coast rivers do not have aids to navigation for any appreciable length. Granted, the St. Marks, Homosassa, Crystal, Carrabelle, Steinhatchee, and Pithlachascotee rivers have relatively short sections containing navigation aids, but even the Suwannee River, which had paddlewheelers plying 126 miles up the river less than a century ago, has no navigation aids today. Local knowledge is very helpful here. For instance, even without navigation aids, it's easy for a big displacement-hull boat to make it 37 miles, or perhaps even 80 miles, up the Suwannee River, but you should hear (from local marinas, other boaters, or even unofficial 'charts') about Jack's Sand bar before you start your trip up the Suwannee and, just as important, about what side of the river to stay on in order to avoid Jack's Sand bar.

There are a few rules of thumb you should heed when navigating rivers. Around curves or bends, the deeper water will invariably be found on the outside of any bend. The inside of a bend is more likely to have a shoal. The is

because there is more scouring by the faster river current occurring on the outside than there is on the inside of a bend. The slower-moving water on the inside of a bend may actually be depositing sediment and slowly building a sand bar. But river shoals can be found just about anywhere. If other cues aren't real strong, the center of the river might be the safest bet. But there can be shoals in the center of a river, too. In a river, a shoal in the center usually means that there is deep water only to one side of that shoal. If you choose the wrong side, the water will only become shallower.

The Apalachicola-Chattahoochee-Flint River System is the only long Corps of Engineers-maintained waterway on our Big Bend. And navigation aids on this river system are reasonably good. There are a few nuances to reading the buoys and, especially, daymarks. Floating buoys, like buoys in tidal waters, are placed close to the channel's edge. Red nun buoys should be passed on your starboard side when going up any river, and the green can buoys passed on your port side. Fixed daymarks are a tad more interesting. Your typical green square or red triangle post-daymark means that the deeper water is found close to that mark, very similar to the floating red nuns and green cans. But on the Apalachicola-Chattahoochee-Flint system (and other inland rivers), you'll see red and green "diamond" daymarks. A diamond daymark may or may not have four smaller diamonds nested within the larger diamond placard. In any event, the interpretation of a diamond daymark is slightly different from a green square or red triangular daymark. A diamond daymark indicates that the deepest water can be found by steering *toward* that diamond daymark. Diamond daymarks are usually slightly bigger, in more noticeable places, and

Green diamond marker on the Apalachicola River

more eye-catching than square or triangular daymarks. These diamond daymarks are aiming points, like range marks, for their side of the river—until, hopefully, you spy the next navigation aid farther up the route.

Riverbank and Mileage Methodology

As you enter a coastal river from the Gulf of Mexico, you need to be able to differentiate one side of the river from the other, whether heading north, east, south, or west. One riverbank is called the LDB (or left descending bank), and the opposite bank is called the RDB (or right descending bank). By using this well-established convention—labeling one bank the LDB and the other bank the RDB—it's less important to relate whether you are describing something from the point of view of going up or down the river. The LDB will

always be on your *left* side if you are going *down* the river. If you are going *up* the river, like you will be initially doing for all of the rivers in this book (unless you launched your boat from well up that particular river), the LDB will always be on your *right* side. Conversely the RDB will always be on your left side as you ascend a Gulf river. We will use this LDB or RDB convention from now on to indicate to which bank we are referring. You may have previously heard the expression "left bank" (e.g., off the Seine River in Paris) or "right bank." The elucidating word "descending" is sometimes omitted. Oftentimes, we will extend this LDB-RDB logic past the river entrances and into the river channels in the Gulf of Mexico. The logic is still the same.

Our mileage measurements for river navigation are in statute miles, unlike the nautical miles we used for Gulf Coast navigation. If your GPS is calibrated for nautical miles, please be mindful of this difference. There are mile markers on the Apalachicola, Chattahoochee, Flint, and Suwannee rivers. In our river tables in the latter chapters of this book, we generally tried to present shoreside locations to the nearest tenth of a mile. Different mileage sources (e.g., mile numbers posted on nearby daymarks, buoys, and locations extrapolated from Corps of Engineers photos, or mileage numbers posted from other sources) often do not agree, but they are generally close. And only God knows which one is closer to the "actual mark." We hope that the river-mile indices that we presented in this guide are within, plus or minus, a tenth of a mile from any actual location. Given our wish to synthesize this information from other sometimes-conflicting sources (e.g., river daymarks that don't agree with information presented on Corps of Engineers publications), it's the best we could do.

Rocks

Besides those occasional sand bars, there are submerged rocks in a few of these rivers. Some rivers are worse than others. We thought that the Econfina and upper Steinhatchee rivers were the worst two. If you find yourself in submerged rock or boulder territory, you may wish to turn around and head back out. But, like finding yourself in a minefield, you probably were already in a precarious situation for some time before you ever "noticed" you were in such a plight. If

A stack of hauled-out river buoys (Note the "fins.")

you find that you have to negotiate through an uncomfortable rock area, proceed very *slowly* and keep an eye on that depth finder. If there is enough clarity to see through the water, a second set of eyes on the bow of the boat, panning beneath the surface of the water is very helpful. If you are able to do this, establish some prearranged hand signals (e.g., signals for slowing down more, hard to port, hard to starboard, etc.). If the bow person has to shout to the helmsman, by the time the message is comprehended over the engine noise, it will likely be too late for the helmsman to react.

In a few places, you could be in 14 feet of water one second and find your keel smacking a huge underwater boulder two seconds later. This actually happened to me on the upper Steinhatchee River. Luckily, I was going *slow* and only sustained some deep scratches and superficial gouges to my thick fiberglass hull. A recently fabricated aluminum outboard propeller guard also saved my propeller on more than one occasion. The nonrotating prop guard was the first thing to encounter underwater river boulders, small rocks extending from the river shore, and even oyster-shell beds miles from the shore out on the Gulf of Mexico. A slightly mangled aluminum prop guard is a much better option than a ruined propeller.

Bridge and Overhead Clearances

Bridge clearances on tidal rivers and waterways are presented on NOAA charts. On "NOAA bodies of water," the overhead clearance is presented at the mean high water level (MHW)—the general worst-case (or least-room-for-error) scenario during a typical tidal day. Yes, the MHW level can be exceeded. I have little doubt that, over the course of a year, the MHW levels (and MLW for depths) are exceeded a fair number of times. But these deviations are usually caused by unpredictable environmental factors (e.g., floods, storms, strong winds from one direction over a long period of time, etc.). Citing the MHW level for bridge clearances is a good way to express it. The nontidal Apalachicola, Chattahoochee, and Flint rivers have another convention known as "Bridge Reference Elevation for Navigation Clearance" or "BRENC." This is somewhat like MHW. The BRENC level is defined as "that water stage which on average is exceeded only twice annually and whose duration is less than five days." A seagoing salt can think of BRENC like MHW. Yes, the water level does occasionally exceed the BRENC or MHW level , but, again, when it does exceed this level, it's the result of peculiar or unusual circumstances.

Nearly all of the bridges over these rivers are fixed. Hence, there are very few bridge tenders to worry about and haggle with. When there was no official overhead-clearance information, we generally tried to provide you with our best guess, and we tried to factor in the MHW. If overhead obstructions were not on NOAA charts, we just made our best estimate. We didn't have the tools to measure these overhead clearances even close to precision. Generally, a power line will have more overhead clearance than any previously negotiated nearby fixed bridge. But there are a few power lines that could be encountered before a fixed bridge (e.g., on the upper St. Marks, Withlacoochee, Homosassa, and Salt rivers, the many small arms of Lake Eufaula, and others). Sometimes, these power-line clearances are depicted on NOAA charts or mentioned in the *U.S. Coast Pilot.*

Over some of the many bays, creeks, and inlets of Lake Seminole, and especially Lake Eufaula, we found no source stating overhead power-line clearances. Here again, we were only able to provide you with our best guess. And this is far from gospel. Furthermore, the water levels on these two large lakes fluctuates significantly. If you are "pushing the envelope" on overhead clearances, especially for dangerous power lines, please use extreme caution and prudence.

River Traffic, Dams, and Locks

The only places you might encounter commercial barge traffic are on the Apalachicola-Chattahoochee-Flint River System and on the lower St. Marks River. Most of the tows are small and not bigger than one-by-twos (i.e., two barges deep by one barge wide). But don't let those small tows and the infrequent amount of commercial traffic lull you into complacency. Granted, if there were more barge traffic, you'd likely be more vigilant. In 1987, there were an estimated 920 tows on the Apalachicola River. That is an average of between two and three towboats per day, plying that 106-mile-long river. Towboat captains refer to us smaller vessels, or recreational vessels, as "RVers." We highly recommend establishing VHF radio contact when going to meet

Petroleum tow on the St. Marks River

a tow. Port-to-port passing is the conventional first choice in a meeting situation, but be extremely flexible here. Many times, a starboard-to-starboard encounter with a tow is the better option. A towboat may be taking, or anticipating the need to take, a bend in a river wide, and starboard-to-starboard passing might be much easier for him and his less mobile cargo. You should attempt to ascertain, via radio contact with a tow, which side is best for the encounter. Towboat captains will often reply something like, "I'll meet you on the one whistle" or "I'll pass you on the two whistle." One whistle means *their port* side or a port-side-to-port-side encounter when meeting bow to bow. A two whistle means *their starboard* side or a starboard-to-starboard-side bow-to-bow encounter.

Waking is always discourteous behavior. A large, planing-hull recreational boat waking a tow can be dangerous. A wake can place a tremendous strain on the hawsers connecting the tow and the barges. Wakes also endanger fellow recreational boats. While being waked, it is much more difficult to control a moving boat in a narrow channel. Being waked at a dock can also cause damage to a boat and a dock. There are many documented instances, resulting in claims of millions of dollars, where discourteous or oblivious boaters have had to pay the piper because of their thoughtless wakes.

There are only three working locks and dams in this area. All three of those locks are on the Apalachicola and Chattahoochee rivers. Before entering the locking pit, all crew on deck should be wearing life jackets. This is a legal requirement while in the pit. Boat fenders should be out to protect the sides of the boat from the rough slimy concrete walls.

When entering or leaving a locking pit, stay in the channel, away from any orange-and-white danger buoys and 800 feet away from any dam area. In a locking pit with floating bollards, place a line wrap around the bollard from a cleat amidship. If you don't already have them, it's best to install some amidship cleats, with solid metal or Delrin cleat-backing plates.

When locking up, the front of the lock sometimes has less turbulence when the pit is filling. More often than not, there is more turbulence in the pit near the back when locking up. When locking down, it generally matters less. Many times the lock tenders will direct you where to tie up—on your port or starboard side and at the front or middle of the pit. When you make radio contact with the lock tender, ask him where you should tie up. Don't ever tie up your vessel to a ladder or to other immovable objects in a locking pit. Engines should be turned off because it's difficult to dissipate the exhaust fumes in the locking chamber. Any movement aboard the deck should be limited to that which is essential. Always enter and leave a locking pit at a "no wake" speed.

In the first two locks on the Apalachicola and Chattahoochee rivers, neither lock gates opened completely during our visit. In the Woodruff Lock, only one gate opened. In the George Andrews Lock and Dam, both gates opened, but neither opened fully. Nevertheless, there was still plenty of room to slide my boat through in both instances. I have generally found that lock tenders are the most knowledgeable and helpful folks on their portion of the river. They are undoubtedly one of the best reservoirs of local river knowledge. If you treat them respectfully, they will often

Walter F. George Lock, Chattahoochee River

answer many of your local-knowledge or river questions.

Anchoring in Rivers

The biggest challenge when anchoring in these rivers—especially in the Apalachicola, Chattahoochee, Ochlockonee, and St. Marks—is the water depth. These rivers are often too deep for safe anchoring. Many creeks off the Chattahoochee had no less than 20 feet of water depth. The anchor rode that needs to be deployed, given the normal 7:1 scope ratios, could easily have your boat swinging into the shoreline if for some unlikely reason the direction of pull reversed in the middle of the night. Hence, you may wish to anchor on a scope shorter than generally recommended (e.g., 5:1 or less). In rivers,

I like anchoring in depths with, ideally, between four and eight feet of water beneath my keel. This way, on a 5:1 scope, not counting the additional freeboard height to the anchor cleat, I need to only deploy about 20+ to 40+ feet of anchor line. And if the wind shifts—my anchoring holding direction shifts in the middle of the night—I will hopefully only swing within a relatively tight 40-foot radius plus the length of my boat. To anchor "properly" in 30 feet of water, you should pay out at least 150+ feet of anchor line on a 5:1 scope. That's too much line to pay out in a narrow river. When you anchor on short scope, you improve your odds of a safe anchoring experience with a heavier anchor and heavy chain at the end of your anchor rode.

A river-beach-style hybrid of the Mediterranean Mooring is a very good technique if you can find a fairly deep accessible and clear spot on a sandy beach. And there are many fairly deep accessible spots on the sandy beaches of these rivers. For more on this Mediterranean Mooring technique, please read that section in chapter 17. A beach-style Mediterranean Mooring is about the only way a large boat can access enchanting Branford, Florida, on the Suwannee River. If the boat is too big, or the boat's draft does not permit bow beaching (e.g., a deep-keeled sailboat), near-circumnavigator and world-class sailor Karl Edler suggests anchoring in deep enough water, parallel and close to the river's bank, employing both a bow and a stern anchor. Of course, using a dinghy or wading ashore would be necessary.

In boating, whatever decisions you make, it's best to integrate information from several sources beforehand (e.g., NOAA or other charts, local-knowledge reports, VHF weather forecasts, and other sources). The Portuguese navigators of yesteryear used to say, "Knowledge [about the sea] is power." This is absolutely true. Obtain as much information as you can, including by talking to other boaters, and feel free to solicit opinions from your more capable crew. Once you've garnered "sufficient" knowledge, synthesize it and act decisively. In the end, it is the captain who must decide upon the course of action and then not be wishy-washy about it. Nevertheless, if a bad decision has been made (and this happens) by a good captain, don't be afraid to reverse that decision. Not being flexible, and not reversing an earlier flawed decision, can sometimes compound what was once only a minor predicament. Boating catastrophes seldom occur as the result of one bad decision. They occur as the result of a bad decision compounded by another bad decision, further compounded—until the situation becomes so deep that even the most able captain and crew cannot extricate themselves.

CHAPTER 5

The Apalachicola Region

Apalachicola

Historic Apalachicola anchors the western end of the area covered in this guide. Although small in comparison to the modern Port of Tampa, or even nearby Tallahassee, Apalachicola is a vital city near the western end of Florida's Big Bend. With a population of about 2,500, it is the largest town sitting on this 300-mile stretch of the coast between Panama City and the coastal-development sprawl northwest of Tampa. Besides being a busy commercial hub for modern fishing, oystering, and crabbing, Apalachicola is steeped in rich history.

In the nineteenth century, shipping was a major business here. In 1822, the first shipment of cotton left Apalachicola, bound for New York. By 1840, Apalachicola was Florida's largest, and America's third largest cotton-exporting port on the Gulf of Mexico. In this region, only New Orleans and Mobile exported more cotton. Apalachicola ranked nineteenth in the entire country in terms of steamboat cargo tonnage, ahead of such heavyweights as Boston, Wilmington, Norfolk, and Newark. Cotton plantations in Alabama and Georgia shipped cotton on the rivers and transferred it to oceangoing ships anchored near St. George and St. Vincent islands. Much of the cotton was shipped to Liverpool, England.

Cotton warehouses and brokerage houses dominated the Apalachicola waterfront. One cotton warehouse still stands today. The navigable Apalachicola and Chattahoochee rivers—passable to the middle of Georgia and Alabama—were a big reason for this commercial port's success. And money flowed into Apalachicola. Many nice homes, including the still-standing Raney House, were built during the 1830s. The Raney House is on the National Register of Historic Places, and legend states it is the site where Franklin County's Confederate soldiers were mustered out of the service at the end of the Civil War. Today, Apalachicola is the seat of Franklin County.

In 1833, John Gorrie, a thirty-one-year-old doctor, moved to Apalachicola. Gorrie was born an illegitimate child in the West Indies but had traveled and studied extensively from South Carolina to New York. After his mother died in Sneads, Florida, Dr. Gorrie moved his practice about 110 miles downriver to Apalachicola—the nearby bustling cotton port on the Gulf. By 1837, the affable Gorrie was serving as postmaster, and would later serve as mayor, of Apalachicola.

Apalachicola was wracked with malaria and yellow fever. It was especially severe in 1841. It would still be another forty years before the dastardly mosquito would be correctly implicated as a controllable vector in these awful diseases. Nevertheless, Dr. Gorrie correctly deduced that there was some connection between these diseases and the hot, humid climates along with the stagnant swamp water. To lessen the suffering of those afflicted with the diseases, and to create a contrary-type environment, Gorrie

Downtown Apalachicola

THE APALACHICOLA REGION 63

started experimenting with ice, compressors, condensers, and piping. In 1849, after several experiments, Gorrie "made ice" and invented the major principles leading to refrigeration and air conditioning. Unfortunately, Gorrie couldn't find any backers to put his new "ice machine" into commercial production. And to make matters worse, the powerful monopoly of northern ice packers and shippers thwarted his efforts with cruel advertisement campaigns with such sayings as, "There is a crank down in Apalachicola who claims he can make ice as good as God Almighty." Ridiculed and dispirited, Dr. Gorrie died in 1855. A cohort fought hard for nearly fifty years to keep Dr. Gorrie's invention from falling into oblivion. In 1902, Willis Carrier advanced Dr. Gorrie's ideas and machinery, and the "Age of Air Conditioning" officially began. After the twentieth century had dawned, Dr. Gorrie of Apalachicola, Florida, was finally recognized as one of the world's great inventors of the nineteenth century!

The Gorrie Museum is near the corner of Sixth Street and Avenue D and open all week, except Tuesdays and Wednesdays. We also recommend that you visit the St. Vincent National Wildlife Refuge Visitor's Center, the very well done Apalachicola National Estuarine Research Reserve exhibits, and the nearby aquarium. All three of these excellent exhibitions are very close to the Scipio Creek Commercial Marina. Every November, Apalachicola hosts one of Florida's oldest maritime festivals, and they also host seafood festivals.

Besides a handful of marinas, the John Gorrie State Museum, and an historic Episcopal church, downtown Apalachicola has more than a half-dozen restaurants, two posh inns, many bed and breakfasts and gift shops, a half-dozen

banks, two service stations, two pharmacies, a library, and a post office. The Gibson Inn, (850) 653-2191, two blocks off the water, is a couple of blocks west of the Apalachicola River Inn. The well-known, Victorian Gibson Inn was built at the turn of the twentieth century. A Piggly Wiggly grocery store and an Eckerd drugstore are about eight blocks west on the main road—Avenue E—heading toward Panama City. A few other motels and restaurants and an auto parts store are farther out on the highway, toward Panama City. Croom's is the local taxi/transportation service in Apalachicola, but Enterprise Rent-A-Car, out of Panama City, has been known to pick up and discharge rental-car clients as far away as Apalachicola.

Apalachicola can be approached via four distinct waterborne arteries, and that's two more approachable directions than from the roadways! The Gulf ICW, coming all the way from south Texas, reaches Apalachicola from the west. The Chattahoochee-Apalachicola River, flowing from the north, is navigable for about 260 miles to Columbus, Georgia. To the east, Apalachicola Bay gives way to St. George Sound and water routes leading to Carrabelle and St. Marks, Florida. For those wishing to quickly jump out into the Gulf of Mexico, Government Cut—on the south side of Apalachicola Bay, is seven nautical miles south of town.

Governmnent Cut and St. George Island

Government Cut, sometimes known as Bob Sikes Pass, was created by the Corps of Engineers in 1952. Two rock jetties mark the outside entrance to this cut, which slices St. George Island into two pieces. The western island, Little St. George Island, houses the abandoned Cape St. George Lighthouse. This nine-mile-long island is inaccessible by vehicle.

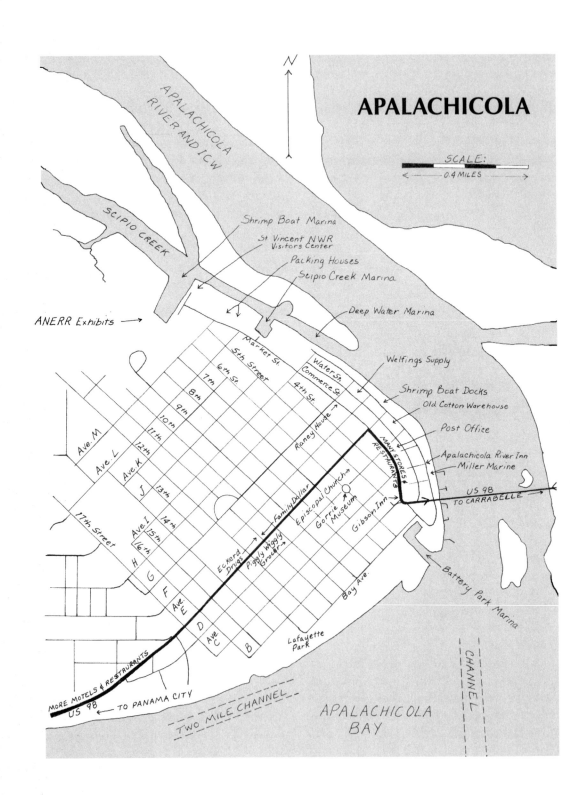

APALACHICOLA

SCALE:
0.4 MILES

N

APALACHICOLA RIVER AND ICW

SCIPIO CREEK

Shrimp Boat Marina
St Vincent NWR Visitors Center
Packing Houses
Scipio Creek Marina
Deep Water Marina

ANERR Exhibits →

Market St.
5th Street
6th St.
7th
8th
9th
10th
11th
12th
13th
14th
15th
16th

Water St.
Commerce St.
4th St.

Welfings Supply
Shrimp Boat Docks
Old Cotton Warehouse
Post Office
Apalachicola River Inn
Miller Marine

Raney House

Ave. M
Ave. L
Ave. K
J
Ave. I
H
G
F
Ave. E
D
Ave. C
B

17th Street

Eckerd Drugs
Piggly Wiggly Grocer →
Family Dollar
Episcopal Church
Gorrie Museum
Gibson Inn

MANY STORES & RESTAURANTS

US 98
TO CARRABELLE

Bay Ave.

Lafayette Park

Battery Park Marina

CHANNEL

MORE MOTELS & RESTAURANTS
US 98 ← TO PANAMA CITY

TWO MILE CHANNEL

APALACHICOLA BAY

St. George Island proper is to the east and about 20 miles long. There is a bridge to St. George Island and its hundreds of residents. Much of the area, especially in the western parts, is very exclusive and off-limits to the public. I was unable to visit the Government Cut area with my car. A long state park now takes up almost all of the space within that easternmost nine miles of the island.

Our way point in the Gulf of Mexico off Government Cut is 29.36.075N/84.57.184W. This way point is in between the sea buoys. Both the sea buoys "G1 and R2", off Government Cut, are flashing lighted beacons and are in about 22 to 23 feet of water at MLW. The cut is an estimated 100 yards wide and the tidal current coming through can be very strong. The water shallows to between 13 and 14 feet before the rock jetties, then deepens to 22 to 23 between the jetties. The shallowest place in the cut's channel is at 9 to 10 feet deep at MLW. Most of this cut is 13-14 feet deep. There is a building on the east side of Government Cut and an attractive beach on the west side. A boat ramp sits on the east side of the cut on the Apalachicola Bay side. There is a very visible pair of range marks, bordered with green outside bands, seen upon entering Apalachicola Bay from Government Cut.

Apalachicola Bay

Apalachicola Bay covers about 210 square miles and is one of the most productive estuaries in the United States. Estuaries are vital parts of our ecosystem. Scores of species of fish, crustaceans, and shellfish are dependent on healthy estuaries as either a juvenile nursery ground or overall habitat area. Estuaries also provide breeding and nesting grounds for many coastal birds. Annually, the Apalachicola Bay estuary produces about 90 percent of Florida's oyster harvest and about 10 percent of the national oyster harvest. Shrimp and crabs thrive here. Many fish that live in the Gulf of Mexico return to Apalachicola Bay to spawn.

The bay is hemmed by the barrier islands of St. Vincent Island (to the west), Little St. George Island (to the southwest), and St. George Island (to the south and east). St. George Sound is to the northeast of Apalachicola Bay. The bay averages about nine feet deep. The Gulf ICW runs down the last six miles of the Apalachicola River before entering Apalachicola Bay and then heads east toward St. George Sound and Carrabelle. Only two of the four passes out of Apalachicola Bay are recommended for safe navigation: Government Cut between Little St. George and St. George Island, and the route to the northeast into St. George Sound and toward Carrabelle. Looking south from Apalachicola, low-lying St. George Island and Little St. George Island sometimes can't even be seen across this seven-mile-wide bay. Needless to say, despite being in a "protected ICW," during bad weather, the water in Apalachicola Bay can become quite rough.

The Apalachicola Municipal Marina, or Battery Park Marina, may have the most wet slips in this area, about 40, and the marina may be able to accommodate 30-footers. But their entrance channel is shallow at low tide. There are plans to deepen this entrance channel to four to five feet at MLW. Nice piers are on both sides of the channel going to the Battery Park Marina. The southernmost pier has a gazebo near the end. Transient boats should side-tie to one of these piers. This municipal marina is the only recreational facility south of the John Gorrie Bridge. Two-Mile Channel begins near

Shrimp fleet in Scipio Creek Commercial Marina

Apalachicola River near Battery Park Marina

the Battery Park Marina and initially heads to the west into Apalachicola Bay.

Battery Park Marina (850) 653-7274

Approach depth—2 feet

Dockside depth—less than 4 feet

Accepts transients—yes

Fixed wooden pier and docks—yes

Dockside power connections—some 15 amp

Dockside water connections—yes

Boat ramp—yes

Restaurant—several nearby

Two-Mile Channel

The Two-Mile Channel extends from near the City of Apalachicola Municipal Marina and the ICW channel to the western parts of Apalachicola Bay. This channel, shallower than the main ICW channel, has about a three-foot controlling depth and is used primarily by workboats. Outbound (i.e., with the channel numbers decreasing) and from near the John Gorrie Bridge, the channel hugs the mainland for about two miles. North of two small islands, the main part of this channel makes a turn to the south at "R10," splitting the islands and heading into the heart of Apalachicola Bay. A short spur continues to the west, between the westernmost island and the mainland. The channel is well depicted on NOAA strip chart 11402.

The Apalachicola River and Scipio Creek

The 65-foot vertical-clearance John Gorrie Bridge crosses the Apalachicola River north of the Battery Park Marina. The next half-mile of the Apalachicola River, on the RDB (i.e., right descending bank) and upriver from the bridge, houses a handful of small facilities and a fishing pier. Miller Marine has the big Chevron gas sign, and the Apalachicola River

Inn is just upriver from Miller. Both are small facilities, but if they have space, they can handle a few large and deep-draft vessels. Miller has a nice ship's store, sells gasoline and diesel, and has about 100 feet of side-tie dockage at their fuel dock. The Apalachicola River Inn is connected to a fine waterfront restaurant. Boss Oyster Restaurant is another waterfront eatery nearby. Boss Oyster has fixed wooden docks about 30 feet long, with no utilities. Also on this RDB, there are a handful of private shrimp docks and seafood-packing houses both downriver and upriver from Miller and the Apalachicola River Inn. Benign Boat Rental and Fishing Charters, (850) 653-8214, is between Miller and Deep Water Marina. Benign also has a boat ramp. Wefing's Marine Supply, (850) 653-9218, (Web site: www.wefings.com) is one block south of Benign on Water Street at Avenue F. Wefing's is a modest-sized but well-stocked ship's store catering to both commercial and recreational vessels and has been around since 1909.

Miller Marine (850) 653-9521

Approach depth—14 feet

Dockside depth—14 feet

Accepts transients—yes, limited to space

Fixed wooden docks—yes

Dockside power connections—30 and 50 amp

Dockside water connections—yes

Gasoline—yes

Diesel—yes

Ship's store—yes

Restaurant—several nearby

The Apalachicola River Inn (850) 653-8139

Approach depth—8-13 feet

Dockside depth—8-13 feet

Accepts transients—limited

Fixed wooden docks—yes

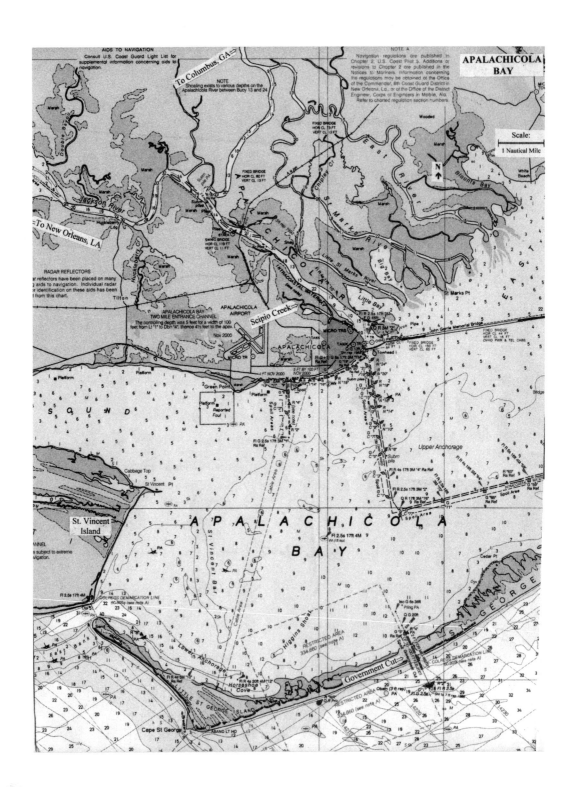

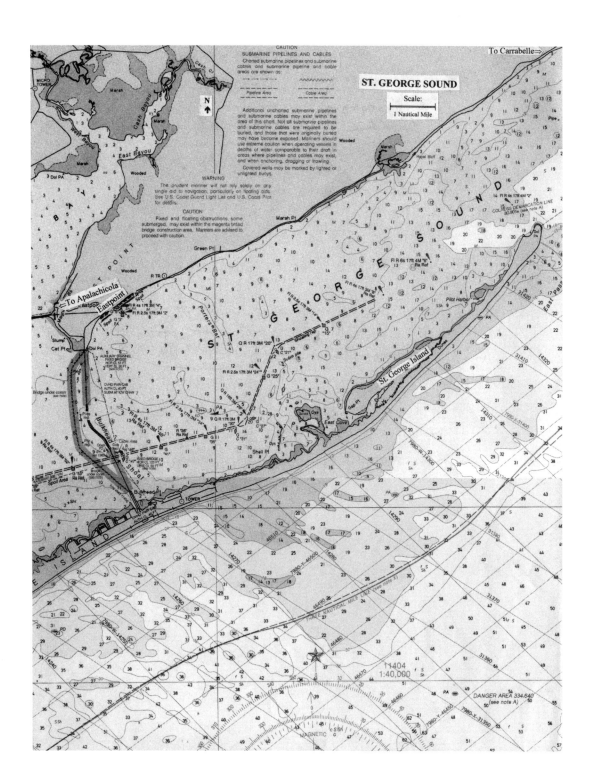

Dockside power connections—15 and 50 amp
Dockside water connections—yes
Restaurant—on site

Scipio Creek

Scipio Creek branches off the RDB side of the Apalachicola near Wefing's. The creek carries about a nine-foot water depth in the center of the channel and for about one mile into the basin housing the Scipio Creek Commercial Marina. If you are entering well-protected Scipio Creek from the upriver portion of the Apalachicola River (i.e., from the west), be careful. You need to give the point of land off the RDB of the Apalachicola River plenty of room. HAZARD *There is a long, submerged sand bar off this point of land between Scipio Creek and the Apalachicola River.* Scipio Creek holds eight- to ten-feet depths at MLW all the way to the shrimp docks. But about 150 yards past the municipal shrimp dock, the water depths shallow to four to five feet. The next three facilities are in Scipio Creek and all are on the RDB side.

Deep Water Marina has about two dozen slips but very few transient spaces. Deep Water has a modest-sized haul-out yard and offers Boat/U.S. discounts.

Scipio Creek Marina is the newest and perhaps the most accommodating full-service marina in Apalachicola. Besides a nice restaurant, ship's store, Laundromat, and fuel, Scipio Creek Marina has about 400 feet of side-tie docking area (and about 180 feet is reserved for transients). The marina can accommodate up to an 80-footer. Scipio Creek also has a large high-and-dry boat-storage building. Professionally

Scipio Creek Marina ship's store

run and clean, Scipio Creek Marina has two forklifts for hauling boats. An Eco-Tour boat, (850) 653-2593, the MV *Osprey,* conducts Apalachicola estuary excursions from Scipio Creek Marina. There are a handful of seafood-packing houses beyond Scipio Creek Marina.

The city's commercial shrimp docks, the Scipio Creek Commercial Marina, are about a third of a mile past Scipio Creek Marina on the RDB. This colorful working facility is full, with about three dozen large shrimp boats—some a big as 50 feet. Scipio Creek significantly shallows beyond the commercial marina and soon ends in Turtle Harbor.

Deep Water Marina (850) 653-8801

Approach depth—7-8 feet
Dockside depth—6-8 feet
Accepts transients—yes
Floating wooden docks—yes
Dockside power connections—30 and 50 amp
Dockside water connections—yes
Showers—yes
Below-waterline repairs—yes with 25-ton
  open-ended travel lift
Restaurants—several within walking distance

Scipio Creek Marina (850) 653-8030
www.scipiocreekmarina.com

Approach depth—8-9 feet
Dockside depth—8 feet
Accepts transients—yes
Fixed wooden docks—yes
Dockside power connections—30 and 50 amp
Dockside water connections—yes
Waste pump-out—yes
Showers—yes
Laundromat—yes
Gasoline—yes

Diesel—yes
Mechanical repairs—yes
Below-waterline repairs—yes, with 10-ton forklift
Boat ramp—yes
Ship's store—yes
Restaurant—on site, others in fair walking distance

Scipio Creek Commercial Marina (850) 653-7274

Approach depth—8 feet
Dockside depth—7 feet
Accepts transients—no
Fixed wooden and concrete docks—yes
Dockside power connections—30 amp
Dockside water connections—yes
Waste pump-out—yes
Showers—yes
Gasoline—yes
Boat ramp—yes

There are also two other small marinas three and a half to four miles up the Apalachicola River. You can learn about these two facilities in chapter 13, when we start heading up the Apalachicola River. Chapters 13, 14, 15, and 16 address the Apalachicola, Flint, and Chattahoochee rivers, Lake Seminole and Lake Eufaula, and the navigable water route as far north as Columbus, Georgia. If you are heading west on the ICW toward Panama City or New Orleans, we recommend *Cruising Guide to the Northern Gulf Coast,* by Claiborne Young.

The Eastern Route through Apalachicola Bay and St. George Sound

ICW East Channel and St. George Sound

At the Gorrie Bridge, the ICW heads south in Apalachicola Bay. The channel is straight and well marked in this four-mile section. The main ICW channel makes a 90-degree turn (if Carrabelle -bound—from south to east or to the port) in between navigation aids "G1 and R2" and "R76 and G77." At this turn, Government Cut is another four miles off the ICW channel. To reach Government Cut, at "G1 and R2" and at that 90-degree turn, you would continue south toward the direction off the cut. You should be able to spy the cut before this 90-degree turn. If you turn to the east near "G1 and R2," the navigation aids continue to be good. A new bridge is being constructed about 200 yards west of the old St. George Island Bridge. HAZARD *We passed through this area twice, and there were many dangerous unfinished pilings that may not be easily seen at night.* The new bridge construction is west of Bulkhead Shoal. And there are shoal patches all around. The St. George Island Bridge and Bulkhead Shoal mark the transition between Apalachicola Bay and St. George Sound. HAZARD *The old St. George Island bridge has a vertical overhead clearance of only 50 feet; however, the new bridge is to be 65 feet high.*

Like Apalachicola Bay, St. George Sound is a large body of water. If there are small-craft advisories, it can be rough here, too. We were unable to locate any good anchorages on the St. George Island side of this big sound. The aids to navigation on ICW channel in St. George Sound don't match the NOAA chart that well, either. There are marks in the channel that aren't printed on the NOAA charts. In the sound, the ICW makes a couple of pronounced dogleg turns. The eastern tip of St. George Island is about 20 miles east-northeast of Government Cut. In St. George Sound, the East Pass Channel between St. George Island and the next island, Dog Island, is a wide and safe approach to the Gulf of Mexico.

Eastpoint

Eastpoint, a small village of watermen, is located at the east end of the Gorrie bridge and causeway. Many small seafood wholesalers are located in town. Eastpoint is on a point of land that juts between St. George Sound and East Bay. East Bay is north of the John Gorrie Bridge, and this shallow bay feeds Apalachicola Bay. With the towns of Apalachicola and Carrabelle nearby, there is little reason for a recreational boat to go into Eastpoint. Nevertheless, in St. George Sound, and near way point 29.44.090N/84.52.262W, the channel to Eastpoint is marked by four buoys—two red and two green.

HAZARD *There are shoals on both the east and west sides of the entry.* The *U.S. Coast Pilot* indicates depths of five feet in the entry channel, two and a half feet in the east arm, and three feet in the west arm. All docks in Eastpoint are very rickety, and much debris (e.g., sunken boats and stumps) can be found in these two, small, side channels. One arm extends to the east and the other to the west. Both extend about the same distance from the Eastpoint entry channel. That-Place-on-98 Restaurant is in the east arm but the facility has no accessible dock. Likewise, the seafood market dock of the Bay Steam Bar is in the west arm, but it also has no good boat dock. The shallow narrow basins in Eastpoint wouldn't be very good for anchorages.

Sportsman's Lodge Motel, RV Park, and Marina (850) 670-8423) is on the northwest side of Eastpoint, near the mouth of extremely shallow East Bay. This tightly packed trailer park has a very small boat basin that contains an unimproved boat ramp. Nearby, in the basin, there are a few floating wooden docks and motel rooms. If you were able to get ashore in Eastpoint, you'd find gas stations, a supermarket, a hardware store, a post office, and a library.

CHAPTER 6

The Carrabelle Region

This chapter covers the eastern part of St. George Sound, Dog Island, the town of Carrabelle, and the Carrabelle, New, and Crooked rivers. The safest passage from Carrabelle to the Gulf of Mexico (or vice versa) is the well-marked channel in between St. George Island and Dog Island. Even though there is a wide opening to the Gulf east of Dog Islands, there are shoals, some deeper than others, southeast of Dog Island. In any event, familiarize yourself with NOAA chart 11405. Carrabelle is a boater's town with about 250 wet slips for recreation boats and many additional docks for shrimp boats. Carrabelle hosts an annual Riverfront Festival in late April. Inland from Carrabelle, both the Carrabelle and the New rivers are worthy of exploration.

Dog Island

Dog Island is the large island in St. George Sound about four miles south of Carrabelle. It's also a sea turtle nesting area. There are shoals and reefs east of Dog Island and the best and safest channel to Gulf of Mexico from Carrabelle is the East Pass Channel, which passes just west of Dog Island. This channel, between Dog Island and St. George Island, is well marked, but once again, the marks don't correspond very well to the depiction on the NOAA chart. Coming from seaward, the green side (i.e., the left or St. George Island side) has more shoals; hence there is a preponderance of green buoys in this channel. A fair way into this channel, we captured a GPS way point right off unlighted green can buoy "C7"—an aid to navigation not shown on the NOAA chart. Our way point off "C7," with at least 20 feet of water depth, is 29.46.005N/84.40.028W. The aids to navigation continue to be out of step with the presentation details of NOAA chart 11405 all of the way into the Carrabelle River. Closer to Dog Island and near "R12," there is a partially submerged, wrecked shrimper.

In Shipping Cove, on the western side of Dog Island, there are some nice houses on piles and a few long extended docks in the cove. But in our view, the only safe anchorage at Dog Island is in the cove near the eastern end of the island—Tyson Harbor Cove. Upon entering the channel to Tyson Harbor Cove, you will notice a marked channel with a dog-leg to the right after the first pair of marks. The unlighted navigation aids are often in pairs. MLW depths are about six to eight feet. There are sand bars on both sides of this channel, so heed these navigation aids. There are also pretty beaches on both sides of this cove.

Spencer's Landing, at the head of this cove, houses some wooden rickety docks belonging to the Dog Island Yacht Club. The docks at the yacht club have about a score of slips, but most of the slips are less than 25 feet long. A sign indicates that transients need to pay, but there wasn't a soul around, and neither was there anything that whiffed of a commercial operation. There were many not-so-great cars and pickup trucks also parked in the area. It looked like many of the cars had not been run in years. It was a rather eerie scene—rickety

Sandy road on Dog Island

Tyson Harbor Cove and Yacht Club, Dog Island

dock, a few small boats and abandoned cars, and nobody around. The cars obviously arrived, perhaps long ago, transported on some sort of ferry. There are sandy roads on the island. A handful of raised bungalows face the Gulf of Mexico, but the island appeared deserted.

HAZARD *Dog Island Reef, with two to six feet of water over it, sits five miles east of the east side of Dog Island.* Local fishermen sometimes cut west of Dog Island Reef in between the reef and close to Dog Island. Duer Channel is another unmarked channel nearby. Duer Channel runs east of Dog Island Reef and west of South Shoal. If you need more draft and are leaving Dog Island or Carrabelle for a run in the Gulf of Mexico, it may be best to depart the Dog Island area from the very well marked East Pass Channel, west of Dog Island.

Carrabelle and the Carrabelle River

Carrabelle started out as a fur-trading center. After the Civil War, pine and cypress logging entered the economy. During the Great Depression, contraband liquor, sailing in from the Caribbean, was often hidden in the swamps around Carrabelle. Carrabelle is somewhat smaller than Apalachicola, but there are three restaurants and many services in town. Near the

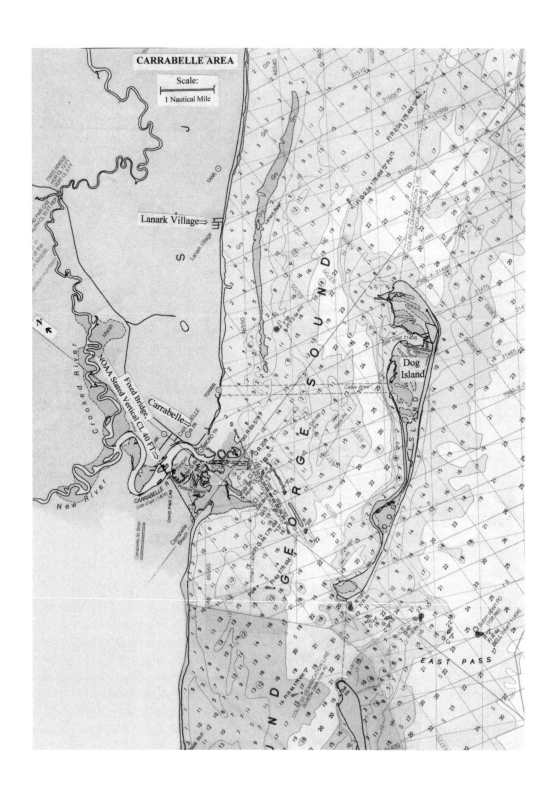

CARRABELLE AREA

Scale:

1 Nautical Mile

Lanark Village ⇒

Carrabelle

Fixed Bridge;
NOAA Stated Vertical CL. 40 FT⇒

Dog
Island

EAST PASS

main intersection in Carrabelle, there is a motel, Gander's hardware, a Chevron gas station, a Laundromat, a Subway restaurant, and a post office. Toward the Coast Guard station, you'll also find a pharmacy. There is also a Texaco gas station, an ACE hardware store, and a CarQuest auto parts store closer to the Carrabelle River Bridge. The IGA grocery store burned down between our first and second visit, but construction was underway to rebuild a new store on the same site during our third visit.

The numbers on channel aids from Dog Island to the mouth of the Carrabelle River sometimes don't coincide with the NOAA charts. However, the turns and bends in this channel are correctly depicted. The land northeast of the Carrabelle River and south of the Crooked River is actually an island—St. James Island. The Crooked River connects to the Ochlockonee river and bay. Hence, the Carrabelle River and the Crooked River can have quite a strong tidal current. The first development on the LDB of the Carrabelle River will be a small marina with a ramp, then a Coast Guard station, followed by a large pavilion. Vicked Willie's Restaurant, (850) 697-488, sits behind this pavilion. Continuing on the LDB, there is a condominium and a docking area. Shrimp boats are scattered at private docks all around Carrabelle, especially on the LBD side.

There is a ramp across the river from the Coast Guard station on the RDB. Timber Island Marina is one of the first facilities on the RDB. However, Timber Island is no longer a marina. The marina operation is going (or perhaps by now has gone) condo—Timber Island Condo Resort. When we twice visited, there were still scattered boats hauled out. By the time you visit, the Timber Island boat ramp may be the only thing left behind, marina-wise. Pirates Landing and Saunder's seafood-processing house are upriver from Timber Island. Both Pirates Landing and Saunder's cater more to commercial shrimping operations. Dockside Marina has only about a dozen wet slips, and six additional slips are planned. This marina has a large yard and a marine railway and soon plans to have a travel lift.

Pirates Landing Marina and Saunder's Seafood (850) 697-2778

Approach depth—12 feet
Accepts transients—no, primarily commercial docks
Fixed wooden docks—yes
Dockside power connections—limited 50 amp
Gasoline—yes
Diesel—yes
Tiki bar—yes

Dockside Marina (850) 697-3337

Approach depth—11 feet
Dockside depth—9-10 feet
Accepts transients—yes
Fixed wooden docks—yes
Dockside power connections—30 amp
Dockside water connections—yes
Mechanical repairs—yes
Below-waterline repairs—with a marine railway
Boat ramp—yes
Ship's store—limited

C-Quarters Marina is broken into two sections on the LDB of the Carrabelle River. Several deep-sea fishing charter boats operate out of C-Quarters as well as the Moorings. The Blue Crab Lounge is next to the C-Quarters Marina. This marina restaurant is seasonal. Marine Systems Shop, (850) 697-2660, is in between the two docking areas of C-Quarters.

CARRABELLE

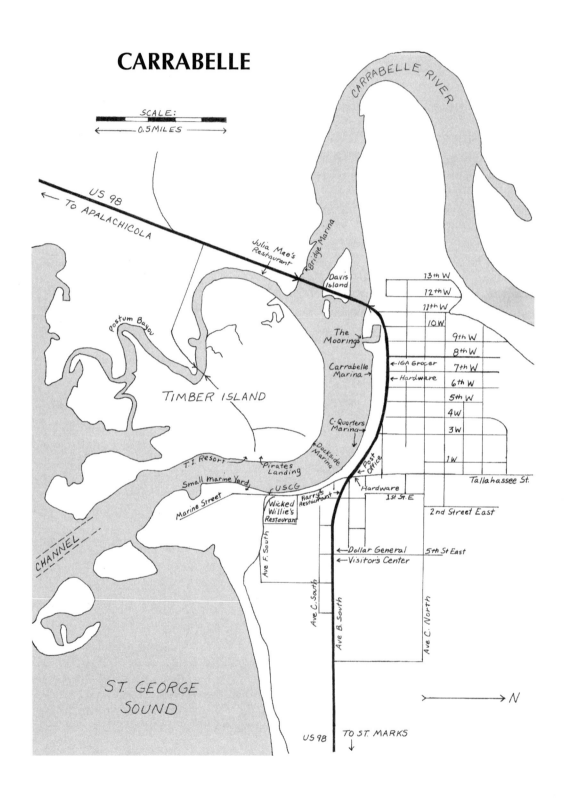

SCALE:

0.5 MILES

US 98
TO APALACHICOLA

CARRABELLE RIVER

Bridge Marina

Julia Mae's Restaurant

Davis Island

Postum Bayou

The Moorings

13th W
12th W
11th W
10 W
9th W
8th W

Carrabelle Marina

IGA Grocer
Hardware

7th W
6th W
5th W
4 W
3 W

TIMBER ISLAND

C. Quarters Marina

1 W

Dockside Marina

Post Office

Tallahassee St.

T.I. Resort
Pirates Landing

Small marine Yard

USCG

Hardware
1st St. E

Marine Street

Harry's Restaurant

2nd Street East

Wicked Willie's Restaurant

Ave F. South

CHANNEL

Dollar General

5th St East

Visitor's Center

Ave C. South

Ave B. South

Ave C. North

ST. GEORGE SOUND

N

US 98
TO ST. MARKS

The transient area of C-Quarters is more upriver and near the restaurant and lounge. Professionally run C-Quarters has 68 slips and can accommodate up to a 65-footer.

Carrabelle Marina has a blue-and-white striped high-and-dry storage building, about 15 slips, and can accommodate up to a 40-footer. The first-class Moorings at Carrabelle has about 140 slips and can accommodate about an 85-footer. Besides many amenities, like a transient lounge with Internet hookups, there is also a reasonably sized boat-trailer storage area. A Boat/U.S. towboat also parks in this marina. There is a narrow channel in the Moorings leading to many slips just past the store and fuel dock. Two large boats meeting head-on in this channel would be an interesting sight, as maneuverability is rather limited, especially for a single screw boat.

C-Quarters Marina (850) 697-8400

Approach depth—15 feet
Dockside depth—12 feet
Accepts transients—yes
Fix wooden docks—yes
Dockside power connections—30 and 50 amp
Dockside water connections—yes
Waste pump-out—yes
Showers—yes
Laundromat—yes
Gasoline—yes
Diesel—yes
Tackle store—yes
Restaurant—yes, seasonal (and three others within a mile)
Motel—yes

C-Quarters Marina, Carrabelle

Carrabelle Marina (850) 697-3351
www.carrabellemarina.com

Approach depth—8 feet
Dockside depth—6 feet
Accepts transients—yes, limited and during the week
Fixed wooden docks—yes
Dockside power connections—15, 30, and 50 amp
Dockside water connections—yes
Gasoline—yes
Mechanical repairs—limited to certain outboards
Boat ramp—yes
Parts store—yes
Restaurants—three within a mile

The Moorings at Carrabelle (850) 697-2800
www.mooringsCarrabelle.com

Approach depth—10-12 feet
Dockside depth—10 feet

Accepts transients—yes
Fixed wooden docks—yes
Dockside power connections—30 and 50 amp
Dockside water connections—yes
Waste pump-out—yes
Showers—yes
Laundromat—yes
Gasoline—yes
Diesel—yes
Boat ramp—yes
Swimming pool—yes
Ship's store—yes
Dive shop—for air fills and tank rentals
Restaurants—three within a mile
Motel—yes

The Carrabelle River forks around Davis Island—the island upstream from the Moorings. The navigable channel is across the river near the RDB. HAZARD *A 40-foot (stated by NOAA*

The Moorings at Carrabelle

and U.S. Coast Pilot) *clearance highway crosses over the Carrabelle River and touches down on Davis Island.* Postum Bayou is on the RDB, just downstream from the bridge. This 30-yard-wide bayou leads back out to St. George Sound on the western side of Timber Island. HAZARD *The water depth in Postum Bayou becomes very shallow, and there is a 12-foot overhead-clearance fixed bridge.* Nevertheless, there is about four feet of water depth in the first half-mile of the bayou. Highly recommended Julia Mae's Seafood Restaurant, (850) 697-3791, is less than one-quarter of a mile up the bayou in a yellow building with a few slips off the bayou. Beyond Julia Mae's restaurant, and up to the 12-foot-high clearance bridge, the water depth shallows to about three feet.

The Bridge Marina is on the RDB just beyond the Carrabelle River Bridge. There are a few sand bars in the river near this marina. Many small and mid-sized trailerable boats are stored at the Bridge Marina. The Bridge Marina has about a dozen slips, and the facility was recommended as a good place for mechanical repairs.

Bridge Marina (850) 697-3502

Approach depth—4-6 feet
Dockside depth—3-4 feet
Accepts transients—yes
Fixed wooden docks—yes
Dockside power connections—15 amp
Dockside water connections—yes
Mechanical repairs—yes
Below-waterline repairs—with a trailer
Boat ramp—yes
Ship's store—yes
Restaurant—one nearby

The Carrabelle River has no less than six to seven feet of water in the main channel at MLW, with some areas of much deeper water. Residential development on the banks of the Carrabelle River is tasteful. There are overhead power lines on the river slightly downriver from marker "G59." HAZARD *The overhead clearance of these power lines is stated to be 50 feet by the* U.S. Coast Pilot. There is a hard, sand boat ramp on the LDB between markers "G63" and "G65." The Crooked and the New rivers connect just beyond marker "R68." There is also another cul-de-sac waterway in between the mouths of the New and Crooked rivers.

New River

There are no aids to navigation on this river. If you are heading up the New River, the RDB side initially has more water depth (i.e., about eight feet at MLW) than the Crooked River side. As you go farther up the New River, there are a few patches where the water depth shallows to about four feet, although much of the river remains over eight to ten feet in depth. Typical of river bends, the outside of the bend generally has deeper water. The river water, like many rivers in the Big Bend, is very brown in color. This is not pollution but tannin coming from all the rich decaying vegetable material. About two miles up the river, the marsh grasses give way to more palmetto scrubs and longleaf pine plantations. Further upriver, the pine plantations give way to lovely live oak trees. There is also scattered residential development on the RDB. Some of those homes have boat docks and dry storage. Boats as long as 40 feet, with three-feet drafts, can be seen at some of these private docks.

HAZARD *About four miles into the New River, Burnt Bridge has an overhead clearance of about nine to ten feet at MHW. If you cannot*

Homes on the Carrabelle River

New River

negotiate beneath this steel-deck bridge, this is the end of the line on the lovely New River. A few shrimpers indicated that the New River has the best local places to hole up during an impending hurricane. And if you can negotiate beneath the Burnt Bridge, you will likely have this great and lovely hurricane hole all to yourself. The river becomes devoid of residential development, while live oaks border the riverbanks. Soon the live oaks give way to a longleaf pine forest. The river also remains deep (e.g., eleven to fourteen feet) and even widens somewhat after Burnt Bridge. In the next six miles of New River's RDB side, there are three nice picnic areas with hibachi grills and canoe landings.

Crooked River

After Carrabelle River marker "R68," the Crooked River forks off on the LDB side. This southwestern end of the Crooked River is much more shallow than the nearby New River. Finding enough water to enter the Crooked River was difficult. Treat the two small islands near the mouth as LDB (i.e., pass them on your right side going into the Crooked River). Initially aim for that cul-de-sac between the New and Crooked rivers. As you approach the sand bar near the mouth of the cul-de-sac, make a hard right turn into the Crooked River. You will likely only have four to five feet of water at MLW in many places. There are a few unofficial navigation aids in the Crooked River. The three standing pipes, along with an exposed sand bar, should be treated like RDB. HAZARD *The southwesternmost three miles of the Crooked River are shallow, loaded with sand bars and a hard-to-follow, shifting river channel.* Furthermore, the lower three or four miles of this river are nothing more than unattractive salt marshes. The river is fairly wide, at about 60 yards. If you

are not discouraged by the numerous shallows of the Crooked River, you'll surely be thwarted by a five-foot overhead-clearance bridge six miles upriver.

Lanark Village

Lanark Village is a small coastal community about four to six miles northeast of Carrabelle. Between 1942 and 1946, Lanark Village was quite a busy place. At nearby Camp Gordon Johnston, entire army divisions trained before overseas deployment during World War II. In late 1943, the 4th Infantry Division practiced assault landings at nearby Dog Island and Carrabelle Beach. This was the 4th Division's last training on U.S. soil before assaulting Utah Beach in Normandy about six months later—on D-day. Unit camaraderie was developed here, and heavy hearts departed. A nearby museum commemorates our World War II heroes.

A narrow, six-mile-long, partially submerged bar, Lanark Reef or Bird Island, parallels the shore less than a mile offshore. There is a shallow-draft access route to Lanark Village on the southwest side of this long bar. HAZARD *An unlighted red and an unlighted green daymark show the narrow passage southwest of Bird Island and northeast of another sand bar.* Follow this passage, favoring the port daymark and port side of the channel, until near shore and near an RV park and campground on the mainland. A red buoy should also be spied. Make a 90-degree turn to your starboard (or the northeast) after that red buoy. The next leg is the shallowest part of this run at about three feet deep. There are two jetties about a mile to the northeast, flagging the entrance of the Lanark Village Boat Club basin. The longer jetty, about 300 yards long, is on the LDB side of the entrance channel. The boat basin has floating wooden docks and a boat ramp. A covered picnic pavilion, convenience store, and gas station are also nearby. Besides requiring less than three feet of draft, this well-protected basin fits nothing much larger than 26 feet.

Lanark Village Boat Club (850) 697-8246

Approach depth—3 feet
Dockside depth—shallow
Accepts transients—yes
Floating wooden docks—yes
Dockside water connections—yes
Boat ramp—yes
Variety store—nearby

Turkey Point

The Turkey Point Channel is about five miles northeast of the eastern tip of Dog Island, and it is our easternmost channel in this chapter. The Florida State University Marine Laboratory is about six miles northeast of Lanark Village and at the head of this channel. All of the navigation aids in Turkey Point Channel are red and even numbered. The red paint on the daymarks was almost bleached out when we visited in October 2001. HAZARD *An intermittent spoil area is on the green side (i.e., west side) of the channel and starts across from aid "R6."* Large Turkey Point Shoal sits on the eastern side of the channel. The marks go from "R2" to "R14," and the water depths in the entire channel are good, at six to nine feet. A small pool, housing the Florida State University Marine Laboratory Research Facility on the LDB, sits at the head of this channel. The pool is about 60 yards across, with reasonably good anchoring depths even close to shore (e.g., six to nine feet, MLW) and before a very low-clearance highway bridge. I would consider this pool at the head of Turkey Point Channel a very good emergency anchorage. The Florida State University Marine Laboratory Research Facility has one serious offshore boat and three much smaller pontoon boats. This facility provides the support (i.e., with the boats and the dormitories) for a wide variety of oceanographic educational groups—from middle school to elderly groups. Their typical programs last anywhere from a weekend to a week.

CHAPTER 7

Western Apalachee Bay and Alligator Harbor

This chapter covers an irregularly shaped part of the Florida coastline from about west longitude 84° and 13 minutes to 84° and 28 minutes and on the western side of Apalachee Bay. Even though we are only covering about fifteen nautical miles of longitude, there are more than 25 miles of Gulf Coast shoreline, six channels, four bays, and one major river—the Ochlockonee—and numerous shoals in this area. There are also six marinas in this area. An educational, open-to-the-public aquarium is located in Panacea.

Due to the nature of the coastline and the many shallow areas offshore, the distance between these marinas and the "safe open water" (i.e., shoal-free water) is sometimes considerable (i.e., sometimes over five miles). Apalachee Bay is notorious for being rough. However, these western arms and fingers that extend through the many shoals and to the west can be quite protected. If your boat's draft and/or the tide permit, you might even find a few passages through some of the calmer waters along this western shore of Apalachee Bay. But first, study NOAA chart 11405 carefully.

Alligator Harbor

Alligator Harbor is a large body of water, about one mile wide and four miles long, with a narrow entry that is not easily spied from the Gulf of Mexico. Arrive at way point 29.55.270N/84.27.141W off "R2." From the multiple-pile "R2" structure, head in a northeast direction toward "R8." The buildings seen ahead of you are on the mainland (i.e., on the

RDB of Alligator Harbor) near St. Teresa. Only when you near "R8" will the entrance to Alligator Harbor become obvious. The channel makes a near hairpin right turn at "R8," in nine to eleven feet of water, toward the harbor. In the Alligator Harbor Channel, most of the navigation aids will be red, forewarning of a long, submerged, then partially submerged, and then partially exposed sand bar extending miles out from Alligator Point. Initially, the Alligator Harbor Channel depths vary between five to seven feet at MLW. In Alligator Harbor Channel, there are many more navigation aids than those depicted on the NOAA chart. Once inside Alligator Harbor, none of the aids are lighted. The water depths also decrease to as little as four feet as the navigation-aid numbers get larger (i.e., around aid "R30"). The bottom characteristic of Alligator Harbor is a layer of about two inches of soft muck over a layer of harder mud.

The last navigation aide is "G39," slightly past Pelican Bay Yacht Club and Marina (formerly Alligator Bay Marina). The short channel leading to Pelican Bay Yacht Club and Marina is on the LDB near "R36 and G37." This channel has about five feet of water at MLW. The most visible building at the marina facility is the large, faded-green-colored, high-and-dry boat-storage building. This facility has about 45 slips and can accommodate boats as large as 35 feet. The Pelican Bay Yacht Club and Marina can pull smaller boats with a seven-ton forklift and the larger boats with a 40-ton open-ended travel lift. The facility

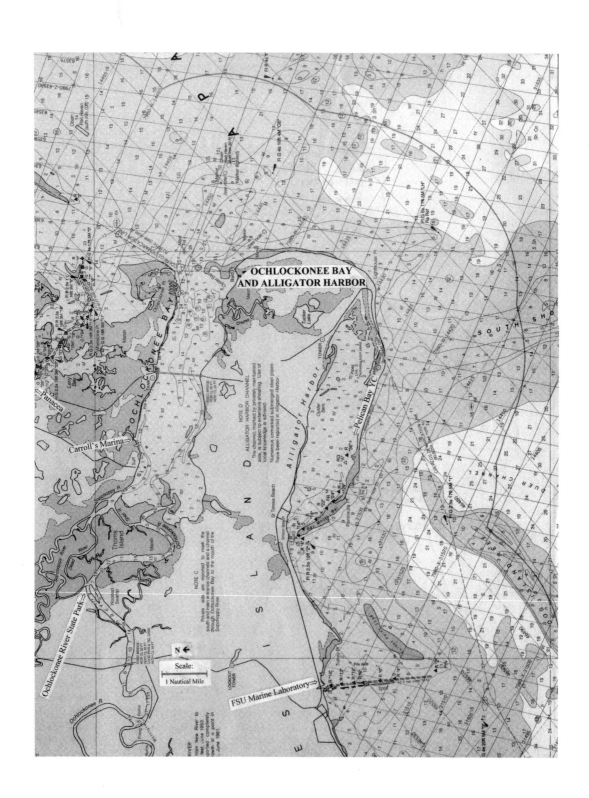

**OCHLOCKONEE BAY
AND ALLIGATOR HARBOR**

Panacea

Carroll's Marina →

Ochlockonee River State Park →

FSU Marine Laboratory →

Pelican Bay YC

NOTE D

ALLIGATOR HARBOR CHANNEL
The channel, marked by privately maintained aids, is subject to extensive shoaling. Use of local knowledge is advised.
Numerous unmarked submerged steel pipes have been reported in Alligator Harbor.

NOTE C:
Private aids are reported to mark the south and main entrance channels and a channel through Ochlockonee Bay to the mouth of the Sopchoppy River.

N ←

Scale:

1 Nautical Mile

LOOKOUT
TOWER

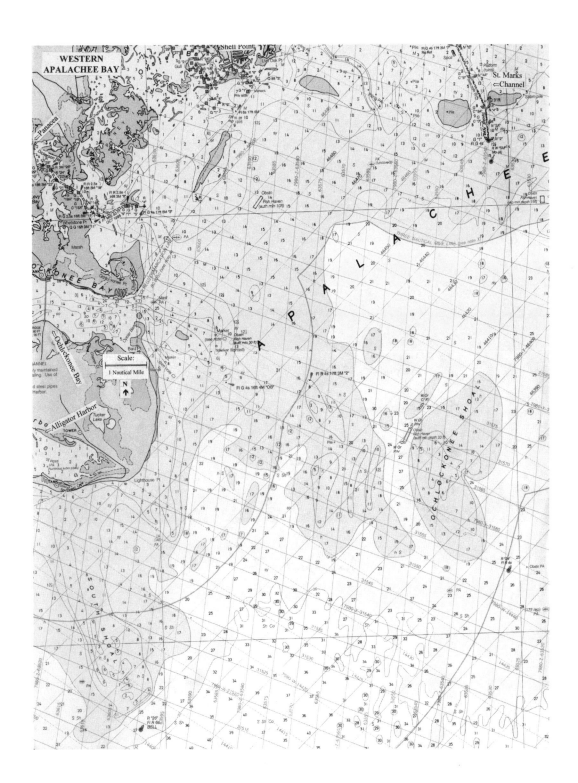

WESTERN
APALACHEE BAY

Scale:

1 Nautical Mile

N

Ochlockonee River and Ochlockonee River State Park

has a reasonably sized shipyard. Their Club House restaurant serves meals but operates on a limited schedule, and it's closed all day on Monday and Tuesday. The restaurant/club-house is available to transient boaters.

Pelican Bay Yacht Club and Marina
(850) 349-2511
www.pelicanbayweb.com

Approach depth—4 feet
Dockside depth—4 feet
Accepts transients—yes
Floating and fixed wooden docks—yes
Dockside power connections—15 and 30 amp
Dockside water connections—yes
Showers—yes
Gasoline—yes
Diesel—yes
Mechanical repairs—limited (with nearby con tractor)
Below-waterline repairs—yes (with 40-ton travel lift)
Boat ramp—yes
Variety store—yes
Restaurant/clubhouse—yes

HAZARD *Outside of Alligator Harbor, from the southwest to the east, there are scattered shoals.* Turkey Point Shoal is about two to four miles southwest of the Alligator Harbor entrance. Dog Island Reef is about four to six nautical miles south and southwest of the Alligator Harbor entrance. South Shoal extends south-southeast of the southernmost point near Alligator Harbor (i.e., Southwest Cape). There is another short shoal extending southeast from Lighthouse Point. This shoal has a few daymarks close to shore. In Apalachee Bay, Ochlockonee Shoal is about 10 miles east of Alligator Harbor. Water depths over Ochlockonee Shoal range from

three to 17 feet. There are also a series of smaller shoals in between Ochlockonee Shoal and the entrance to Ochlockonee Bay. Depending on your boat's draft requirement, you may or may not be able to compromise with (some of) these shoals. In this regard, you need to study NOAA chart 11405 very carefully.

Ochlockonee Bay and River

Ochlockonee Bay is about the same size as Alligator Harbor (i.e., over a mile wide and four miles long). The name Ochlockonee means something like "yellow water." The Sopchoppy and Ochlockonee rivers feed into Ochlockonee Bay. The Ochlockonee River extends over 100 miles from the coast, past Tallahassee, and well into Georgia. A small boat with limited overhead-clearance require-ments can sail, in the most scenic Apalachicola National Forest, from Ochlockonee Bay to the dam at Lake Talquin—or about 65 miles up the beautiful Ochlockonee River.

In the Gulf, a good navigation aid to Ochlockonee Bay is "OB." At way point 29.56.091N/84.17.987W, treat "OB" like a green daymark. "OB" is in seven to eight feet of water at MLW. A marked channel with about six feet of water depth, and with many unlighted marks, starts after "OB," and this is not shown on the NOAA chart. Also, the *U.S. Coast Pilot* indicates "craft drawing up to six feet experienced no trouble." The first marked pair of aids is "G1 and R2," on a heading of about 345 degrees from "OB." The next pair of marks is on a heading of 295 degrees, and the water depth is about six to seven feet at MLW. This sinuous channel makes several doglegs. The first dogleg to the left is at "G7 and R8." There is a dogleg to the right at "G9 and R10." After "G11," and near junction marker "B," our channel connects to another channel entering Ochlockonee Bay from the south. We are in the "preferred channel," hence we should be treating this "B" like a green navigation aid (and those in the other intersecting channel should be treating this "B" like a red aid). This second channel runs much closer to the shore. If you lose your bearings in this area—and it's easy to do—look for the turquoise water tower on the north shore and near the Ochlockonee Bay Bridge as a landmark.

Some channel water depths are quite deep, but there are some patches as shallow as five to seven feet of water. Often ripples on the surface of the water (i.e., if the tide is strongly ebbing or flowing) are an indication of these abrupt changes in water depth. There also may be fishermen in small boats fishing over these underwater ledges. "G21" is just inside the fishing pier and public beach off Ochlockonee Point. There is a residential development with five narrow and shallow canals. None of these channels are recommended for larger seagoing vessels.

The Ochlockonee River Channel continues to be chock-full of reversing doglegs. HAZARD *There are still many shoals to be avoided.* One of the bigger shoals is west of "G25." The shoals start thinning out about one mile before the bridge. The last mark before the 35-feet-high Ochlockonee Bay Bridge is "R36." Water depth in this area is about eleven to thirteen feet at MLW. After the Ochlockonee Bay Bridge, the channel veers to the RDB (or north) side of the bay and shallows considerably to four- to five-foot readings at MLW. Closer to Carroll's Bayside Marina, the water depth increases to eleven to twelve feet of water. Carroll's Bayside Marina is located in a small cove across from

"G57" and west of a highly visible large tan-colored condominium complex. The marina channel has its own set of private navigation aids on white posts with red-painted color bands in about four to five feet of water. Carroll's has about 30 slips and can accommodate 30- to 40-footers. The marina also has a small high-and-dry storage building.

Carroll's Bayside Marina (850) 984-5548
www.baysidemarina.net

Approach depth—4 feet
Dockside depth—4-5 feet
Accepts transients—limited
Floating wooden docks—yes
Dockside power connections—no
Dockside water connections—yes
Gasoline—yes
Diesel—yes
Mechanical repairs—nearby contractors
Below-waterline repairs—with forklift and lim-
    ited to nine tons
Bait shop—yes
Café—seasonal and open on weekends

There is a small private harbor about one-fifth of a mile up the bay from Carroll's, on the bay's LDB. About one mile beyond Carroll's, near marker "G63," there are two river routes out of Ochlockonee Bay. The channel that we've been in is the Sopchoppy River Channel. If you wish to find the Ochlockonee River Channel, you must depart the Sopchoppy Channel in a south-westerly heading from "G63." There is about ten feet of water near "G63," and much more water than is indicated on the NOAA chart 11405. The "best" chart for depicting the location of channels in Ochlockonee Bay (and near the mouth of the bay) is not the NOAA chart but the *Boating and Angling Guide to Apalachicola*

Bay, published by McShane Communications, Inc., and several state of Florida agencies. The last navigation aid on the Sopchoppy River is "R66," about a half-mile farther than the connecting route to the Ochlockonee River.

The Sopchoppy and Ochlockonee Rivers generally parallel each other for more than 15 miles. In the first three miles of both rivers, there are no less than three side-spur bayou routes (e.g., the Shell River and the Dead River—twice) connecting them. None of these bayou routes is more than two miles in length. We explored the uppermost Sopchoppy-Ochlockonee Dead River-connecting bayou and found a comfortable six to twelve feet of water depth, MLW. In most places, this connecting bayou is about 40 yards wide.

HAZARD *There is a low, six-foot, overhead-clearance bridge on the curvy Sopchoppy about ten miles beyond the end of the Ochlockonee Bay.* The *U.S. Coast Pilot* indicates that "four feet can be carried on the Sopchoppy River to this low bridge." The Ochlockonee River is generally "more navigable" and about 150 yards wide nearer the mouth. The first four or five miles of the Ochlockonee are rather bland unless you are into salt marshes and savannas. But this part of the river belies the beauty farther up.

At Ochlockonee River State Park, on the LDB and about four miles from the bay, the savanna grassland turn into a more picturesque pine forest. In the park, and on the upper Dead River bayou, there is a fishing pier in about five feet of water. But the park doesn't permit vessels to tie up to this dock.

Narrow private channels off Ochlockonee Bay

Vessels can visit the park only if they can beach at one of the several nice sandy beaches on the LDB of the Ochlockonee River and use one of the three "walk-up" stairways to access this beautiful park. If you do this, you ought to throw out a stern anchor. Please read our section in chapter 17 on setting a Mediterranean Mooring. The picnic area is one of the prettiest anywhere. The park also has a lovely campground and canoe rentals.

Farther up the Ochlockonee River, some residential development starts to sprout on the RDB about a mile past Ochlockonee River State Park. HAZARD *A U.S. Coast Pilot-and NOAA-stated ten-foot vertical-clearance bridge is two miles past the park.* There are only two more bridges over the Ochlockonee

River all the way to the dam at Lake Talquin—almost another 50 miles upstream. These two upcoming bridges have no less than 15 feet of vertical clearance. So if you can squeeze beneath this first ten-foot-clearance bridge, there should be no more significant height obstacles until that dam 50 miles upstream.

In parts of the lower Ochlockonee River, water depths are usually no less than six feet, and there are several deeper holes (e.g., over 20 feet and even a few patches with over 40 feet of water depth). The river remains very wide, but there are a few submerged trees and large limbs lurking beneath the surface. If you are unsure where to navigate, and you are not in a river curve, the center of this wide river is likely the best place to be. This rule of thumb applies to all of these rivers,

Dead River near Ochlockonee River State Park

but especially to the Ochlockonee River. The longleaf pines start to slowly thin out and are being replaced with a hardwood forest, containing much cypress, along the shoreline. HAZARD *The remains of an old railroad trestle appear to block the river about two miles up from the highway bridge.* Nevertheless, near the RDB side, there is a 30-foot-wide gap in these old overrun-with-vegetation bridge ruins. There is also a boat ramp on the RDB side in a large pool beyond the railroad-bridge ruins.

The Crooked River soon veers off on the LDB side. This is the same Crooked River that meets with the New River to become the Carrabelle River (see chapter 6). This eerie, very sparsely inhabited, and deep part of the tidal Crooked River is quite different from the shallow tidal-flats section 25 miles away near Carrabelle. HAZARD *Two miles from the Ochlockonee River, the remnants of another long-abandoned railroad trestle cross the Crooked River.* It's about ten more miles on this prettier part of the Crooked River to that low five-foot vertical-clearance highway bridge northeast of Carrabelle. Besides the low bridge, river overgrowth and shallows make the Crooked River impassable back to Carrabelle. But this might be a most interesting canoe or dinghy trip.

Continuing on the Ochlockonee River, the Tallahassee Boating Club is on the RDB about a mile past the Ochlockonee railroad trestle ruins. This club has a ramp, dock, trailer park, and pavilion. On just about any day, many small, bass, fishing boats can be found in this part of the Ochlockonee River. Overhead power lines cross the Ochlockonee River, but the clearance is notably more than the Ochlockonee River highway bridge. The river remains wide and depths are very comfortable—sometimes at over a dozen feet deep. This comfortable water depth is usually sustained for much of the river's width. The many enchanting wide bends in the Ochlockonee constantly pique your curiosity to explore the scene just around the next bend. The trees along the shore become mostly mixed hardwoods. Unlike the sometimes swift-flowing Apalachicola River, there is only about a knot of current in the Ochlockonee. Like the New and Crooked rivers, the Ochlockonee contains much tannin. And like the New River, much of the Ochlockonee extends into the Apalachicola National Forest. About 20 miles west of Tallahassee, the Jackson Bluff Dam on Lake Talquin limits small-boat navigation coming up from the Gulf of Mexico. There are over a half-dozen boat ramps and a handful of small fish camps along this upper part of the Ochlockonee River. Ed and Bernice's Fish Camp, on the RDB, is the last fish camp before the dam. This fish camp also has a boat ramp.

Panacea

The town of Panacea is on Dickerson Bay and north of Ochlockonee Bay. In western Apalachee Bay, and in about ten feet of water (MLW), arrive at way point 30.00.362N/ 84.18.653W, off unlighted aid "R2." After "R2," head 265 degrees to the next distant pair of marks—"G3 and R4." "G3" is a lighted navigation aid. There is a pleasantly surprising number—about six—of lighted navigation aids in this channel. A boat ramp should be seen on the LDB, off marker "G19A." Soon you'll be in Dickerson Bay. The last marker before Panacea Harbor Marina is "G29." At MLW, we read about ten to eleven feet of water depth nearly all of the way in this channel. The *U.S. Coast Pilot* only stated a 5.3-foot depth in the middle of the channel. A large condominium complex sits just south of the marina. Panacea Harbor Marina was a bit bedraggled when we first visited. But the facility had just come under new management when we arrived. On our second visit, about four months later, many notable improvements had already been made. They had about 44 slips and were expanding. They can accommodate up to about 40-footers. Boats up to 26 feet can usually be hauled out with their forklift. The marina has a large beige-colored high-and-dry storage building.

Panacea Harbor Marina (850) 984-5844

Approach depth—6-7 feet

Accepts transients—yes
Fixed wooden docks—yes
Dockside power connections—30 amp
Dockside water connections—yes
Waste pump-out—yes
Showers—yes
Gasoline—yes
Diesel—yes
Mechanical repairs—with contractors
Below-waterline repairs—yes (with forklift up to 10 tons and less than 30 feet)
Boat ramp—nearby
Ship's store—under refurbishment
Restaurants—two nearby

The town of Panacea has two motels and two restaurants—the Harbor House Restaurant (right next to the marina) and Posey's

Old railroad trestle across Ochlockonee River

Panacea Harbor Marina

Restaurant (also a motel). An IGA grocery store is about ten blocks north of the marina and on the main highway. The post office is a couple blocks farther north. A Laundromat, liquor store, and small marine-supply store are also in town.

The Gulf Specimen Marine Lab Aquarium, (850) 984-5297 (www.gulfspecimen.org), has about 30,000 gallons of seawater. There are about 50 fish tanks in four separate buildings. This aquarium is open to the public. The laboratory is only about two and a half blocks north of the Panacea Harbor Marina. This facility emphasizes biodiversity and displays some of the unique smaller creatures of our seas, as well as a few of the typical larger marine animals (e.g., shark, grouper, and large sea turtles). If you're in Panacea, this educational facility is definitely worth the visit.

Shell Point and Spring Creek

Hazard *The hodgepodge of numerous unlighted navigation aids within a mile and a half south and west of Shell Point is most confusing.* The area looks like "daymark city." In some instances, you might find the nearest aid to your position is not "in" the current navigation-aid "numbering sequence." This could be because of either a nearby intercepting channel or because your channel is doubling back. Confusing? Yes. Basically, there are three separate winding channels guiding you around the many small tidal flats and shoals in this area. The

NORTHWESTERN
APALACHEE BAY

Scale:

1 Nautical Mile

N ←

Shell
Point

←To St. Marks

Panacea→

CHANNELS NEAR SHELL POINT

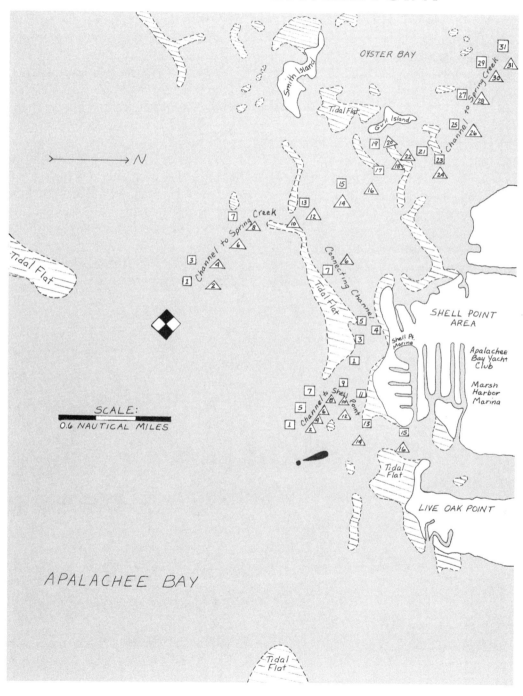

southernmost, and by far the longest, channel extends northwestward from Apalachee Bay into Spring Creek. The northernmost channel extends from Apalachee Bay to the protected waters inside the Shell Point head of land. Near Shell Point proper, a third channel connects from the Shell Point Channel, generally in a westward direction, back toward that Spring Creek Channel.

Although not to the NOAA scale, and missing many of the doglegs, we have included a rough sketch of these three channels to assist you—especially near where they connect to each other. On the positive side, many of the navigation aids are paired (e.g., "G23 and R24"). When the gap between a pair of aids is especially narrow, that is a strong indication to strictly honor those cues and don't take any shortcuts in this area.

Spring Creek

The Spring Creek navigation aid in Apalachee Bay is a lighted daymark with four diamonds (two vertically oriented green and two horizontally oriented white diamonds) all nested on a larger diamond placard at way point 30.02.341N/84.17.623W. This navigation aid should be treated like a green marker (i.e., passed on the left side upon leaving Apalachee Bay for Spring Creek). The depth at this marker is ten to eleven feet at MLW. The initial heading after this daymark is about 300 degrees magnetic. Near "G3 and R4" there is the first of many doglegs. This first dogleg is to starboard. After that first lighted navigation aid in Apalachee Bay, no other aids in this long Spring Creek Channel are lighted. Somewhere between "R10" and "R12," that "connecting channel" meets this

Spring Creek Marina

Spring Creek Channel. That connecting channel heads in an easterly direction toward Shell Point. Water depths in the Spring Creek Channel are about three to four feet at MLW. HAZARD *After "R20" there is a hairpin turn to starboard and toward "R22."* After "R22 and G21," there is a right-angle turn back to port and toward "G23 and R24." Again be careful at "G23 and R24." This is the shallowest spot in Spring Creek Channel, at only about three feet of water at MLW. The next several daymarks will be fairly tightly packed together—and a giveaway signal that you should heed them closely.

Back at "G27 and R28," the water depth increases to seven feet and holds that depth for the remainder of Oyster Bay. Somewhere after "R30," we make the transition between Oyster Bay and Spring Creek. The water depths, once in Spring Creek proper, are about four to nine feet at MLW. Spring Creek Marina is on the LDB of Spring Creek and about three-quarters of a mile past the last official navigation aid, "R38." The marina has about 32 slips and can possibly handle a few 40-footers. There are two slightly off-parallel entry canals to Spring Creek Marina. The farther-upcreek entry, angling away from the southern entry, has about four to six feet of water depth. This canal also leads to a small workboat area and another boat ramp. With all of the twists and turns to get in here, these two canals are well protected from any inclement sea and weather conditions that may be occurring in seemingly distant Apalachee Bay.

Spring Creek Marina (850) 926-6035

Approach depth—4-5 feet
Dockside depth—2-4 feet

Accepts transients—very limited
Floating and fixed wooden docks—yes
Dockside power connections—30 amp
Dockside water connections—yes
Showers—yes
Laundromat—yes
Boat ramp—only private use

The navigable portion of Spring Creek continues about a half-mile past Spring Creek Marina. A few floating and fixed wooden docks, Spears Seafood Distributor, a boat-launch ramp, and a nearby trailer park are near the head of navigation of Spring Creek.

Shell Point

In order to arrive at the entrance to Shell Point in northwestern Apalachee Bay, arrive at way point 30.02.825N/84.17.070W—off the outside Shell Point Channel daymark. This daymark is a "spider daymark" structure with a flashing red light. The channel starts out with about eight to ten feet of water and then the depths drop to about five to seven feet at MLW. After navigation aids "G7 and R8," this Shell Point Channel has an intersection. The aids veering off to your right, "G9 and R10," are the continuation of the Shell Point Channel leading to Shell Point. The last set of daymarks in this channel, leading behind the head of land behind Shell Point, is "G15 and R16." Beyond these official marks, there are more unofficial navigation aids. Most of these are fairly easy to figure out (e.g., the ones with a red stripe should be treated like red aids).

Back at "G9" in the Shell Point Channel, the aids bearing off to your left, or to the west, are in that channel connecting to the Spring Creek Channel. This is where the connecting channel "begins," and the navigation aids at this end of the connecting channel are the aids with the "lower" numbers. (See our sketch.) The first navigation aid in this channel is "G1" and the general initial heading is close to due west. Depths in this connecting channel are five to eight feet at MLW. This connecting channel is the most straightforward of the three channels in this area. The last set of navigation aids in this connecting channel, "R6 and G7," is in four to ten feet at MLW. At this point the aids outlining the Spring Creek Channel are easily seen. Leaving this connecting channel, we intercept the Spring Creek Channel between Spring Creek navigation aids "R10 and R12." The *U.S. Coast Pilot* indicated five-foot depths in the channel.

When we twice arrived at Shell Point Marina, there had been no management for about a half a year—and it showed. The place was becoming quite run-down and there were no services. By the time you read this, hopefully somebody will have purchased this potentially nice marina and started fixing things up. The marina has the potential to dock several 40-footers in its protected basin. A nice swimming beach off Shell Point is barely 50 yards from the marina basin. There is no town or village on or near Shell Point. The Shell Point area is just a residential beach development with no commercial services. The U.S. Coast Guard Auxiliary does have a flotilla building on Shell Point west of the marina.

There are another four "residential boat canals," with numerous private docks, north of the main Shell Point Marina canal. An unofficial channel with unofficial markers, having about five to seven feet of water depth at MLW, heads north to these four other east-west channels. The last, and northernmost,

east-west channel houses Marsh Harbor Marina and Apalachee Bay Yacht Club. These are two private facilities. Marsh Harbor Marina is much larger, with about 110 slips, and is capable of accommodating 40- and 50-footers. Farther up this channel, the docks of the smaller Apalachee Bay Yacht Club connect to Marsh Harbor. Donaven's Cove Restaurant, (850) 926-9711, is the nearest eating establishment to any of the boating facilities in the Shell Point area. This fine-dining restaurant is about a mile down the road from Apalachee Bay Yacht Club.

Shell Point Resort Marina, Motel, and Waterfront Restaurant (out of business)

Approach depth—4-8 feet
Dockside depth—3-5 feet
Accepts transients—unknown
Floating wooden docks—in disrepair
Dockside power connections—no
Dockside water connections—no

Marsh Harbor Marina (850) 926-7811

Approach depth—4-7 feet
Dockside depth—4-5 feet
Accepts transients—yes
Floating wooden and concrete docks—yes
Dockside power connections—30 amp and
    twin 30 amp
Dockside water connections—yes
Waste pump-out—coming
Showers—yes
Laundromat—nearby
Gasoline—coming
Diesel—coming
Clubhouse—yes

Apalachee Bay Yacht Club (229) 377-7728
www.tfn.net/abyc

Approach depth—4-7 feet
Dockside depth—4-5 feet
Accepts transients—yes
Floating wooden and concrete docks—yes
Dockside power connections—30 amp
Dockside water connections—yes
Showers—yes
Clubhouse—yes

Fenholloway River

CHAPTER 8

The St. Marks Region and Eastern Apalachee Bay

This chapter covers eastern Apalachee Bay and the four rivers flowing into it—the St. Marks, Aucilla, Econfina, and Fenholloway. On this swath of the Gulf of Mexico, there is virtually no development, residential or commercial, along the coast. Furthermore, the rivers covered in this chapter have almost no commercial development and very little residential development on their banks—there's more likely to be a few outposts. This is truly the heart of Florida's Nature Coast And this coast—so far, spared from human encroachment—is quite beautiful.

Over 460 years ago, in 1539, Hernando De Soto made a trip from his winter outpost near Tallahassee and visited the present-day St. Marks Lighthouse area. De Soto hung a banner on some trees to mark the location of the St. Marks River for the Spanish fleet that was to possibly pick up his army at a later date. That never happened, because De Soto went wreaking havoc throughout the entire southeast in his insatiable search for gold.

In 1829, construction of the present limestone-block lighthouse was started. In 1842, eroding shoreline forced the structure to be relocated to its present site. In 1863, Union troops burned a large portion of the building's interior and rendered the beacon inoperable to the Confederates. In 1866, soon after the Civil War, the lighthouse was restored to service. It soon resumed its critical role in Gulf Coast navigation. Today, this 80-foot tower,

with its 15-mile-visible beacon, is a watchful sentinel orienting us boaters on Apalachee Bay.

St. Marks Channel

From northern Apalachee Bay, arrive at way point 30.01.480N/84.10.530W and continue on a northerly heading (slightly west of due north) in well-marked St. Marks Channel. There are more official navigation aids in this channel than are depicted on NOAA chart 11406. There is also a good set of range marks. Slightly past St. Marks Lighthouse, near "G11 and R12," the Gulf channel becomes more like a river channel. On the LDB side, at "R12," there is about a one-third-mile-long side channel, about 25 yards wide, leading to a small turning basin. In this turning basin there is a wide concrete boat ramp with ample parking and a steel floating dock about 15 feet long. Water depths in this side channel are about three to four feet at MLW.

The easily navigable St. Marks River Channel continues for about another five miles to the junction of the Wakulla River. The *U.S. Coast Pilot* indicates a 10-foot midchannel controlling depth and a five-and-a-half-foot depth off midchannel to the fuel terminals beyond St. Marks. The St. Marks River has an ample number of navigation aids. A handful of these aids are lighted, making day or night navigation into the St. Marks River a calm and easy proposition. Markers

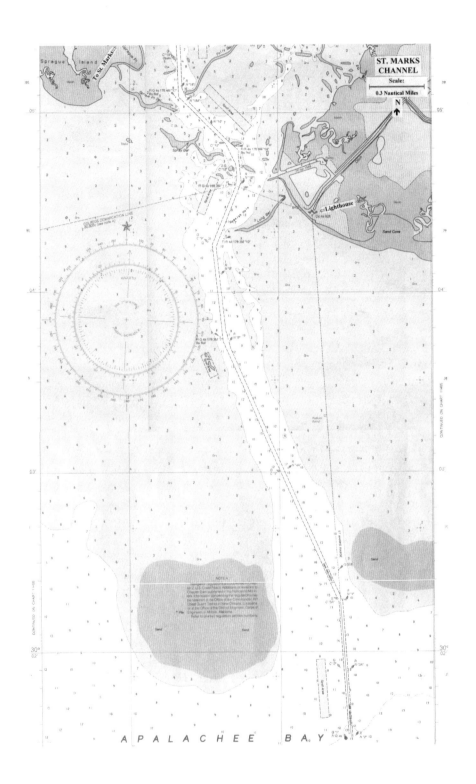

ST. MARKS
CHANNEL

Scale:

0.3 Nautical Miles

N

Lighthouse

A P A L A C H E E   B A Y

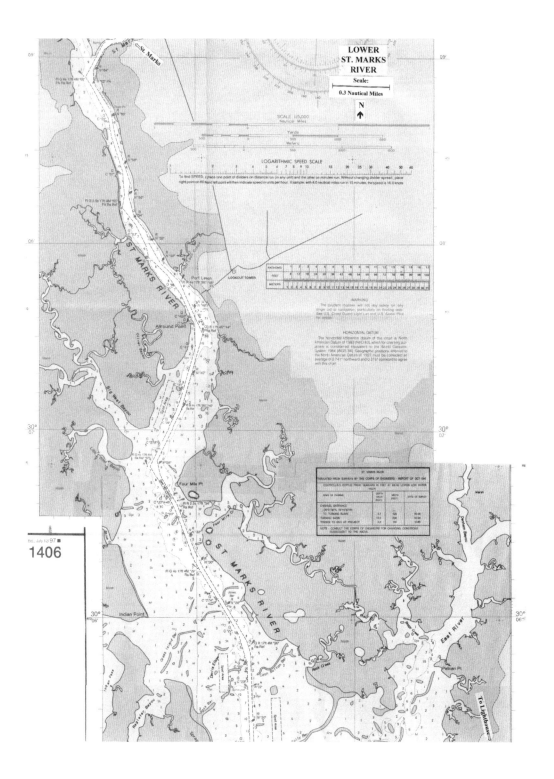

LOWER
ST. MARKS
RIVER

Scale:

0.3 Nautical Miles

N

1406

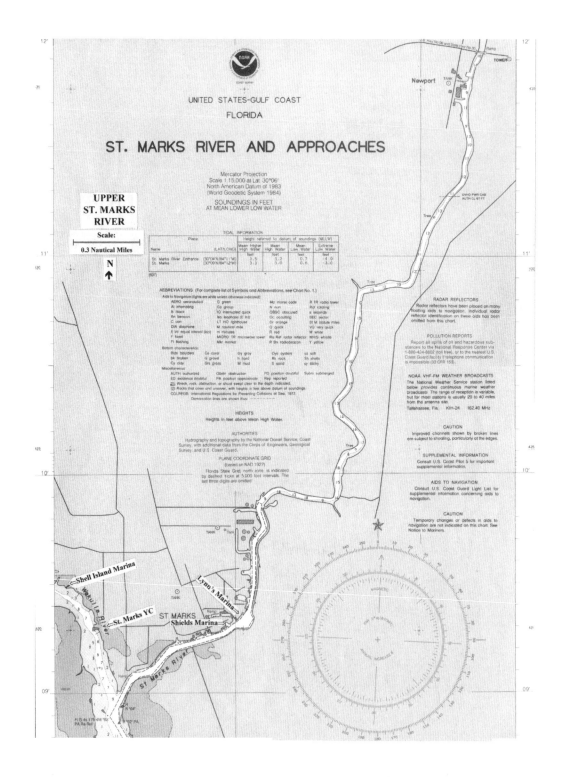

UNITED STATES-GULF COAST

FLORIDA

ST. MARKS RIVER AND APPROACHES

Mercator Projection
Scale 1:15,000 at Lat. 30°06'
North American Datum of 1983
(World Geodetic System 1984)

SOUNDINGS IN FEET
AT MEAN LOWER LOW WATER

**UPPER
ST. MARKS
RIVER**

Scale:

0.3 Nautical Miles

N

ST. MARKS

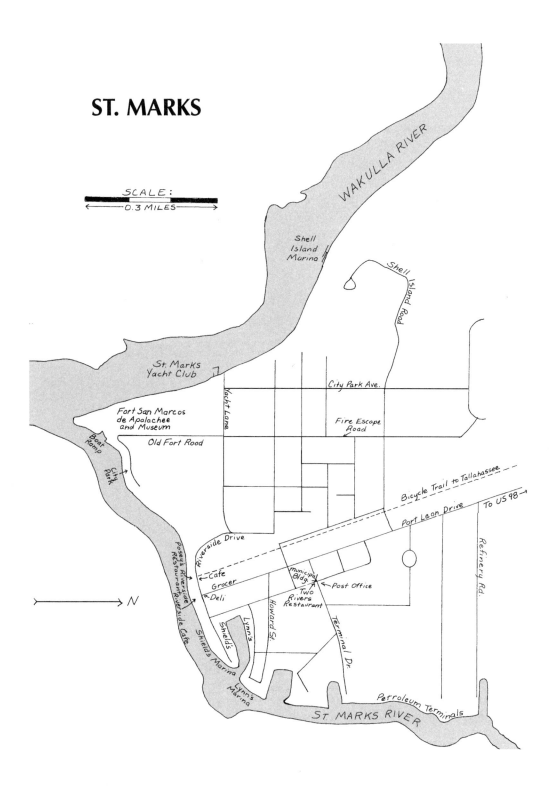

Central St. Marks

St. Marks Lighthouse

"G63 and R64" are just before the Wakulla and the St. Marks rivers split, and we found about 15 feet of depth at MLW.

Wakulla River

The Wakulla River, entering from the RDB side of the St. Marks, is the wider river. It is not difficult to find the Wakulla's channel for the first mile past the junction with the St. Marks River. And within this mile section of the Wakulla, there are two boating facilities. On the Wakulla's LDB, the St. Marks Yacht Club is the first facility and Shell Island Fish Camp and Marina is the second. Shell Island Marina houses many workboats and has a high-and-dry storage building and a trailer park. Some slips are covered and others are open. Shell Island Marina has about 40 slips and can accommodate up to about a 55-footer. The St. Marks Yacht Club has about a dozen and a half slips, many covered docks, and a few 40-footers berthed.

St. Marks Yacht Club (850) 925-6606

Approach depth—5-6 feet
Accepts transients—no
Fixed wooden dock—yes
Dockside power connections—15, 30, and 50 amp
Dockside water connections—yes
Pool—yes
Showers—yes
Clubhouse—yes

Shell Island Marina, Wakulla River

Shell Island Fish Camp and Marina (850) 925-6226

Approach depth—5-6 feet
Accepts transients—yes
Floating wooden docks—yes
Dockside power connections—15 amp
Dockside water connections—limited
Showers—yes
Gasoline—yes
Mechanical repairs—only outboard motor work
Below-waterline repairs—with a forklift to 28 feet
Boat ramp—yes
Variety/ship's store—yes
Motel and cottages—yes

Lacking navigation aids, it's not easy to find the deep channel on the Wakulla River after the Shell Island Fish Camp and Marina. We couldn't find the channel upstream from Shell Island. But Alan at Shell Island Fish Camp says, "It's there." It's closer to the RDB side. The *U.S. Coast Pilot* states, "A draft of seven feet can be taken upriver for 0.4 miles, and [a draft] of about three feet taken to [the second bridge]." There is also much sea grass and hydrilla in the shallow Wakulla River—and this has a potential to foul your propeller. So it's not surprising, with all of the sea grasses, that the Wakulla River is home to many manatees. Various species of hardwood trees grace the shores of the Wakulla River.

If you can make it beneath the first low bridge (i.e., with about eight to ten feet of overhead clearance at MHW), about two miles beyond Shell Island, there is another beautiful three miles to a second low bridge. The Wakulla River is almost crystal clear here. A fence across the entire river just past this second bridge intentionally restricts all waterborne navigation. Inaccessible Wakulla

Springs, one of the largest springs in the world, pumps about 250,000 gallons per minute into this river. The Apalachee Indian name "Wakulla" roughly translates to "mysterious waters."

St. Marks River and St. Marks

Back at markers "G63 and R64," making a right turn and following the LDB will lead you into the St. Marks River. A small dock and a boat ramp are just inside the entry to the St. Marks River, on the St. Marks RDB. There is ample boat-trailer parking in this area. The St. Marks River City Park and covered pavilion are less than a quarter mile upstream from the boat ramp on the RDB of the St. Marks River.

This boat ramp is also very near the Fort San Marcos de Apalachee Florida State Park and Museum (and more on the LDB of the Wakulla River). Around 1633, Spanish Franciscan friars arrived in this area and constructed seven missions. In 1639, waterborne commercial traffic aboard a Spanish frigate connected St. Augustine to the Port of Apalachee (soon to be known as the Port of St. Marks). In 1679, about 150 years after the Narváez visit, the first fort, San Marcos de Apalachee, was built by the Spanish. But in 1682, this wooden fort was raided and burned by pirates. In 1718, the fort was rebuilt. In 1758, after a hurricane drowned 40 men in the garrison, the first masonry fort was constructed on the present-day site. In 1764, the British seized control of the fort at San Marcos de Apalachee and renamed the outpost St. Marks.

By 1769, the British had abandoned the entire region. In 1783, after the Treaty of Paris, the Spanish once again claimed possession of the fort. Andrew Jackson seized the fort in 1819. About ten years later, some of the limestone

St. Marks River City Park and pavilion

blocks of the old fort were used in the construction of the St. Marks Lighthouse. With the looming confrontation in America between the North and the South, and with both sides jockeying for position—trying to acquire new sympathetic states—Florida joined the Confederacy. During the Civil War in 1861, the Confederates manned the fort at St. Marks and renamed it Fort Ward. But they surrendered the fort to the Union in 1865. Today the area is a pleasant, historical, state-run museum. This worthwhile museum is open from 9:00 A.M. to 5:00 P.M. daily, but it's closed on Tuesdays and Wednesdays. The present-day town of St. Marks sits another half-mile northeast of the museum and old fort, on the RDB of the St. Marks River.

In March 1865, one of the last major military engagements of the Civil War took place near St. Marks. Sixteen Union vessels carrying Blue soldiers sailed into Apalachee Bay. They planned to blow up the railroad bridges over the St. Marks, Aucilla, and Ochlockonee rivers, and they threatened Tallahassee. Tallahassee was the last capital east of the Mississippi River still in the hands of the Confederate army. Fourteen Union vessels, with between 900 and 1,000 soldiers, landed near Port Leon (southeast of St. Marks). The Union, forgoing an attempt to cross the St. Marks River at Newport (i.e., present-day U.S. Route 98), decided to try to cross the river six miles farther up stream and at a natural bridge, where the river goes underground. But the Union troops were repulsed at the Battle of Natural Bridge. And Tallahassee remained the only Confederate capital east of the Mississippi River to remain in Southern hands until the end of the war.

St. Marks is about 16 miles from Florida's capital, Tallahassee. In 1834, the oldest railroad in Florida, the third oldest railroad in the entire nation, a 16-mile link connected Tallahassee to St. Marks and then later to Port Leon. Before steam locomotives, mules pulled these first rail cars. The cars shipped cotton from Tallahassee to St. Marks. In 1841, Port Leon had a population of about 300, but much of the town was washed away by a hurricane in 1843. The railroad was later refurbished with a route only to St. Marks. The remaining inhabitants of old Port Leon relocated farther inland to New Port Leon (later shortened to Newport). Today that old railroad bed is a splendid bicycle trail connecting Tallahassee at St. Marks. Besides Port Leon (and even Newport much later), there are two other "ghost ports" on the St. Marks River—Magnolia and Rock Haven.

Today in St. Marks, besides four marinas, there is a deli, a grocery store, a post office, and a municipal building. There are four restaurants; two are also taverns. Posey's is one of the more colorful restaurants at taverns in the Big Bend. Back on the St. Marks River, Shields Marina is beyond a few shrimp-boat docks and a couple of those waterfront restaurants. Shields is doing many things right and there is much new construction taking place. The marina has about 40 slips and can accommodate 50-footers. Shields also has a reasonably well-stocked ship's store on site and a high-and-dry boat-storage facility. We also noted that the lowest marina fuel prices found anywhere on the Big Bend were in St.

Posey's Restaurant, St. Marks River

Shields Marina sign, St. Marks River

Marks. Lynn's Riverside Marina is beyond Shields on the RDB. This facility has about 50 wet slips, with many covered slips, a high-and-dry boat-storage building, and room for about a 70-footer on the waterfront. They can haul large, mostly commercial, boats (i.e., up to about 90 feet) out of the water on a marine railway. Lynn's also operates a nearby seafood-packing house and they have been known to sell fresh seafood to transient boaters. A new boat basin is being constructed upriver from Lynn's.

Shields Marina (850) 925-6158

Approach depth—10 feet
Dockside depth—8-9 feet

Accepts transients—yes
Floating and fixed concrete docks—yes
Dockside power connections—30 and 50 amp
Dockside water connections—yes
Waste pump-out—yes
Showers—yes
Laundromat—yes
Gasoline—yes
Diesel—yes
Mechanical repairs—yes
Boat ramp—yes
Ship's store—yes
Restaurant—four nearby

Lynn's Riverside Marina (850) 925-6157

Approach depth—10 feet

Marine railway at Lynn's Riverside Marina, St. Marks

Dockside depth—5-6 feet

Accepts transients—yes

Floating and fixed wooden and steel—yes

Dockside power connections—30 and 50 amp

Dockside water connections—yes

Showers—yes

Gasoline—yes

Diesel—yes

Mechanical repairs—with contractors

Below-waterline repairs—marine railway

Ship's store—yes

Restaurant—four in town

The greatest tides anywhere in the Big Bend are likely to be on the St. Marks River. Four-foot—and sometimes greater—tidal swings are typical. Gulf Coast ICW barge traffic extends all the way to St. Marks, as petroleum tows trek between St. Marks and Mobile, Alabama. There are three petroleum terminals on the RDB of the St. Marks River beyond the town. The St. Marks River also holds considerable water depth—with many areas over 15 to 20 feet deep—upriver from town. The river also holds a width of about 70 yards for much of the way to the U.S. Route 98 highway bridge. About a mile beyond the last petroleum terminal on the RDB, you feel like you're in the wilderness, except for a handful of scattered private docks housing boats—some are 50 feet long. There are wooden walkways connecting these boat docks to isolated houses, which you usually cannot see because they're hidden away in the woods. In other places, the pleasing shoreline is often lined with tall cypress and other hardwoods interspersed with a few scattered pines. There is no development on the LDB side because we are in the St. Marks National Wildlife Refuge.

The first overhead obstruction on the St. Marks River is a power line about two miles beyond the petroleum terminals. The NOAA chart indicates that the power-line overhead clearance is a comfortable 67 feet at MHW. Today Newport on the LDB is nothing more than the remnants of World War II landing-craft manufacturing ruins with silted-in coves and broken pilings. The U.S. Route 98 highway bridge crosses the St. Marks River within sight of abandoned Newport. HAZARD *We'd estimate the overhead clearance beneath this highway bridge to be about a tight nine to eleven feet at MHW.* The *U.S. Coast Pilot* states nine feet of overhead clearance. On the upriver side of the bridge, there is a concrete boat ramp with two short piers on the LDB. Behind this ramp there is a small park with bathrooms and a soda machine. Ouzts' Oyster Bar Restaurant is on the west side of the river (on the RDB), near the U.S. Route 98 bridge.

The water depths, although still comfortably deep, drop to about seven to ten feet at MLW as the river narrows to about 40 yards wide on the upriver side of this highway bridge. As we continued farther up the St. Marks, the river continues to narrow, and we sometimes had to dodge large overhead tree limbs protruding from the shores. Even though we were a fair distance away from the coast, we would not consider this part of the St. Marks River a great hurricane hole. Much anchor scope would need to be paid out in order to reach the river's deep bottom, and the river is not wide enough to permit sufficient swinging room at anchor. Furthermore, if some of those large overhanging branches broke off during a storm and fell into the river, that river could become blocked with

debris and you might not be able to get back out. Rapids about a half-mile downstream from the natural bridge further limit boating.

The Natural Bridge, made famous during a Civil War battle, crosses the St. Marks River about six miles upriver from the U.S.. Route 98 bridge. In this area, the St. Marks River sort of gets lost in a series of sinkholes. And there is a not-so-well-defined dry-land route over the St. Marks River. Union forces also knew this in March 1865. Aware of the advancing Union troops, a quickly assembled group of motley Confederates from Tallahassee, ranging from 14 to 70 years old, set out to defend this land bridge twelve miles from their state capital. In their defensive positions, 595 Confederate soldiers held off about 500 advancing Union troops. In the three-and-a-half-hour battle, the Union force was repulsed and lost 21 men; another 89 were wounded. The successfully defending Confederates lost three men, with 23 wounded.

It has been reported that many of the rivers of eastern Apalachee Bay, including the St. Marks River, are chock-full of rocks. More rocks are reported in the rivers farther south—and usually at a distance removed from the Gulf. We did find merit in these reports. Although some rivers weren't bad at all, others were much worse. In this section of the Big Bend, the Aucilla wasn't bad, but we found the shallow Econfina loaded with rocks.

Aucilla River

Crossing the Aucilla River was sometimes problematic for the conquistadors of yesteryear. We should have far fewer problems with this river because we are entering this historic river by boat. The Aucilla is deeper and easier to enter and navigate than the Fenholloway

Boat ramp area on the Aucilla River

and Econfina rivers farther to the south. In eastern Apalachee Bay, position yourself at way point 30.04.070N/84.00.254W. You'll be right off a small, red, triangular mark on an eight-foot-tall wooden post (NOT shown on NOAA chart 11405) in four feet of water depth at MLW. From this way point, take a heading of 50 degrees to another daymark on a marshy point of land (shown on NOAA chart 11405 off Gamble Point). This mark has a light and sits on a 20-foot-tall quadrapod (which is used as a bird stand). The water depths between these two marks should be about five feet at MLW. If you can get over this "shallowest spot," you should have no problem going up another three miles on the Aucilla River. After Gamble Point, the Aucilla

River Channel turns more toward the north and then slightly west of north. Don't enter the wide bay on the LDB side. Water depth in the channel holds about five feet at MLW, with some spots as deep as nearly 15 feet. There is an island in the river about a mile up. We passed on the west side, treating this island like LDB, and found no less than six to eight feet of water depth at MLW. The *U.S. Coast Pilot* states, "The Aucilla . . . [has] depths over five feet . . . and boats drawing four feet will have little difficulty."

The reasonably deep Aucilla is about 120 yards wide, and the shore is lined with palms and live oaks. The Aucilla is the boundary between Jefferson and Taylor counties. Taylor County has the longest county coastline in the state of Florida. Unlike many rivers that we've so far encountered, the lower Aucilla has few bends. There is a very nice, wide, boat ramp, a floating dock, and ample parking on the LDB about two miles from the river's mouth. The concrete ramp area has plenty of trailer parking and a 30-foot floating concrete dock. Although there were no serious shallows, the bottom of the Aucilla River is very uneven. My depth finder was fluctuating wildly between four and fifteen feet in some of the lower portions of the Aucilla River!

In this region of the Aucilla, the shoreline becomes indistinct. Trees, draped in Spanish moss, are swamped by the water's edge, and still water extends past these trees into the forest. The solid-ground shoreline is seldom seen. Large turtles (i.e., with shells about a foot in diameter) might be seen sunning on some of the larger low limbs extending just above the water's surface. The Aucilla River is also one of the richest sites in Florida for finding fossils of prehistoric mammoths and mastodons. The Aucilla flows about 70 miles south from its source in Georgia.

The rural residential hamlet of Mandalay is about three miles up the river on the LDB. Mandalay probably does resemble something from the wilds of Burma. Actually, this river and the encroaching vegetative shoreline reminded me of a certain part of coastal Ecuador (i.e., Manabi), where I once served as a Peace Corps volunteer. The Wacissa River branches off on the RDB of the Aucilla about a half-mile upriver from Mandalay. The mouth of the Wacissa was strewn with several downed trees when we visited, and we couldn't proceed very far into this river. HAZARD *An overhead power line crosses the Aucilla about a quarter mile before the U.S. Route 98 bridge.*

We'd estimate the power-line clearance to be about 40 to 50 feet. Just before the U.S. Route 98 bridge, water depths shallow to about four feet, and the river starts producing many bends and curves. The U.S. Route 98 bridge clearance has only about five to seven feet of clearance at MHW. If you have a very low overhead-clearance vessel, you can continue beneath the bridge. The little residential hamlet of Nutall Rise is about a quarter mile upstream from this bridge on the LDB. If you find a way to park a boat around here, there is an unimproved boat ramp with no dock, a small convenience store, and a gas station about a half-mile to the southeast on U.S. Route 98.

Econfina River

The Econfina River, along with the Waccasassa, was about the shallowest river that we were able to explore on the Big Bend. Nevertheless, if one were able to enter and depart this river on high tide, there would be about another three and a half feet of tidal water depth beneath your keel. HAZARD *Be especially careful in this part of Apalachee Bay because there are many shoal patches near the mouth of the Econfina River, particularly to the southwest of the river's opening.* From comfortable water depths in Apalachee Bay, taking a northerly heading toward the mouth of the Econfina is the best way to avoid shoals. There is a quadrapod about three miles from shore, near the mouth of the Econfina. These quadrapods are used as bird stands, and there are many of them in this part of the Gulf of Mexico. It could be disastrous to run into one of these large unlighted structures at night! However, during the day, these structures can make reasonably good reference points. Some quadrapods are correctly

Low tide on the Econfina River

Boardwalk near Econfina State Park

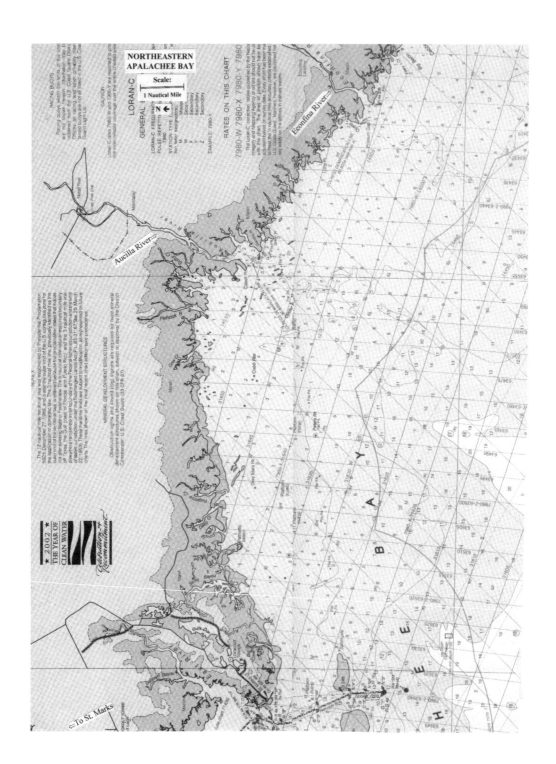

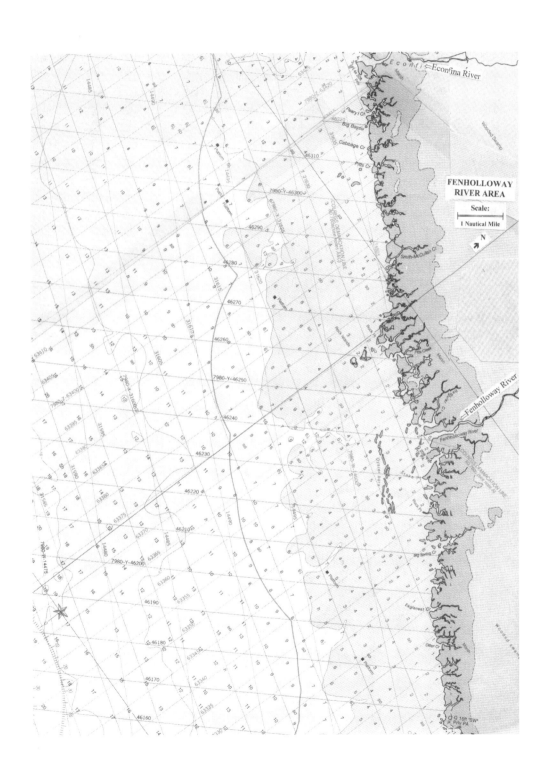

FENHOLLOWAY
RIVER AREA

Scale:

1 Nautical Mile

N

depicted as "platforms" on the NOAA charts. But beware, others are not depicted, and a few others may be mispositioned on the NOAA charts.

In Apalachee Bay, the quadrapod labeled "T12" is a good mark in signaling the entrance to the Econfina River from about three miles out. Our way point off this quadrapod is 29.58.546N/83.55.972W. The water depth at the quadrapod is six feet at MLW. From this way point, a heading of about 25 degrees should enable you to spy the 20-foot-tall daymark on a tripod off the marshy point of land on the Econfina's LDB. On this route we were only reading three feet of water depth at MLW. After reaching this tripod daymark, we treated a PCV plastic post, like a green daymark, and we were only able to get three to four feet of water at MLW. If you can successfully negotiate the shoals at the river's mouth, the river deepens slightly to about five feet at about three-quarters of a mile from the mouth. The *U.S. Coast Pilot* indicates "the Econfina is shallow and navigable by boats drawing two feet at half tide or better; although lesser depths may be found during protracted periods of offshore winds." HAZARD *There are also many submerged and partially submerged rocks in the Econfina.* If you do encounter rocks, the confrontation might not be too destructive to your boat if you travel at a slow speed. We entered this river on a low tide and had a few light brushes with the bottom. But the next morning, when we departed the Econfina on one of those REAL low tides, we had some problems. We became more than momentarily stuck, and a few times, I had to jump overboard to push us over shoals near the mouth of the Econfina River. Please go very slow in here, especially on a low tide.

Better yet, go in and out of this river only on the high tide!

Many parts of the Econfina shoreline are mostly studded with tall palm trees, giving us our first authentic tropical backdrop. The Seminole name "Econfina" translates to "earth bridge." The Econfina is also one of the narrower rivers and is only about 40 yards wide. There is a small settlement on the LDB comprised of a few rustic homes and trailers and some dilapidated small docks about a mile and a half from the river's mouth. The Aucilla Wildlife Management Area constitutes much of the region in between the Aucilla and Econfina rivers. The Econfina River State Park is also on the Econfina's RDB (i.e., the Aucilla River side), less than a half-mile up from that rustic settlement. This area has a double boat ramp and docks, another small area of covered dock, ample parking, and a boardwalk. Econfina River State Park has a seasonal snack bar. Econfina River RV Resort and Fish Camp, (850) 582-2135, is about a third of a mile up the road from the Econfina River State Park. This RV resort and fish camp has a reasonably stocked camp store, a gas pump, a public telephone, and a swimming pool.

Fenholloway River

The Fenholloway River divides two U.S. Coast Guard Search and Rescue and law-enforcement districts. The Seventh District, based out of Miami, is south of the Fenholloway. The Eighth District, based out of New Orleans, is north and west of the Fenholloway. We have heard reports that the Fenholloway was a rather polluted river. There is a pulp and paper mill about 25 miles up the Fenholloway that supposedly contribute to this pollution. We didn't observe any noticeable

Bird-roost tree on the Fenholloway River

pollution, or smell any foul river odor, but the Fenholloway River did have a very high level of natural tannin, which darkened the water. And with a northeast wind, we could get an ever-so-slight whiff of that huge pulp mill near Perry, Florida. Many local fishermen seemed to be enjoying themselves on the river. And there might have been more crab traps in the Fenholloway than in any other river in the Big Bend.

HAZARD *A long oyster bar sits in Apalachee Bay about a mile from the mouth of the Fenholloway.* We successfully passed on both the northwest side and the southeast side of

this oyster bar. On the northwest side, we found about three to five feet of water depth at MLW. On the southeast side of the bar, we encountered about three to four feet of water depth at MLW. A line of four stakes, spaced 30 to 60 yards apart, runs parallel to the shore and across the mouth of the Fenholloway. Near the middle and southeastern end of this stake line, we found only two feet of water depth in a couple of places. The Fenholloway River light should be spied on a marshy point of land on the river's RDB. This 20-foot-tall mark has a placard with two green vertical diamonds nested on a larger diamond placard

Locals on the Fenholloway River

labeled "Fenholloway River Approach Light." This lighted aid should be treated like a green daymark (i.e., passed on the port side) when entering this river. For about three miles up the Fenholloway, the water depth varies between two and nine feet at MLW. The *U.S. Coast Pilot* indicates that "three feet can be taken into the river on a favorable tide."

There is a fork in the river about one mile from the Gulf. Favor the RDB side of this fork (i.e., take the left fork). The river is about 80 yards wide and many decapitated palm trees stand along the shore, where the salt marsh slowly gives way to a hardwood forest. Live oaks, garlanded with Spanish moss, predominate in this hardwood forest. And the forested shoreline gradually becomes denser and darker. There is an unimproved boat ramp on the LDB about three miles from the Gulf. In the Fenholloway, and off the main channel, there are a number of wide bends in this river, and if the water depth permitted, these would make nice anchorages.

CHAPTER 9

The Steinhatchee Region, from Keaton Beach to Horseshoe Beach

There are three well-marked channels in this section of the coast—Keaton Beach, Horseshoe Beach, and Steinhatchee. Steinhatchee (the *Stein* rhymes with *bean*) is the center of things on this part of Florida's Nature Coast (from Wakulla to Pasco counties). Steinhatchee and the Steinhatchee River are situated in a broad indentation on the Gulf of Mexico called Deadman Bay. Supposedly, the bay received its name after Indians found some floating corpses. In these waters, Gulf navigation is fairly straightforward. If you need deeper water beneath your keel, turn away from the coast. Here, you need worry less about the numerous distant shoals than you would in many of the western parts of Apalachee Bay. The mean tidal range in this area of the Gulf is about three and half feet between high and low tide—and slightly less than the four-foot range around St. Marks. You also have to be slightly mindful of the many quadrapod bird-roosting platforms in this part of the Gulf of Mexico. Many folks rent diving equipment for spearfishing, artifact hunting, and scalloping. This entire area has been highly touted for scallops. The scallop season runs from July to mid-September. Supposedly, the best scalloping is from about three miles north of Keaton Beach to Steinhatchee. Eight miles northwest of Keaton Beach, the first coastal development since Shell Point, more than 30 miles ago, occurs at Spring Warrior Creek. There is also a boat ramp in Spring Warrior Creek. At Dekle Beach, six miles south of Spring Warrior Creek, there is a 500-foot-long fishing pier. In March 1993, the "storm of the century" wreaked a northbound path of death and destruction from Florida to New England. That storm first slammed ashore on the U.S. mainland here. In Keaton Beach and Dekle Beach, many homes were totally destroyed and ten people lost their lives.

Keaton Beach

In the Gulf of Mexico, position yourself at 29.48.811N/83.37.850W, and you'll be off the Keaton Beach Channel and very near lighted aid "G1" in about five to six feet at MLW. After reaching this seaward daymark, head about 75 degrees to the next group of navigation aids. We encountered channel depths of about four to six feet, MLW. However, the *U.S. Coast Pilot* indicated a controlling depth of only two and a half feet. This channel has no sharp turns but a few easy doglegs. About a half-dozen of the channel navigation aids are lighted (although the light on "G11" was extinguished when we passed it). After lighted aid "G19," you'll come to a small bay. The shallow water straight ahead, and a channel marked by PVC plastic pipes, leads to Cedar Island. The only marina in this area, Keaton Beach Marina, is tucked into the first canal to the north (or the left) side. From "G19," look for that canal on a heading of about 345 degrees. You will need to make a

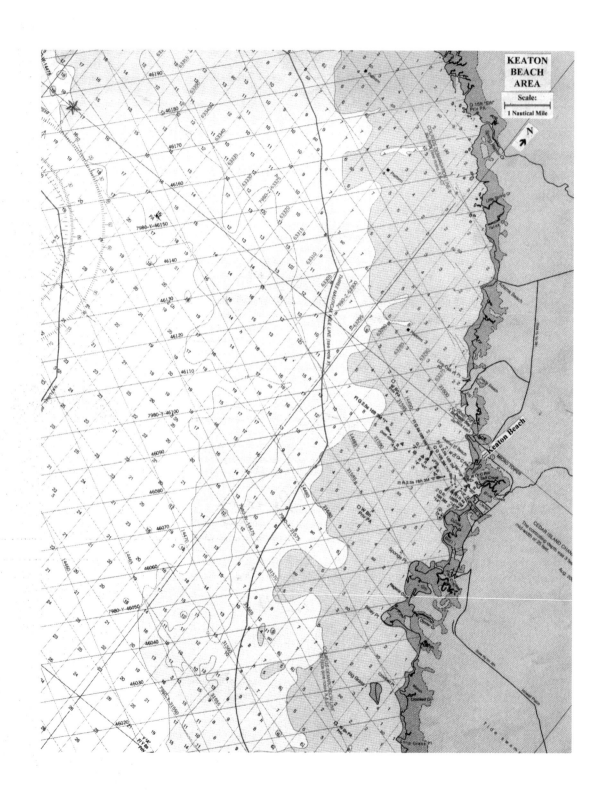

KEATON
BEACH
AREA

Scale:
1 Nautical Mile

N

Keaton Beach

sharp turn around the spit of land and the 500-foot-long fishing pier to your left (or northwest). HAZARD *There is a shallow patch of water not far from this spit.* Hug the spit-of-land side of the channel fairly closely. Two white and orange can buoys warn of submerged rocks on the LDB side of this channel. When entering, pass these danger buoys on your starboard side. Work your way into the first, and main, canal on the RDB.

The two canals in the Keaton Beach area are chock-full of boats—everything from small shrimpers to airboats. Keaton Beach Marina is in a small arm on the RDB side of

this westernmost canal and less than a half-mile away from the 500-foot-long fishing pier. This helpful marina can accommodate at least a 30-footer. Keaton Beach Marina employs a unique docking system, utilizing as much as about 500 feet of floating dock. There are no slips in the narrow canal. Boats are supposed to nuzzle and secure their bow to the floating dock while throwing out a stern anchor in the canal to keep that stern of the boat from wagging (at least from not wagging too much). This is true Mediterranean Mooring. Keaton Beach Marina has motel and cottage rooms and a boat dry-storage yard.

Road sign at Keaton Beach Marina

Keaton Beach Marina (850) 578-2897

Approach depth—1-4 feet
Accepts transients—yes
Floating wooden and concrete docks—yes
Dockside water connections—yes
Gasoline—yes
Mechanical repairs—nearby contractors
Below-waterline repairs—limited to forklift and about 35 feet
Boat ramp—yes
Boat hoist—yes
Convenience store—yes
Restaurant—nearby hot-dog (and burger) stand
Motel and cottages—yes

Hodge's Park Beach and the Keaton Beach Hot Dog Stand are near the 500-foot-long fishing pier. Hodge's Park also has a beach bathhouse. The busy Taylor County public boat ramp is at the head of the canal and beyond Keaton Beach Marina. There are also floating wooden docks and paved parking for boat trailers in this ramp area. Keaton Beach hosts an arts-and-crafts festival during the month of May.

There are a few coastal settlements immediately southeast of Keaton Beach. Both Cedar Island and Dark Island have a few canals, and the canals in Cedar Island connect directly to the main Keaton Beach Channel. Dark Island, south of Cedar Island, has about a half-mile-long swath of nice homes along the beach.

Steinhatchee and the Steinhatchee River

South of Keaton Beach, Deadman Bay is a large indentation in the Gulf of Mexico between latitudes 29° 30' N and 29° 45' N. The Steinhatchee River empties near the center of Deadman Bay. This river channel should be fairly easy to negotiate at night, if the need ever

arose. By far, most of the channels to the south of this one are strewn with rocks along the edge of the channel. To enter the Steinhatchee River and visit Steinhatchee, position yourself at way point 29.39.353N/83.27.452W in Deadman Bay. You should be in nine feet of water at MLW and just ahead of lighted Steinhatchee Channel marker "G1." After "G1," take a heading of 75 degrees most of the way in. This is a fairly long, but straight, channel. There are many more lighted navigation aids than depicted on NOAA chart 11407. In the channel, navigation aids "G5," "G9," "R14," "G17, "R22," "G29," "R32," and "G35" are lighted in addition to the three lighted aids depicted on the NOAA chart.

We observed that most water depths in this channel, from "G1" to after "G7," range between eight to ten feet at MLW. After "R8 and G9," there are spots where the water depth decreased to six to eight feet at MLW. The *U.S. Coast Pilot* indicated a midchannel controlling depth of only five and a half feet. After "G14 and R14," we experienced water depths increasing to about eight to nine feet and then to about seven feet at "G19 and R20." After "G23," the channel makes its first of four dogleg turns—a slight turn to the port side. After "G25 and R26," the water depths begin to make some fluctuations. But after "R28 and G29," the water depths once again deepen and level off to around eight to twelve feet at MLW. The channel makes its second dogleg—this time to starboard—after "R28 and G29." The channel makes a third dogleg—back to port—after aids "R32 and G33." A fourth dogleg—back to starboard—is made after "R34 and G35." Channel water depths continue to hold between ten and sixteen feet to "R40" at MLW.

Boats along the Steinhatchee River

STEINHATCHEE

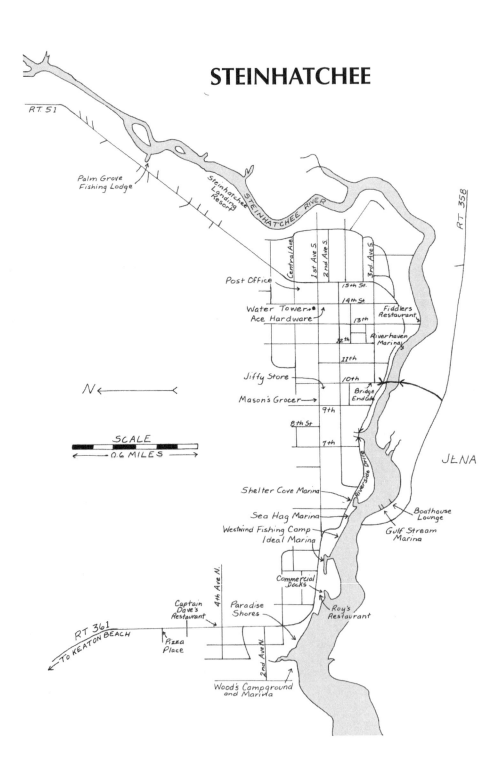

RT. 51

Palm Grove
Fishing Lodge

Steinhatchee
Landing Resort

STEINHATCHEE RIVER

RT 358

Post Office

Central Ave.
1st Ave S.
2nd Ave S.
3rd Ave S.

15th St.
14th St.

Water Tower
Ace Hardware

13th

Fiddlers
Restaurant

12th

Riverhaven
Marina

11th

Jiffy Store

10th

Bridge
End Cafe

Mason's Grocer

9th

8th St.

N

7th

JENA

SCALE
0.6 MILES

Shelter Cove Marina

Sea Hag Marina

Westwind Fishing Camp
Ideal Marina

Riverside Drive

Boathouse
Lounge

Gulf Stream
Marina

Commercial
Docks

4th Ave N.

Captain
Dave's
Restaurant

Paradise
Shores

Roy's
Restaurant

RT 361
TO KEATON BEACH

Pizza
Place

2nd Ave N.

Wood's Campground
and Marina

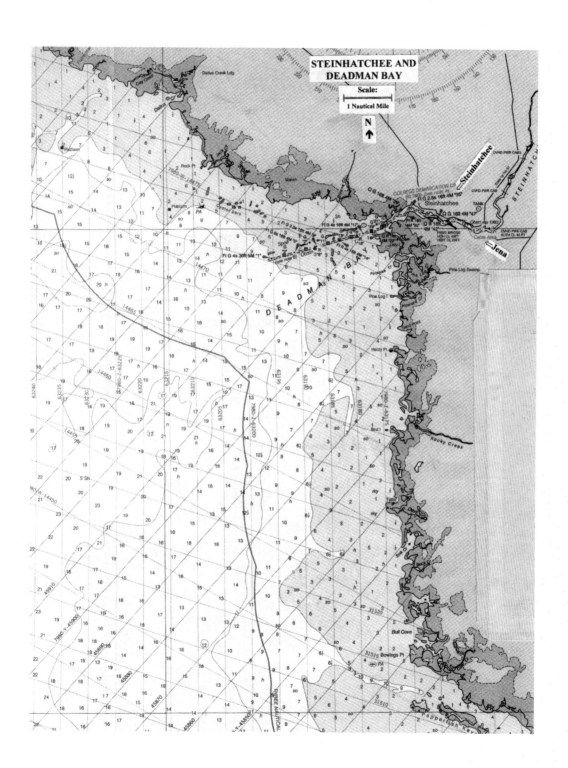

STEINHATCHEE AND
DEADMAN BAY

Scale:

1 Nautical Mile

N

Commercial boat basin, Steinhatchee

Many local fishing boats, some quite large, come barreling in and out of the Steinhatchee Channel. We got rudely waked several times in this channel. Generally, the larger commercial fishing boats displayed more wake etiquette (i.e., slowing down) than the smaller recreational boats.

Besides diving for scallops, spearfishing is very popular in and around Deadman Bay. Diving gear is sold and/or rented at many of the local marine stores around Steinhatchee. Furthermore, to accommodate this expanding local recreational demand, the majority of the boating facilities in the Steinhatchee area are attached to a motel. Steinhatchee hosts a seafood festival every April.

The first of many Steinhatchee recreational marine facilities, Wood's Gulf Breeze Campground and Marina will be seen on the RDB slightly beyond "G35." Wood's, four other nearby marine facilities, and the town of Steinhatchee are on the RDB (or north shore). The town of Jena and the new Gulfstream Motel and Marina are on the opposite LDB side of the river. Wood's is more of a trailer park than a marina, with about 20 slips on a shaky-looking floating dock. A 15- to 20-footer is probably the biggest thing Wood's is capable of handling. The long pier upriver from Wood's belongs to Sweet Paradise Charters. Roy's Restaurant, directly on the river, is about a half-mile past Wood's. Roy's is the most upscale dining establishment in Steinhatchee. Captain Dave's Restaurant is on the main road about one-half of a mile north of Roy's, but Dave's was closed and for sale the second time we visited. Fiddler's is the third restaurant in town, and it is located in the eastern part of Steinhatchee and slightly east of River Haven Marina. The fourth restaurant, the Bridge End Café, is located near the bridge to Jena.

A commercial basin housing some of the local shrimp fleet is immediately after Roy's Restaurant. A boat hoist can lift some fairly large boats in and out of the water here. Steinhatchee Fish, a wholesale and retail fish house is located behind and slightly to the north of this commercial basin. Friendly Ideal Marina and Motel is situated in a small L-shaped channel about one-quarter of a mile past this commercial basin, also on the RDB.

Ideal Marina has about 20 slips and can easily accommodate a 25-footer, if a low tide doesn't drain all of the water out of their basin. Westwind Fishing Camp and Motel, (352) 498-5254, sits upstream from the Ideal Marina channel. Westwind also has one long floating pier, a boat hoist, boat rentals, a dry storage, a bait-and-tackle shop, and gasoline. Although many marinas don't have do-it-yourself boat ramps, boat hoist lifts/small cranes are very popular for launching small boats in the Steinhatchee area. Many small and large marinas in Steinhatchee have these hoist/sling boat-launching systems. Besides motel units, many marinas in Steinhatchee also rent small boats.

Gulfstream Marina, Jena

Sea Hag Marina, Steinhatchee

Wood's Gulf Breeze Campground and Marina
(352) 498-3948

Approach depth—2-5 feet
Dockside depth—1-4 feet
Accepts transients—yes
Floating wooden docks—yes
Showers—yes
Laundromat—yes
Gasoline—yes
Mechanical repairs—yes (with local contractors)
Boat ramp—unimproved
Variety store and dive shop—yes
Restaurants—two within a half-mile walk

Ideal Marina and Motel (352) 498-3877

Approach depth—shallow (may not be
    approachable at low tide)

Dockside depth—very shallow
Accepts transients—yes
Floating wooden docks—yes
Showers—yes
Gasoline—yes
Diesel—yes
Mechanical repairs—local contractors
Below-waterline repairs—limited to 4,500
    pounds and forklift
Boat hoist—yes
Ship's store and dive shop—yes
Restaurant—within a third-of-a-mile walk
Motel—yes

The Sea Hag Marina is about one-third of a mile beyond Ideal Marina. Sea Hag is recognized as one of the better-known facilities in Steinhatchee. This facility has about 42 slips and can easily accommodate a 40-footer. The Sea Hag also offers Boat/U.S. discounts. Besides being a comprehensive boating facility, Sea Hag has high-and-dry boat storage as well as a dive shop.

Shelter Cove Marina, next door to Sea Hag, has about 20 covered slips and might be able to accommodate a 25-footer in their small well-protected cove. A nice, large, public boat ramp sits across the river from Sea Hag on the LDB. This corrugated concrete boat ramp, with a small floating dock, is at the end of the road in Jena.

Gulfstream Motel and Marina, the only marina on the LDB in Jena, is just upstream from this public ramp. It is also located across from Sea Hag near marker "R48." Gulfstream was brand new and sections were still being constructed during our second visit. They have a few slips and had future plans for about 500 to 600 feet of dockage by the summer of 2002. They soon hope to be selling fuel and can accommodate about a 50-footer. Gulfstream has a brand-new motel and operates Sportsman Den Tiki Bar. This marina will also provide a courtesy vehicle to reach Steinhatchee on the other side of the river. The seasonally opened Boathouse Restaurant and Lounge is also on the LDB and two *T*-docks upriver from Gulfstream. Transient tie-up is allowed for restaurant or lounge patrons. The aquamarine-colored Quonset hut sandwiched between Gulfstream and the Boathouse restaurant has another floating *T*-dock," but this is private property.

Sea Hag Marina (352) 498-3008

Approach depth—6 feet
Dockside depth—4 feet
Accepts transients—yes
Floating wooden docks—yes
Dockside power connections—30 amp
Dockside water connections—yes
Showers—no
Gasoline—yes
Diesel—yes
Mechanical repairs—yes
Below-waterline repairs—limited to 13,000 pounds and forklift
Ship's store and dive shop—yes, well stocked
Restaurants—three within a mile walk
Motel—yes

Shelter Cove Marina (no published telephone number)

Approach depth—2-4 feet
Floating wooden docks—yes
Dockside power connections—15 amp
Dockside water connections—yes
Restaurants—three within a mile walk
Motel—yes

Gulfstream Motel and Marina (352) 498-8088
www.steinhatcheeinc.com

Approach depth—4-5 feet
Dockside depth—4 feet
Accepts transients—yes
Floating concrete docks—yes
Dockside power connections—limited 30 and 50 amp
Dockside water connections—yes
Waste pump-out—coming
Showers—coming
Gasoline—coming
Diesel—coming
Mechanical repairs—local contractors
Boat ramp—yes
Convenience store—yes
Restaurants—across the river

Tiki bar—yes
Motel—yes

Boathouse Restaurant and Lounge

Dockside depth—4 feez
Accepts transients—yes, with restaurant and/or
    lounge patronage
Floating wooden dock—yes
Dockside power connections—very limited 15
    amp
Dockside water connections—yes
Restaurant—limited to pizza and chicken wings

On the RDB, between Shelter Cove Marina and the 10th Street highway bridge, there are several small private docks. Some of these advertise slips that have few or no utilities. The last navigation aid on the Steinhatchee River is "R50," just downriver from the fixed bridge. River Haven Marina, the only full-service marina beyond the bridge, has about 35 slips and probably can accommodate a very big boat, subject to its draft. Tim Powell at River Haven Marina indicated that he has never seen a time when a boat requiring a four-foot draft was unable to reach his marina, even at the lowest winter tidal conditions (i.e., lower than the MLW). Like many marinas in the area, River Haven is also in the rental-boat business. HAZARD *The water-line marker yardstick for the bridge between Steinhatchee and Jena registers from 20 to 26 feet, depending on the tide level and other factors.* NOAA charts and the *U.S. Coast Pilot* indicate mean-high-water (MHW) clearance under this bridge is 25 feet. When we passed under this bridge, a couple of hours away from low tide, there was another three to five feet on the safe side of that 26-foot yardstick reading.

River Haven Marina (352) 498-0709
www.steinhatchee.com/riverhaven

Approach depth—4 feet
Dockside depth—4 feet
Accepts transients—yes
Floating wooden and steel docks—yes
Dockside power connections—20, 30, and 50 amp
Dockside water connections—yes
Waste pump-out—in the near future
Showers—no
Laundry service—yes
Gasoline—yes
Diesel—yes
Mechanical repairs—local contractors
Below-waterline repairs—limited to 30,000-
    pound hoist lift and 14-foot beam
Boat hoist—yes
Ship's store—yes, well stocked
Restaurants—one nearby and one about a mile-
    walk away
Motel—yes

Besides three restaurants, the town of Steinhatchee has two food stores: a Jiffy Food Store and Mason's Food Market. Mason's, one block west of Jiffy, is the larger food store in town. There is an ACE hardware store near the east end of town, near the town water tower. The post office is also in this neighborhood, next to the Baptist church.

Private docks on both sides of the Steinhatchee River are prevalent after the Jena Bridge. Within the next three miles, three sets of power lines cross the Steinhatchee River. We'd estimate that the lowest power lines are the first set you'll encounter—with about 25 to 30 feet of vertical clearance (but still likely higher than the highway bridge). The second set of power lines has the most clearance—perhaps 50-55 feet. The third set of power lines is estimated to have around 35 feet of vertical clearance. The *U.S. Coast Pilot* states that the clearance beneath these three power cables is respectively 43, 43, and 40 feet. There is a fork in the river about one and a half miles upriver from the highway bridge. The Steinhatchee River goes to the left—follow this RDB side of the river. Steinhatchee Landing Resort is on the RDB a slight way past this fork, in between the first and second sets of power lines. This first-class resort has about a 200-foot-long dock and a small pontoon tour boat. There is also a conference center on the grounds. The resort caters to families with children, and they even have a small petting zoo and a children's playground.

Steinhatchee Landing Resort (352) 498-3513

Dockside depth—3-4 feet
Accepts transients—yes, prior permission
    appreciated
Floating wooden dock—yes
Dockside power connections—limited 15 amp
Resort cottage—yes

Downriver from this resort, the water depth in the Steinhatchee may be 10 to 15 feet, with many deeper holes. But upriver from the resort, the water depths become quite erratic and more of a problem for boaters. Also beyond the resort, the Steinhatchee River significantly narrows to only about 40 yards wide. Heading upriver, you'll encounter the first of two islands. Leave the first island on your port side and treat this island like the RDB shore. But leave the second island on your starboard side and treat it like the LDB shore. Be careful, as you near this second

island. HAZARD *Please stay very close to the RDB shore, because the keel of my boat unfortunately found some huge "unseen from the surface" underwater boulders extending well into the "channel" southwest of this second island.* The Palm Grove Fishing Lodge is off a small canal on the RDB, just before that second island.

Palm Grove Fishing Lodge (352) 498-3721

Dockside depth—shallow
Floating wooden dock—yes
Dockside water connections—yes
Gasoline—yes
Boat ramp—yes
Motel—yes

Beyond the Palm Grove Fishing Lodge, I sometimes found seven to 14 feet of water at MLW, but there are protruding rocks all over this river. HAZARD *The Steinhatchee River becomes completely unnavigable about four miles past the Jena Bridge.* Small rapids can be seen at a distance up the river. There are also tree branches in the river, and rocks are everywhere—in the river and lining the shores. If the rapids weren't there, Steinhatchee Falls is about another four miles further upstream.

Horseshoe Beach

Horseshoe Beach is a colorful coastal settlement about 18 nautical miles south of Steinhatchee. This town likes to consider itself, perhaps, Florida's last frontier. This settlement is in the heart of the Big Bend, and we are about halfway through our coastal trip. In several regards, Horseshoe Beach epitomizes the Big Bend and Old Florida. Horseshoe Beach was settled by squatters who moved in on lumber-company land. To protect the existing residents,

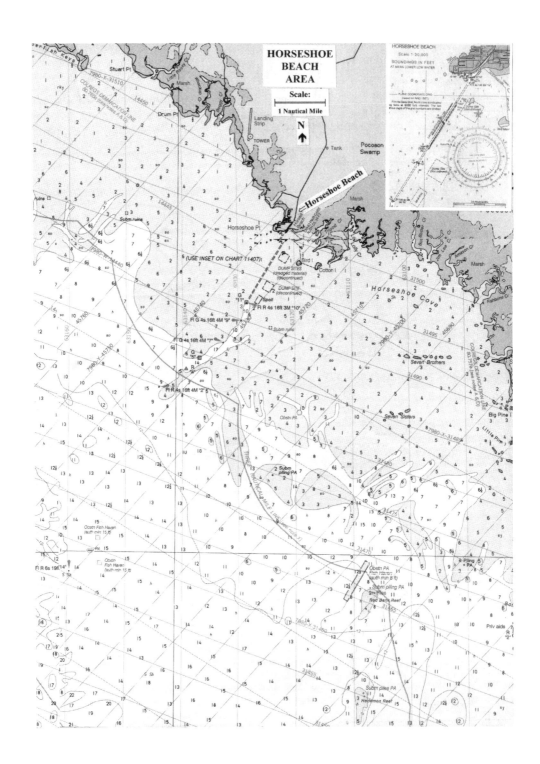

a couple of the better-off and more insightful town members were able to "buy out" this small parcel of the lumber-company land. The community leaders then tried to resell the parcels—without a profit to themselves—back to the squatters. Unfortunately, many of the ungrateful squatters didn't oblige, and the generous town leaders took a financial bath. Nevertheless, off-centered Horseshoe Beach developed into its present mix of outlandish bungalows (one looks like a boat on stilts), modest homes, and trailers—painted on the beautiful Gulf Coast panorama.

A very visible white water tower is spied from out in the Gulf north of Horseshoe Beach. If you become disoriented, you can regain your bearings by sighting on this water tower. Our way point off lighted "R2" to Horseshoe Beach Channel is 29.23.260N/83.20.426W. MLW depth off "R2" is eight to nine feet. Upon entering the Horseshoe Beach Channel, relying only on the Horseshoe Beach NOAA chart INSET could get you in trouble. This "inset channel" actually begins at "R10 and G11," not at "R2." HAZARD *Between "R2" and "R10 and G11," there are several shallows on both sides of this channel.* But there is no less than six to seven feet at MLW in the channel between "R2" and "R10 and G11." The channel also arcs to the southeast (or to the LDB side) here. This marked channel is easy to follow, but if you deviate from it, you may run aground at low tide. "R10 and G11" sit in seven to nine feet at MLW. Nevertheless, we have provided you another intermediate way point off "R10 and G11" for the Horseshoe Beach Channel in the appendix. After lighted "R10," it's a straight shot on a heading of 40 degrees to Horseshoe Beach. The water depth after "R10" holds a steady six to eight feet at MLW. The shallow

spots in this channel were being dredged to six feet when we first visited by boat. In early 2002, we were told the dredging was completed. The spoils from dredging operations are pumped on the sides of this channel, especially the LDB side. Pelicans, cormorants, and other seabirds use these spoil islands as roost. You cannot miss the aroma from all that cumulative guano as you pass by these spoil islands.

There is a small exposed basin with about nine feet of water depth at MLW at the head of the Horseshoe Beach Channel between "R18" and "G23." Tina's Dockside (and Restaurant) is on the north side of this basin. Tina's sells gas and has two rickety slips. Continuing straight past "R18," there is an even smaller sheltered arm. Horseshoe Marina and RV Park has a few private shrimp docks that can be found on the LDB of this small arm. HAZARD *MLW in this arm can be as low as one or two feet.* Before entering this arm, and perhaps even before entering the Horseshoe Beach Channel, you may wish to radio Horseshoe Marina on VHF 16, and then switch to VHF 17, to inquire about the present tidal depths. Friendly Horseshoe Marina has about 10 covered slips and about 200 feet of side-tie docking. They can place a 50-footer in here, but the low tide must be considered. This facility also has a marine railway and they launch small boats with a hoist lift. The good-value Crimson Crest Restaurant is across the street from Tina's and near the entrance to the Horseshoe Marina arm. The town of Horseshoe Beach has a post office, convenience store, public launch ramp, and RV park. The Butler-Douglas Memorial Park is a small campground right on the Gulf of Mexico, due west of Horseshoe Marina.

Butler-Douglas Memorial Park, Horseshoe Beach

Tina's Dockside (352) 498-5768

Approach depth—4-7 feet
Dockside depth—4 feet
Accepts transients—no
Fixed wooden docks—yes
Gasoline—yes
Boat hoist—yes
Restaurant—yes (and one nearby)

Horseshoe Marina and RV Park (352) 498-5687

Approach depth (after head of dredged channel)—
   1-4 feet

Dockside depth—1-4 feet
Accepts transients—yes
Fixed wooden docks—yes
Dockside power connections—15 and 30 amp
Dockside water connections—yes
Gasoline—yes
Diesel—yes
Mechanical repairs—very limited
Below-waterline repairs—on a small marine
   railway
Boat hoist—yes
Ship's store—yes
Restaurants—two nearby

CHAPTER 10

The Suwannee and Cedar Key Region

This chapter covers the Gulf of Mexico between the mouth of the Suwannee River and Waccasassa Bay and Waccasassa River. The Cedar Keys and the town of Suwannee are also covered in this chapter. Except for its mouth, the fabled Suwannee River is covered in chapter 17. There are many shoals, islands, and a fair amount of obstacles in this part of the Gulf of Mexico. Much of these smaller oyster-bar reefs comprise a section in the Gulf of Mexico known as Suwannee Reef. Suwannee Reef is about 20 miles long, extending from south of Horseshoe Beach nearly to Cedar Key. There are about a half-dozen channel breaks, some much better than others, through this uneven reef. Suwannee Sound is the Gulf water inside of this reef. Crab traps and clam and oyster beds dot Suwannee Sound. There are also more than a few wrecks scattered around the reefs in Suwannee Sound. Be vigilant when navigating this area!

Waccasassa Bay is a large indentation east of Cedar Key that is even larger than Deadman Bay. Like Suwannee Sound, Waccasassa Bay is reef-riddled with oyster bars. The Waccasassa River Channel and the channels behind Cedar Key are not suitable for large, transiting vessels. You'll see many airboats operating in this region. These boats, although extremely loud, are well suited for these shallow waters. But don't ever get caught behind one, even by 40 yards, when they are pulling out on a ramp and onto their trailer. Besides the deafening noise, you'll be soaked!

The Suwannee Area

There are three channels leading to the town of Suwannee and the Suwannee River from the Gulf of Mexico. The town of Suwannee has about five boating facilities, but only one of those facilities, Miller's Marina, is really geared up to handle a large amount of transient traffic. The town of Suwannee is woven with canals. The *U.S. Coast Pilot* refers to McGriff Pass as Wadley Pass, and Alligator Pass as West Pass.

Alligator Pass Channel

The middle channel, or Alligator Pass Channel, is no longer being maintained or dredged. We had no trouble negotiating the still well-marked channel in October 2001. The outside way point for Alligator Pass Channel off lighted "R2," in six feet of water at MLW, is at 29.14.577N/83.11.802W. The second mark, "R4," may be difficult to spy from "R2." If you look hard in the direction of 55 degrees, you should be able to see "R4." Between markers "R2" and "G7," water depths ranged between four and ten feet at MLW. The lowest MLW depths in Alligator Pass Channel were between "R8" and "G27." Nevertheless, the water depth, even in this stretch of channel, still registered between

Sunken derelict workboat on Cedar Key

Channel to Miller's Marina, Suwannee

four and six feet. Alligator Pass Channel has a fair number of doglegs. Even though this channel has been officially discontinued, if the navigation aids remain standing, I wouldn't resist using the Alligator Pass Channel again—especially when approaching the Suwannee area from the south.

Derrick Key Gap and the East Pass Channels

Derrick Key Gap is at the southern end of Suwannee Reef and Suwannee Sound and northeast of Cedar Key's Northwest Channel. By far, this is the most dicey and convoluted approach into Suwannee Sound and the Suwannee River. This is the least recommended of the three marked approaches to the Suwannee River, and it's only feasible for

shallow-draft vessels. There are five distinct parts to this approach: 1) the outer Derrick Key Gap Channel; 2) the inner Derrick Key Gap Channel; 3) the five-mile run in Suwannee Sound between the end of the inner Derrick Gap Channel and the beginning of East Pass Channel; 4) the East Pass Channel in Suwannee Sound; and 5) East Pass Creek behind Hog Island. Only East Pass Creek behind Hog Island is easy.

Outside the south end of Suwannee Sound, position yourself at unlighted "R2" near way point 29.09.265N/83.06.255W. "R2" should be in about six feet of water at MLW. This is the beginning of the outer Derrick Key Gap Channel. There are no lighted navigation aids in these channels. After "R2," head north and then northeast, eventually reaching navigation aid "G15." The water depths in outer Derrick Key Gap Channel between "R2" and "G15" are between five and eight feet at MLW. After arriving at "G15," look away from the mainland and in a northerly direction for an unlighted navigation aid—another "R2." Follow this "continuation" of Derrick Key Gap Channel—the inner Derrick Key Gap Channel—from "R2" to "R10." Remember, even though it doesn't seem like it, you are apparently still returning in this second channel, and the red navigation aids should be passed on your right side, the green aids passed on your port side. After you reach "R10," you should be safely in Suwannee Sound near way point 29.12.030N/83.05. 585W. You should encounter about three to five feet of water depths at MLW in the inner Derrick Key Gap Channel between "R2" and "R10." Now head northwest in Suwannee Sound, passing a cultivated shellfish bed to your starboard. This shellfish bed is marked by posts with white and orange placards. After about five miles on a northwest heading in Suwannee Sound, arrive at way point 29.16.030N/83.08.000W.

In Suwannee Sound, the East Pass Channel is the trickiest, especially at low tide. After you have arrived at way point 29.16.030N/83. 08.000W, you should be in two to three feet of water at MLW, off an unofficial-looking tripod. In a general northeasterly heading, you should see more unofficial pilings marking the entrance to East Pass. Initially, this channel makes two doglegs to starboard. HAZARD *After that seaward-most piling, the depth in this channel ranges between three to seven feet deep at MLW.* About a half-mile away from the entrance to East Pass, the channel turns back to port on a heading of 35 degrees. Near

the last set of pilings, the channel turns to starboard to a heading of 85 degrees. Treat the low-lying island ahead like the LDB.

You should find two to five feet of water at MLW as you negotiate on the north side of this island. The *U.S. Coast Pilot* states that this is the shallowest part of the entire Derrick Key Gap route, at one-and-a-half-foot depths. But soon you will be in the safer and deeper waters of East Pass Creek. If you can pick your way through those shallows in Suwannee Sound, East Pass Creek has plenty of water depth (e.g., no less than nine feet) west of Hog Island and beyond Suwannee Sound. Furthermore, if you are contemplating taking this Derrick Key Gap-East Pass channel route, carefully scrutinize NOAA chart 11408 and try to obtain the latest local knowledge beforehand.

McGriff Pass Channel

McGriff Pass Channel is the northernmost, the newest, and the Suwannee River Channel of the future. By the fall of 2002, dredging work should have begun to deepen McGriff Pass Channel to six feet, MLW, and widen the channel to 75 feet. Mostly straight, McGriff Pass Channel is almost half the length of Alligator Pass Channel. To enter McGriff Pass Channel, position yourself off "G1 and R2" and near way point 29.18.570N/83. 12.060W. At "G1 and R2," you should be in about seven feet of water at MLW. Right after you enter the channel, the depth shallows (i.e., pre-fall 2002 dredging observations) to four to five feet and then shallows again to three to four feet at MLW. The *U.S. Coast Pilot* indicated channel controlling depths were three feet in Wadley Pass (i.e., the extension of McGriff Pass Channel). The channel deepens a bit near "R6" to five to six feet. There are spoil shoals on both sides of the McGriff Pass Channel and none of the navigation aids in the channel are lighted. Markers "G11 and R12" are at the end of the straight section in about three to four feet of water depth at MLW. The water depths finally start increasing to about six to seven feet east of Little Bradford Island, near the junction with the Salt Creek Channel. McGriff Pass Channel meets the Salt Creek Channel on the RDB between "R20" and "R24." After "R26," and after the McGriff Pass Channel has already turned into Wadley Pass in the Suwannee River, the channel holds about three to seven feet of water at MLW. At "G31" the Alligator Pass Channel and McGriff (or Wadley) Pass Channel converge in four to five feet at MLW. You are now in the Suwannee River.

Salt Creek Channel

The Salt Creek Channel runs out of McGriff Pass Channel up to and in Salt Creek. Salt Creek is a wide marshy body of water, but the Salt Creek Channel is narrow and pretty much hangs in the center of Salt Creek. None of the navigation aids have lights; nevertheless, the channel is well marked. Depart the McGriff Pass Channel on the RDB side after "R20." The Salt Creek navigation aids begin at "G1 and R2" in about four feet at MLW and end about two miles later at "G29." Salt Creek channel depths generally range from four to seven feet at MLW. The channel starts out in a north-northwesterly direction and then makes a nearly 90-degree turn to starboard at "R12." HAZARD *The shallowest spot in the channel may be near "G17," where the channel depth briefly drops to about three feet.* After "R20," channel depths increase slightly to about four feet, MLW. After "R24," the channel deepens even more to about seven feet. On the LDB,

there are three nice houses on a point of land before the Salt Creek Shellfish Company Restaurant (also on the LDB of Salt Creek). "G29," the last navigation aid in Salt Creek, is just off the seafood restaurant. The restaurant has about 150 feet of fixed wooden dock next to their outside dining area. We were told boaters can side-tie gratis overnight if they patronize the restaurant. Unmarked Salt Creek continues northwest for a couple more miles. There is a wide spot in Salt Creek, about 100 yards upriver from the restaurant, with sufficient water depth and room for anchoring (e.g., four to nine feet at MLW).

Suwannee

Back on the Suwannee River, two miles upriver from Salt Creek and near river mile number three, some residential development will be observed on the RDB (the northwestern shore). The first three canals on this side are more developed and slightly narrower than the fourth canal. These first three canals have many private docks and accommodate some upscale residential development. The wider, fourth canal houses Miller's Marina in the basin at its head. Miller's has about 50 slips—many covered—and is capable of accommodating about a 60-foot transient boat. Miller's also operates an RV park on the premises. Miller's is one of the places most engaged in responsibly developing and promoting the Suwannee River. For many years, Miller's has been renting large (i.e., no smaller than 44 feet) houseboats to folks who wish to take a vacation and ply up the Suwannee River. If you have any questions about the Suwannee River that aren't answered in chapter 17 of this guide, the folks at Miller's are a fine and reliable source of information.

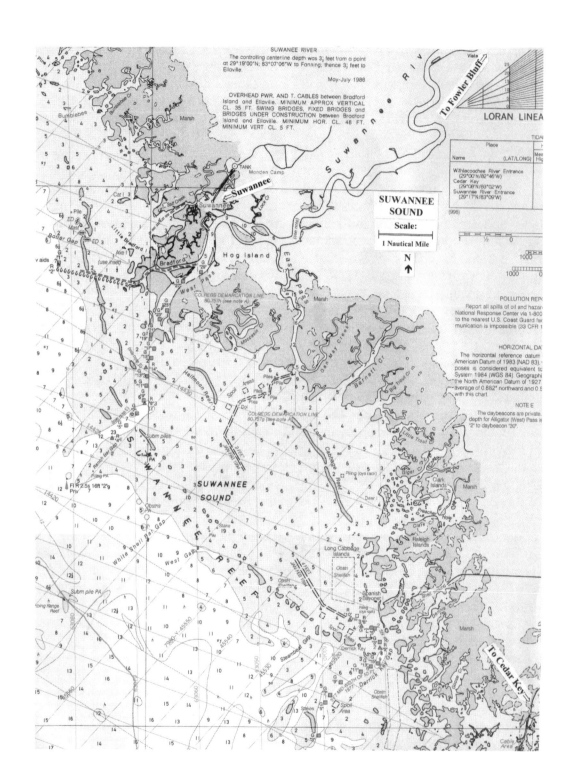

SUWANEE RIVER
The controlling centerline depth was 3½ feet from a point at 29°19'00"N; 83°07'06"W to Fanning; thence 3½ feet to Ellaville.
May-July 1986

OVERHEAD PWR. AND T. CABLES between Bradford Island and Ellaville. MINIMUM APPROX VERTICAL CL. 35 FT. SWING BRIDGES, FIXED BRIDGES and BRIDGES UNDER CONSTRUCTION between Bradford Island and Ellaville. MINIMUM HOR. CL. 48 FT. MINIMUM VERT. CL. 5 FT.

To Fowler Bluff

LORAN LINEA

SUWANNEE SOUND

Scale:

1 Nautical Mile

N
↑

To Cedar Key

POLLUTION REPO

Report all spills of oil and hazard
National Response Center via 1-800
to the nearest U.S. Coast Guard fac
munication is impossible (33 CFR 1

HORIZONTAL DAT

The horizontal reference datum
American Datum of 1983 (NAD 83),
poses is considered equivalent to
System 1984 (WGS 84) Geographic
the North American Datum of 1927
average of 0.882" northward and 0.5
with this chart.

NOTE E

The daybeacons are private.
depth for Alligator (West) Pass is
"2" to daybeacon "30".

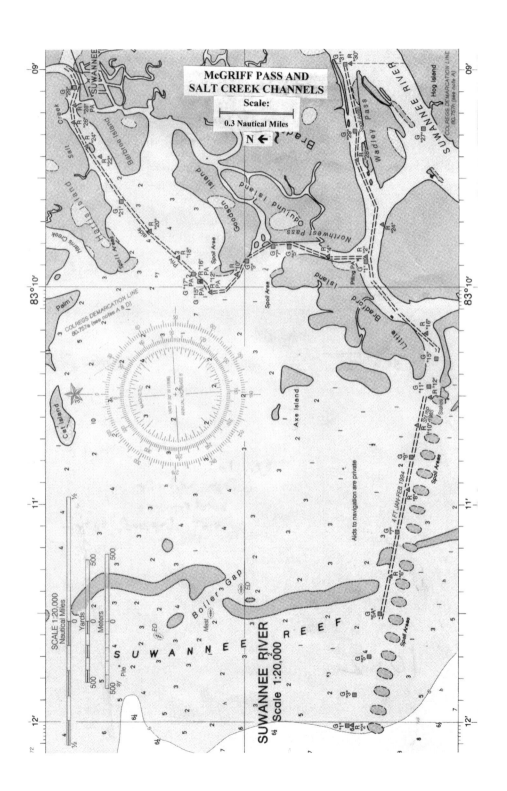

McGRIFF PASS AND SALT CREEK CHANNELS

Scale:

0.3 Nautical Miles

N

Miller's Marina (352) 542-7349
www.suwanneehouseboats.com

Approach depth—3-6 feet
Dockside depth—4-6 feet
Accepts transients—yes
Floating wooden and concrete docks—yes
Dockside power connections—30 amp
Dockside water connections—yes
Waste pump-out—yes
Showers—yes
Laundromat—in town
Gasoline—yes
Diesel—yes

Mechanical repairs—yes
Below-waterline repairs—closed-end travel lift
  and forklift
Boat ramp—yes
Ship's store—yes
Restaurants—two within walking distance

In addition to Miller's, there are four smaller boating facilities in Suwannee. They each have their own unique flavor. All of these boating facilities are off the next Suwannee River canal on the RDB side, one canal upriver from Miller's. This fifth canal is also known as Demory Creek. After entering Demory Creek,

Canal of the Suwannee River lined with boat docks and boat houses

it can be a confusing route with many turns. Please refer to our canal and road sketch of Suwannee. Well-managed Angler's Resort Marina and RV Park has about 35 covered slips and could accommodate about a 30-footer. Bill's Fish Camp and Motel is in the same side canal as Angler's Resort Marina, with about 20 feet of floating dock but with very limited docking space. Starling's Suwannee Marine is in a neighboring canal and very near to the Ship's Wheel Restaurant. Starling's Suwannee Marine has a green-colored high-and-dry boat-storage building,

about 30 covered slips, and probably can accommodate a 30-footer. Jon's Marina (also known as Bum's Marina on a sign facing the water) is in a wide basin and has about 30 covered slips. Jon's can generally accommodate boats smaller than 30 feet. By water, Jon's is in a circuitous, and sometimes very narrow (e.g., 20 feet wide), route from the Suwannee River.

Angler's Resort Marina and RV Park
(352) 542-7077

Approach depth—3-6 feet
Dockside depth—7-8 feet

Basin at Miller's Marina, Suwannee

Accepts transients—yes
Fixed wooden docks—yes
Dockside power connections—15 amp
Dockside water connections—yes
Gasoline—yes
Mechanical repairs
Boat ramp—yes
Bait-and-tackle shop—yes
Restaurants—two within walking distance

Bill's Fish Camp and Motel (352) 542-7086

Approach depth—3-6 feet
Accepts transients—very limited dock space
Floating wooden dock—yes
Dockside power connections—limited 30 amp
Dockside water connections—yes
Variety store—yes
Café—nearby
Cabins—yes

Starling's Suwannee Marine (352) 542-9159

Approach depth—3-6 feet
Accepts transients—limited
Floating wooden docks—yes
Dockside water connections—yes
Gasoline—yes
Mechanical repairs—limited to engine repairs
Boat ramp—yes
Ship's store—yes
Restaurants—one a block away (others nearby)
Motel—nearby

Jon's Marina (352) 542-2833

Approach depth—3-6 feet
Accepts transients—yes
Fixed wooden docks—yes
Dockside power connections—limited 15 amp
Dockside water connections—yes
Gasoline—yes

Boat ramp—yes
Variety store—yes, limited
Restaurants—a fair walking distance away

The town of Suwannee had two nice restaurants: the Ship's Wheel and the Salt Creek Shellfish Company. The Ship's Wheel had a serious fire between our first and second visits. Hopefully, they will be back in operation by late 2002. Also in Suwannee is a quaint café—the Suwannee Café—and a nightclub—Maggie Brown's Eatery and Emporium. Limited groceries can be purchased at Crown's Waterfront Market. A hardware store, Laundromat, and post office are also in town. The town of Suwannee is riddled with canals, and depending on your destination, it may be to your advantage to use your dinghy in the canals rather than walk along the streets.

Cedar Key

The Cedar Keys are a conglomeration of more than 30-40 islands and even more shoals. A few islands are large but most are small. This general region is more commonly referred to as just Cedar Key. Most, but not all, of the "development" in the Cedar Key area is actually on the largest island, called Way Key. In a section of the Gulf of Mexico that is strewn with shallow oyster reefs, Cedar Key has one of those rare and naturally deep channels. Throughout its history, Cedar Key has been host to pirates, spies, blockade-runners, and other outcasts. Deadly smallpox once reigned here.

In 1818 during the first Seminole war, Gen. Andrew Jackson ruthlessly hacked his way south to Cedar Key, destroying as much Indian property as possible and killing many

SUWANNEE

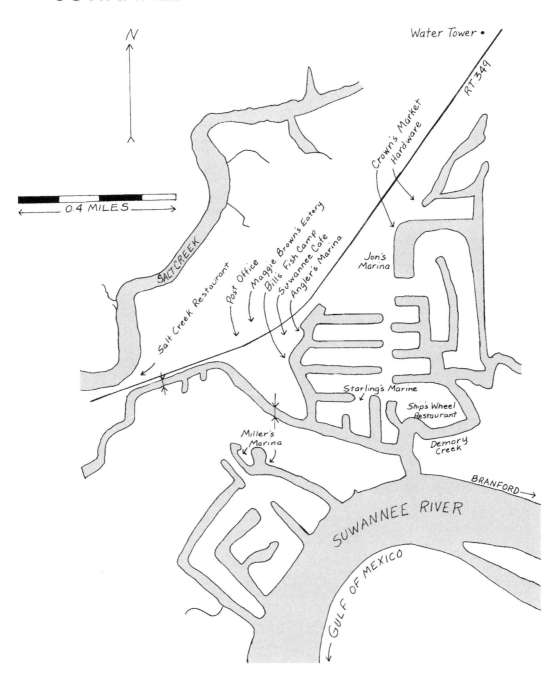

N

0.4 MILES

Water Tower •

RT 349

SALT CREEK

Crown's Market
Hardware

Jon's
Marina

Salt Creek Restaurant

Post Office
Maggie Brown's Eatery
Bill's Fish Camp
Suwannee Cafe
Angler's Marina

Starling's Marine

Ship's Wheel
Restaurant

Demory
Creek

Miller's
Marina

BRANFORD →

SUWANNEE RIVER

GULF OF MEXICO

Triumphant fishermen at Angler's Resort Marina, Suwannee

Indians en route. Near Cedar Key, Jackson encountered two British citizens who he thought were trading goods with the Indians. They probably were. After marching the two men back to St. Marks, Jackson summarily had them executed. One was shot, and the other was hanged. Britain was so infuriated by General Jackson's behavior that it was about to go to war with the Americans for the third time in 40 years! The U.S. House of Representa-tives, in an attempt to be politically correct, condemned Jackson for his actions. However, others in Congress tacitly approved, and Jackson was elected the seventh U.S. president only ten years later.

Cedar Key started to seriously develop around 1835, with the construction of a military depot and hospital. In the 1840s, Cedar Key was an important port for the shipment of cotton, sugar, tobacco, and lumber. However, a hurricane annihilated this early development. In 1853, work was started on Florida's first "cross state" railroad, but the financing and construction was sporadic. In 1861, with the help of Florida senator David Yulee, the 380-mile Atlantic-to-Gulf railroad finally connected Cedar Key to Fernandina Beach (north of Jacksonville).

When Cedar Key was blockaded by Union forces during the Civil War, many locals became skilled as blockade-runners. Block-ade-runners were carrying out cotton, turpentine, rosin, and lumber and sneaking in sugar, coffee, flour, sulfur, and gun powder. Eventually Union troops, coming from the Gulf, sacked Cedar Key, and the locals had to abandon the town.

Also during the Civil War, salt became one of the largest industries in Confederate Florida. In those prerefrigeration days, salt was a precious commodity needed to preserve many foods. The effective Union blockade dried up the pre-Civil War South's salt supply, which was previously imported from England. So these resourceful Confederates began distilling their own salt from the Florida waters of the Gulf of Mexico. Cedar Key and St. Marks were pivotal to the Confederacy as sources of salt. Whenever Union raiding parties attacked coastal settlements, such as Cedar Key and St. Marks, they generally made a point to knock out as much Confederate salt production as possible by rupturing the huge cast-iron boiling kettles.

In 1867, noted naturalist John Muir ended a 1,000-mile hike from Indianapolis to the Gulf of Mexico at Cedar Key. After contracting malaria, Muir needed to recuperate for three months in Cedar Key. The region prospered after the Civil War. In the middle of the nineteenth century, Cedar Key was a major trading port with regular routes to New Orleans, Key West, and Havana, Cuba. By the 1880s, only the Florida ports of Jacksonville, Key West, Fernandina Beach, and Pensacola ranked ahead of Cedar Key. Around 1869, several large pencil factories were built to take advantage of the region's red cedar trees for pencil stock. Cedar Key's population peaked at 5,000 people in 1888. But near the dawn of the twentieth century, the red cedar trees were nearly depleted, and Tampa was selected over Cedar Key as the west-coast rail hub. If that wasn't enough, in 1896, a fierce hurricane, with over a 27-foot tidal surge, killed several hundred people and wiped out the railroad, the pencil mills, and 5,000 square miles of standing timber. Cedar Key was devastated, and its heyday was over. Today, the population of Cedar Key is in the neighborhood of 800 permanent residents.

Throughout the last 150 years, Cedar Key residents have been heavily engaged in fishing, oystering, crabbing, turtling, sponging, and boat building. One on hand, today's Cedar Key—with all the trendy shops, waterfront restaurants, and sunset piers—reminds me of a small-scaled Key West. On the other hand, Cedar Key—with its tidal marshes, mud flats, and "scraping for a living" watermen—reminds me of Maryland's eastern shore of the Chesapeake Bay. In mid-October, Cedar Key hosts its famous annual seafood festival. And in April, there is the sidewalk art festival.

Like Suwannee Sound, there are about three separate approaches to Cedar Key—Northwest Channel (from the west and north), the Main Ship Channel (from the southwest), and South Bar Channel (from the east and Waccasassa Bay). Besides its many islands, the local waters are peppered with small shoals. However, the two main channels are very well marked with many lighted navigation aids. There are a few hairpin turns in these channels, and it behooves you not to take any shortcuts. If you become temporarily disoriented around any of these channels, look for the white water tower on Cedar Key. It's very visible from any direction of approach—from Suwannee to the three Cedar Key channels and well into Waccasassa Bay. Better yet, before you start plying all over these water, try to find a source of local knowledge. Early on, I had the good fortune to befriend Capt. Bill Roberts as we both waited at anchor for a rising tide to negotiate the shallows beneath the city bridge.

Northwest Channel

To arrive at Northwest Channel aid "R2," position yourself at 29.08.500N/83.07.900W.

If you can live with six feet of water depth at MLW, you may be able to head directly for Northwest Channel's "G3," at way point 29.08.471N/83.06.261W. "G3" is a lighted tripod. The initial heading after "G3" is about 110 degrees. We encountered between nine and 12 feet at MLW between "G3" and "G9." After "R6," the channel doglegs slightly to port on a heading of 95 degrees. Near "R6," you'll be passing the north side of North Key. Between "G11" and "R16," the channel holds a seven- to eight-foot depth at MLW. In Northwest Channel, the *U.S. Coast Pilot* indicates a six-and-a-half-foot channel. HAZARD The *U.S. Coast Pilot* states that there is only three feet of water between "G17 and G19." We noted that the water did shallow near "G17A and R18," but we still encountered water depths of five to six feet at MLW. After "G21 and R22," water deepens back to seven to eight feet. Northwest Channel has several lighted navigation aids—"R2," "G3," "R6," "G9," "G11," "R16," "R18," and "G19. After "G21 and R22," head for lighted mark "R30." The Northwest Channel intersects the Main Ship Channel near Main Ship Channel lighted aid "R30." Follow the Main Ship Channel to the fishing pier off Cedar Key or to the anchorage area beyond "R36."

Main Ship Channel

Seahorse Reef sits out in the Gulf of Mexico from about two and a half miles west to nine miles southwest of Main Ship Channel. From this north end, Seahorse Reef extends in a south-southwestern direction for about eight miles. HAZARD *Some places over this reef are as shallow as four to five feet.* The Cedar Key Main Ship Channel begins at "G1," about two and a half miles east of the northern end of

Seahorse Reef—near way point 29.03.988N/ 83.04. 577W, in 12 feet at MLW. "G1" is an unusual-looking green can buoy with a light perched atop. After "G1," look for the next navigation aids in the direction of 35 degrees. You should encounter about ten to twelve feet of water depth, MLW, between "G7" and "G9." Near "R12" and Seahorse Key (on port side while entering), the channel narrows and the water depths shallow to seven feet at MLW. The *U.S. Coast Pilot* states a controlling depth of seven feet for this channel.

Seahorse Key is an enticing key with sandy beaches and calm lagoons. The key is a seabird nesting area and is off-limits between March and June. Seahorse Key is also the center for marine research and environmental education for the University of Florida. There is also a decommissioned lighthouse on Seahorse Key. That lighthouse was built in 1855 by Lt. George Meade. Eight years later, General Meade was commanding the Union forces in a great Civil War battle at Gettysburg, Pennsylvania. About twenty years earlier, Seahorse Key was a prisoner-of-war camp for Seminole Indians.

Past "R12," all the way to "G27," the Main Ship Channel deepens again from eight to 13 feet at MLW. HAZARD *The channel becomes very confusing near the vicinity of "R26, G27, and R28."* Directly ahead, there is a narrow sand bar extending about a half-mile to port and a mile to starboard. You could leave this sand bar on either side, but the Main Ship Channel turns to the port, leaving that sand bar to starboard for the remainder of the way in. After arriving at "R30," you have cleared the southwestern tip of the sand bar, and you can make a hairpin turn back to the northeast toward the fishing pier off Cedar Key. The

Northwest Channel has joined the Main Ship channel at "R30." The last mark in the Main Ship Channel is unlighted "R36." There is eight to 11 feet at MLW between "R30" and "R36." Unlighted "R36" is less than a half-mile from the fishing pier. The Cedar Key anchorage area off Atsena Otie Key will be to your starboard. If you enter the Atsena Otie Key anchorage area, be sure to give the water east of "R36" a wide berth. The northeastern tip of that long sand bar ends near "R36." The lighted navigation aids in the Main Ship Channel are "G1," "G7," "G9," "R18," "G21," "G23," "G27," and "R30." Atsena Otie Key housed a federal military hospital and a supply depot during the Civil War. In the latter part of the nineteenth century, a Faber Pencil Mill shaped the local red cedars into pencil slats on Atsena Otie Key.

There is also another approach to this anchorage area from near "R26." At "R26," instead of turning left toward "R30," turn right toward the northern tip of Atsena Otie Key. On this shorter route to the anchorage, you should be leaving that shallow sand bar on your port side. Study NOAA chart 11408 beforehand. Atsena Otie Key is a national wildlife refuge. A long *T*-dock extends from the northwest side of the island in seven feet of water. The end of the *T*-dock is coated in distasteful and smelly guano.

South Bar Channel

The South Bar Channel is more of an approach than an actual channel. If you are arriving at Cedar Key from the east or southeast (i.e., from the western part of Waccasassa Bay) and you only require about three feet of draft at MLW, this is an acceptable approach. In Waccasassa Bay, position yourself at 29.07.210N/82.58.826W. You'll be off the only

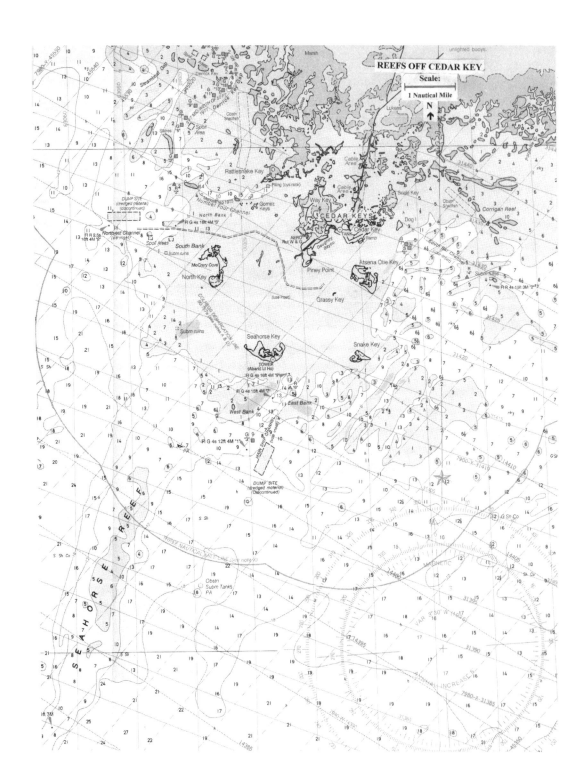

REEFS OFF CEDAR KEY.

Anchorage off Atsena Otie Key

lighted navigation aid in this channel, "R2," in three to four feet at MLW. Head in a northwesterly direction, passing "R4" and "G5 and G7." You should be able to find no less than three feet of water at MLW. After "G7," dogleg to your port slightly and then you should be able see the last marker, "R8." "R8" is in six feet at MLW and about a half-mile east of the main Cedar Key fishing pier. The *U.S. Coast Pilot* stated a controlling depth of two and a half feet in this channel. For all three of these channels, please study NOAA chart 11408 beforehand.

Cedar Key

The village of Cedar Key hosts over a dozen restaurants, a greater number of boutiques, several bed and breakfasts, a few motels, a hardware store, an auto parts store, a Laundromat, and a grocery store. But the town has no easily accessible-by-water deep-draft marinas. Many of the finer restaurants and boutiques are on Dock Street, near the very large fixed wooden fishing pier protruding into the Main Ship Channel. This large intimidating public pier has no utilities and is primarily used by locals for fishing, day and night. There are a few sliplike places on the pier, but the pier is so high over the water, it would be difficult to tie dock lines and clamber off the deck of your typical cruising boat.

This hefty pier was once the terminus of the railroad on the mainland.

The so-called City Marina is located in the small basin on the other side of this large pier. Access to this basin is beneath a road bridge on the southwest side of the basin. At high tide, there may only be six to seven feet of vertical clearance beneath this road bridge. At low tide, there may be less than a foot of water depth beneath the bridge. Nevertheless, the floating concrete dock in this small basin on the inside of the bridge is a good landing area for the dinghies coming from the larger boats anchored out near Atsena Otie Key. There are also two boat ramps near this concrete dock. One ramp is inside the small basin, and the other is a concrete ramp across the street. The ramp across the street (the offshore ramp) has two small fixed wooden piers, and boats need not negotiate in the small basin or beneath the bridge. A few of the local mid-sized tour and commercial boats also have dock space near this offshore ramp.

The highly suspect, very shallow, and marginally marked channel leading to Willis Marina begins near the offshore ramp. Willis Marina is primarily a high-and-dry facility for small local boats and the channel to the marina is unapproachable at mid-tide for even compact-sized

Old railhead and pier at Cedar Key

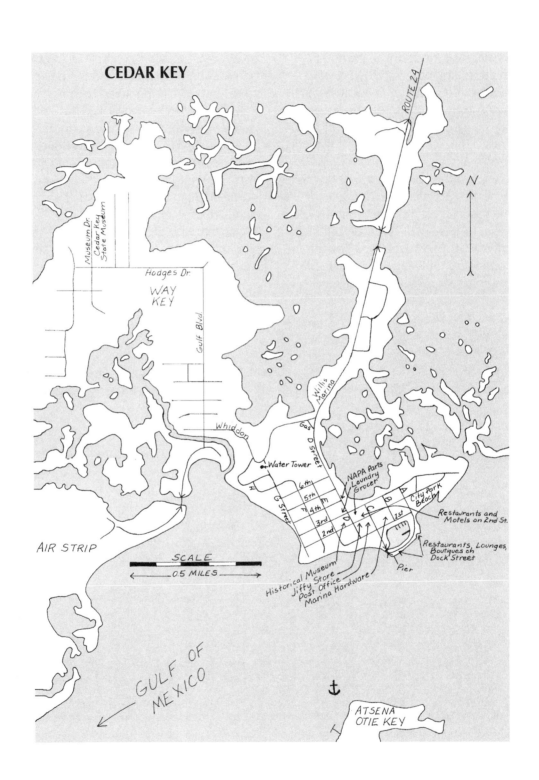

CEDAR KEY

ROUTE 24

N

Museum Dr.
Cedar Key State Museum

Hodges Dr.

WAY KEY

Gulf Blvd

Whiddon

Willis Marina

Gas

D Street

Water Tower

6th

5th

4th

3rd

2nd

G Street

H

NAPA Parts
Laundry
Grocer

City Park Beach

1st

Restaurants and Motels on 2nd St.

Restaurants, Lounges, Boutiques on Dock Street

Pier

AIR STRIP

SCALE
0.5 MILES

Historical Museum
Jiffy Store
Post Office
Marina Hardware

GULF OF MEXICO

ATSENA OTIE KEY

transiting vessels. It is not recommended that transient boats try to find their way though the tidal marsh flats to Willis. If you need fuel or other marine supplies, phone Willis. They may very well be able to accommodate your needs by making a trip to the main city dock. If, for some unusual reason, you had to get a shallow-draft vessel to Willis Marina, this very fluky channel is on the east side of Way Key. Willis Marina has a ship's store, a high-and-dry storage building, and primarily caters to watermen and small boats.

Willis Marina (352) 543-6148

Approach depth—less than 1 foot

Accepts transients—no

Gasoline—yes, with portable containers to fishing pier

Diesel—yes, with portable containers to fishing pier

Mechanical repairs—yes

Below-waterline repairs—up to 30 feet with a forklift

Ship's store—yes

The main part of Cedar Key is only about three blocks wide and about seven blocks long. Dock Street fronts the Gulf. Second Street parallels Dock Street two blocks away from the Gulf. The commercial district and many of the city restaurants (i.e., which have nonwaterfront prices) can be found on Second Street. There is a public beach, with picnic pavilions and outside showers, in a small park on the east end of Cedar Key, near First and A streets. Marina hardware store is at the corner of First and B streets. The very informative Cedar Key Historical Museum is located at northwest corner of D and Second streets. D Street is perpendicular to Second

Street and becomes the only road out of town—State Route 24. A grocery store, Laundromat, auto-parts store, gas stations, and Willis Marina are on D Street, heading out of town. The Cedar Key State Museum is also off this road and about a mile and a half to the northwest. This enlightening museum is closed on Tuesdays and Wednesdays.

What once was the town of Rosewood is about ten miles east of Cedar Key on Florida State Route 24. No one knows with absolute certainty what set off the shameful events in 1923 or exactly what events followed—events that would later be known as the Rosewood Massacre. White mill workers (some were fugitives from far away places) were drawn to gritty sawmills in the Cedar Key region. These low breed sawmill workers regularly drank themselves senseless, and this was very easy because illegal stills were everywhere on the Big Bend. Nearby was an African-American community called Rosewood, and these folks, in the minority, also worked in the mills or the mill support economy. Somewhere between a few dozen and 100 people were murdered—and by far, most of them were African-American. And those African-Americans who weren't murdered, eventually left, never to return.

Here are two versions leading to these tragic events of early 1923. A white woman with a battered face claimed that an intruder had entered her house. Soon tracking dogs followed the "intruder's" scent along the railroad tracks three miles to the community of Rosewood. Another version has a white woman regularly playing around in the black community. When she discovered that she was pregnant, she was cornered by drunken white sawmillers. She *then* cried rape. The looking-for-an-excuse horde of sawmillers, about to be murderers, went to Rosewood and burned down a house, incinerating the six scared black folks inside. And a couple of the white drunks were shot. Soon other blacks from Rosewood tried to leave, but the white train guards (the trains were the only way out at that time) wouldn't let them out of the area. Over the coming months, more blacks were shot, lynched, or just chopped to pieces. As much as many would wish to forget it, Rosewood should be a painful reminder to us all of how ignorance, prejudice, the lack of restraint, and an absence of law and order can lead to such inhumanity—even in the United States and less than a century ago.

Waccasassa Bay and River

HAZARD *Like Suwannee Sound, Waccasassa Bay is strewn with shallow patches, shoals, and reefs.* And to make matters even worse, Waccasassa Bay has many more shallow areas (that are much more extensive) than shown on NOAA chart 11408. Furthermore, this bay is littered with old pilings and floating weeds that could foul a boat's propeller. Unless you want to explore the shallow Waccasassa River, or

Cedar Key waterfront

Waccasassa River

fish the river or bay, you may wish to consider bypassing Waccasassa Bay. It's only about 16 miles on a rhumb line from "R2" of the Cedar Key Main Ship Channel to the "G1" off the Withlacoochee River Channel (or 14 miles on a rhumb line from the "R2" of Cedar Key's South Bar Channel to the Withlacoochee Channel's "G1"). There are two distant horizon features on Waccasassa Bay. The white water tower on Cedar Key can be spied to the west or northwest from just about anywhere on Waccasassa Bay. And even more dominant, and south of Waccasassa Bay, the towers of the Crystal River Nuclear Power Plant can be seen for more than 20 miles. And there are many places in Waccasassa Bay where you can barely see the low-lying shoreline and soon find yourself hard aground. Please study NOAA chart 11408 carefully. The entrance to the Waccasassa River (along with the entrance to the Econfina River) is one of the shallowest ones on the entire Big Bend.

To enter the Waccasassa River Channel, position yourself at 29.06.438N/82.51.235W in Waccasassa Bay. You should be right off unlighted "R2" in two to three feet at MLW.

After arriving at "R2," look for your next navigation aids on a heading of 55 degrees. None of the navigation aids in the Waccasassa Channel or Waccasassa River are lighted. Never try this particular channel at night. There is a relatively long distance between the small navigation aids, and the channel makes slight-angled and often continuously reversing doglegs. There is about three to five feet of water depth, MLW, in between "R2" and "G9." Most of the navigation aids in this channel are of the green persuasion (i.e., they should be passed on your port side while entering). HAZARD *As you near the river's* *mouth (i.e., after "R24 and G25"), there are more and more shoals and navigating becomes trickier and trickier. The U.S. Coast Pilot indicates that the controlling depth should be two feet. We think, near the river's mouth, this depth may be even less at MLW. And to compound matters, some of the red marks shown on NOAA chart 11408 near the mouth of the Waccasassa River were not physically observed in the area.*

Just because you might notice an airboat or two "taking a route" through the patchwork of shoals and islands in this area, don't assume there will be enough deep water for your boat.

Up the Waccasassa River

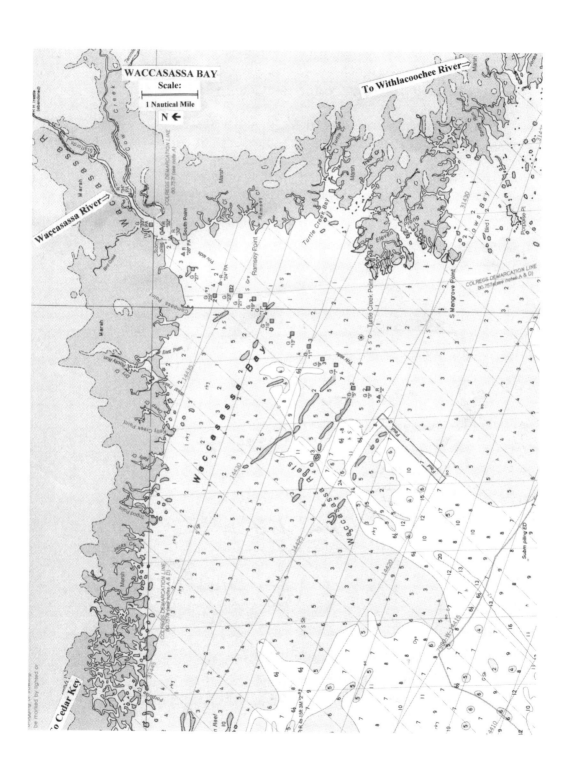

WACCASASSA BAY
Scale:

1 Nautical Mile

N ←

To Withlacoochee River →

Waccasassa River →

To Cedar Key →

After passing the river's mouth, the deeper water seems to be closer to the RDB side (i.e., pass some of the larger islands as LDB). On the bright side, at least the water depth increases to about nine feet at MLW in a few places beyond the river's mouth. The last marker, "R34," is at the junction of Cow Creek and the Waccasassa River. Cow Creek goes off on the LDB shore, while the Waccasassa River follows the RDB shore (or the shore to our port). This area is the Waccasassa Bay State Preserve. In the river after "R34," water depths are ample, at nine to 18 feet at MLW.

The Seminole name Waccasassa means something like "place of cattle." The lower Waccasassa River is picturesque, about 80 yards wide and lined with scattered palm trees. Staffords Island splits the river about a mile past

Cow Creek. We passed the island in the right fork, leaving Staffords Island as RDB, and found four to 18 feet at MLW on this preferred side. In the upper part of the left river fork, near the northern tip of the island, there is some very thin water. Staffords Island is about a mile long. Upriver from Staffords Island, the possibility of encountering partially submerged stumps and branches becomes greater the farther upriver you travel. The river is popular with small fishing skiffs and noisy airboats. The ruins of an old railroad trestle can be seen on both sides of the river about a mile upstream from Staffords Island. Farther up, there is a park with a public concrete ramp. An inviting 40-foot dock sits about two miles upriver from the northern tip of Staffords Island on the RDB. This park also has bathrooms and trash receptacles. The

Near the Waccasassa Fishing Club

Waccasassa Fishing Club is another quarter mile beyond this dock and ramp. This fishing club is situated in a small arm off the Waccasassa's RDB. The private club has a concrete ramp, a nice side-tie dock, a clubhouse, a trailer park, and a small variety store. They generally don't cater to overnight transients, but a boater could purchase gasoline, ice, and other items from their variety store.

Waccasassa Fishing Club (352) 486-6380

Approach depth—less than 2 feet
Dockside depth—4-7 feet
Accepts transients—generally no
Fixed wooden dock—yes
Gasoline—yes
Boat ramp—yes
Variety store—yes
Clubhouse—yes

Cypress trees on the Withlacoochee River

CHAPTER 11

The Crystal River Region, from the Withlacoochee to the Homosassa River

This chapter of the Big Bend has three recreational and two commercial channels. The recreation channels are about five miles long between the sea buoys and the mouth of the river. All of these recreational channels have tricky sections, and often there are rocks along the channel edges. Furthermore, like the channels in the previous chapter, there are many scattered reefs and oyster bars extending well into the Gulf of Mexico. And that is the reason

why these channels likely need to be about five miles long—to pick a way though the mazes of the many offshore reefs. All three recreational channels maintain reasonably good depths when compared to the channels to the north or to the south of this area. The Withlacoochee Channel has a stated controlling depth of five and a half feet, but we'd estimate that there was no less than nine to 12 feet at MLW. The Crystal River Channel has a NOAA-stated controlling

The unfinished Cross Florida Barge Canal

depth of five and a half feet. And the unusual Homosassa River Channel has a stated controlling MLW depth of three and a half feet. Much of the Homosassa channel and river were much deeper; however, we did encounter a few four-foot-deep MLW "shallow patches." The northernmost channel, the Withlacoochee River, begins near another channel—the Cross Florida Greenway.

The entrance to the never-completed Cross Florida Barge Canal sits to the south of the Withlacoochee River Channel. The idea for this canal goes back 400 years to St. Augustine's founder, Pedro Menéndez de Avilés. The idea was later resurrected by Pres. Thomas Jefferson, war secretary (and later to be president of the Confederacy) Jefferson Davis, Robert E. Lee, and presidents Theodore Roosevelt, Calvin Coolidge, Franklin Roosevelt, and John Kennedy. In 1964, during the Lyndon Johnson administration, sufficient funds for digging finally became a reality. Later in 1968, with high inflation and the Vietnam War, funding became restricted. The canal, with digging started at both ends, was to meet somewhere in the middle. By the 1970s, the funding ceased and the digging stopped. During the 1970s, environmental concerns also arose. A deep canal cutting east-west through Florida aquifers could have the potential to divert the north-to-south-flowing underground water out of the natural aquifers and thereby parch the land south of the canal. Today, as it was in 1971, the canal is only one-third completed. Politicians, both at the local and national levels, have argued the merits and shortcoming of this expensive and unfinished project. In 1986, the federal government deauthorized the project

Recreational boats on the Withlacoochee River

and shortly turned the canal right of way over to the state of Florida. That right of way has become the Cross Florida Greenway—a good fortune to hikers, bikers, and horseback riders. Today, the Florida Fish and Wildlife Conservation Commission, and a public boat ramp with a 50-foot floating wooden dock, are housed on the LDB in the westernmost five miles of this unfinished (probably never-to-be-finished) barge canal. There is also a failed Sun Cruz casino operation in the canal. The fixed wooden pier on the RDB used to belong to this casino boat.

Withlacoochee River

Our Withlacoochee River originates about 100 miles from the Gulf of Mexico in the Green Swamp, southwest of Orlando. Believe it or not, there are two Withlacoochee rivers in Florida. The Withlacoochee #2, or Withlacoochee West,

originates in the middle of Georgia, flows past Valdosta, and feeds into Florida's Suwannee River near Suwannee River mile 128. In the Seminole tongue, Withlacoochee translates to "little river." The nearby Cross Florida Barge Canal limits our from-the-Gulf navigation on our Withlacoochee River to a little less than 11 miles. An old lock and dam once permitted us to navigate the Withlacoochee into Lake Rousseau and then farther inland. But an unfinished nine-mile section of that barge canal cut through the Withlacoochee River and an ugly earthen berm wall blocks the Withlacoochee River. A complicated channelization scheme—involving a new lock, an old dam, a new spillway, and a barge canal—severed the upper Withlacoochee from its lowest portion. And now the new lock, the Inglis Lock, on the barge canal is permanently closed.

Spillway on the Withlacoochee River

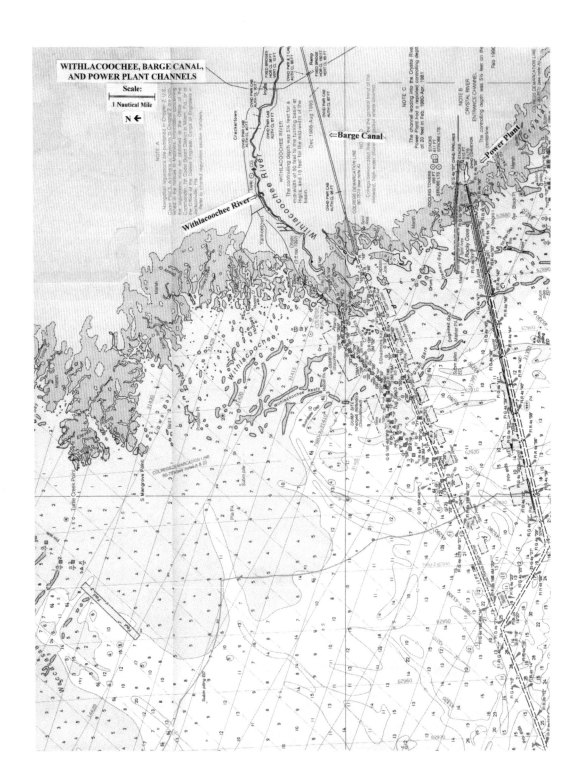

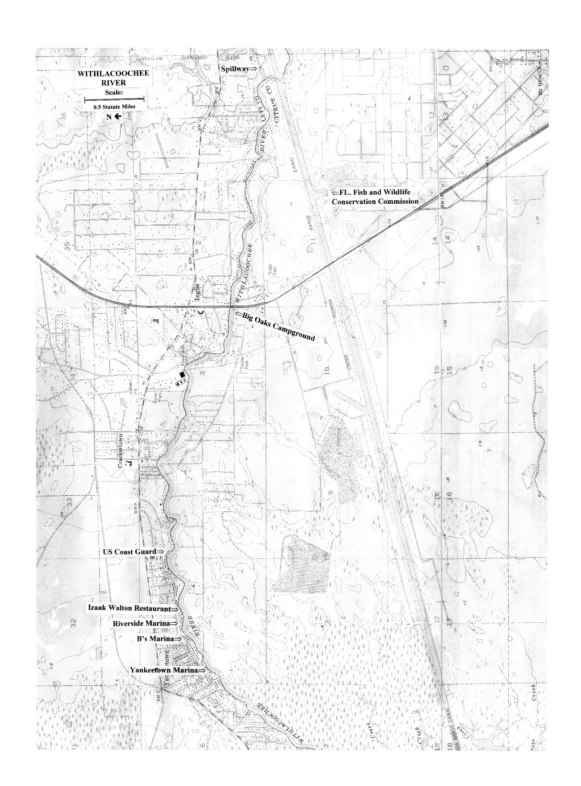

WITHLACOOCHEE RIVER

Scale:

0.5 Statute Miles

N ←

Spillway⇒

⇐FL. Fish and Wildlife
Conservation Commission

⇐Big Oaks Campground

US Coast Guard⇒

Izaak Walton Restaurant⇒

Riverside Marina⇒

B's Marina⇒

Yankeetown Marina⇒

The lower Withlacoochee River is one of the deepest rivers on Florida's Big Bend. No spots are less than ten feet deep, and there are many places as deep as 18 feet. But this is not natural. This deep channel was cut many years ago, allowing barges to supply the power plant six miles from the Gulf. That coal-fired power plant has long been decommissioned in favor of the more efficient, and possibly safer, Crystal River Nuclear Power Plant (also with coal-firing capacity), five miles away. The Withlacoochee River forms the border between Levy and Citrus counties. The developments in Yankeetown (downriver) and Inglis (slightly up the river) are both on the navigable Withlacoochee River's RDB, in Levy County. Inglis doesn't have any marinas, but the town is more commercialized than Yankeetown. A trip up the lowest 11 miles (or lowest eight miles if you can't squeeze beneath the ten-foot-clearance highway bridge) of the Withlacoochee is quite enchanting. There are three reliable marinas, a half-dozen boat ramps, a first-class restaurant and lodge, a friendly little campground with a dock, and a U.S. Coast Guard station.

HAZARD *Out in the Gulf of Mexico, the Withlacoochee Channel has many exposed and many slightly submerged rocks on the edge of both sides of the channel. An encounter with these rocks could be disastrous to a boat. To enter this channel, position yourself off the sea buoy, lighted aid "G1," near way point 28.58.127N/82.49.727W. We were in 12 feet of water at MLW. If you are approaching this way point from the south, be careful. You will need to first cross the Cross Florida Barge Canal Channel. This channel*

Yankeetown Marina on the Withlacoochee River

has a series of spoil islands on its south, or LDB, side. If you can't scoot your boat in between two spoil islands, you'll need to approach this way point from the west rather than from the south. Study NOAA charts 11408 or 11409 carefully. The *U.S. Coast Pilot* indicated a controlling depth of only five feet in the channel to aid "R46" and deeper water beyond "R46." However, we found this channel to be significantly deeper.

The Withlacoochee Channel does have many navigation aids, but only a few of them are lighted. Besides having many aids, there are many navigation aids suffixed with an *A* and sometimes even suffixed with a *B* designation. This is good and bad. It's good because they have that *A*, and sometimes a *B*, supplemental aid. It's bad because they *need* them. Boats have probably previously strayed between navigation aid "xA" and the next navigation aid "x+1" (where *x* is any number) and become grounded on the rocks near the channel's edge. Thus there is a need for a supplemental navigation aid, "xB," in between "xA" and "x+1." (You never know when that old high-school algebra will come in handy.) In any event, always head directly from one navigation aid to the very next navigational aid with minimal deviation in this tricky channel. The Withlacoochee River mouth finally materializes near aid "R36A." There is a public concrete double-boat ramp with a very short pier on the RDB near marker "R40." The lower part of the river is about 80 yards wide and often has a rocky shoreline. A few gnarled cedar trees dot the banks. The last navigation aid is "R46."

There are three marinas within a mile of each other on the RDB in Yankeetown. Yankeetown Marina is beyond the second canal on the RDB. This marina is the largest facility and has about 60 slips, but most of the spaces are taken by shrimpers. B's Marina and Campground has about a dozen slips, and Riverside Marina and Cottages has about two dozen slips. The latter two marinas focus on recreational boaters, and both can accommodate up to about 50-footers. There is a seafood-packing house, also on the RDB, in between Yankeetown Marina and B's Marina. Both B's Marina and Riverside Marina have very nice grounds and docks. The nearby Izaak Walton Lodge and Restaurant serves fine foods for lunch and dinner. This upscale restaurant and lodge is located on the river. There is also a small grocer within walking distance from all three marinas in Yankeetown. At Riverside Marina, Carl and Barbara (who originally hail from coastal Connecticut) twice wouldn't let me leave before I first imbibed a British beer. I liked them both—and the beer. Our boating discussions (with the help of British beers) evolved into a discourse on this new post-September 11 world in which we all live. Carl and I spoke our minds and agreed on many things.

Yankeetown Marina (352) 447-2529

Approach depth—4 feet

Accepts transients—yes

Fixed wooden docks—yes

Dockside power connections—30 amp

Dockside water connections—yes

Showers—no

Gasoline—yes

Diesel—yes

Mechanical repairs—yes (nearby contractors)

Boat ramp—yes

Ship's store—yes, limited

Restaurant—a half-mile away

B's Marina on the Withlacoochee River

B's Marina and Campground (352) 447-5888

Approach depth—6 feet
Accepts transients—yes
Fixed wooden docks—yes
Dockside power connections—20 and 30 amp
Dockside water connections—yes
Showers—yes
Laundromat—yes
Mechanical repairs—with local contractors
Boat ramp—yes
Restaurant—three blocks away

Riverside Marina and Cottages (352) 447-2980
www.yankeetownyachtclub.com

Approach depth—6 feet
Accepts transients—yes
Fixed wooden docks—yes

Dockside power connections—30 and twin 30 amp
Dockside water connections—yes
Showers—yes
Laundromat—yes
Nautical gift shop—yes
Mechanical repairs—with local contractors
Restaurant—next door

A U.S. Coast Guard station, (352) 447-6900, from the USCG Seventh District, is about another half-mile upriver from Riverside Marina on the RDB. This USCG Search and Rescue and Law Enforcement operation covers a large swath of the Gulf of Mexico—from the Fenholloway River to Hernando Beach. Another USCG station out of Clearwater covers the region south of

Riverside Marina on the Withlacoochee River

Hernando Beach. A station from Panama City, in another USCG district, covers search, rescue, and law-enforcement operations west of the Fenholloway River. The Yankeetown USCG station uses three fast trailerable boats, the largest being 27 feet long. About 30 uniformed military personnel work at this operation seven days a week, 24 hours a day.

The attractive Withlacoochee River remains deep but gradually narrows to about 30 to 40 yards wide. Water depths to the highway bridge remain ten to 13 feet, MLW. The Withlacoochee keeps a boater guessing what's around the next bend. There could be some colorful seen-better-days shrimper or a new posh private semi-mansion. And that next bend ain't never going to be very far away! Three sets of overhead power lines straddle the Withlacoochee River several miles from the Gulf and near the old coal-fired power plant. HAZARD *The U.S. Coast Pilot states only 40 feet of overhead clearance, but we thought that the lowest clearances were about ten feet higher.* There is a wide spot in the river, the old turning basin near that old power plant on the RDB, about five and a half miles from the coast. An island is situated about a quarter mile past the old power plant site. Leave this island like the RDB, and there will be ten feet of water depth.

Big Oaks Campground is on the LDB just prior to the highway bridge. HAZARD *The U.S. Coast Pilot indicates a bridge clearance at ten feet, but interpolating between the tidal range, we'd estimate the clearance to be as little as at eight feet at high tide but 12 feet at low tide.*

Big Oaks River Resort and Campground Marina
(353) 447-5333
www.bigoakscampground.com

Approach depth—10 feet
Accepts transients—very limited (to small boats)
Small fixed wooden pier—yes
Small floating aluminum dock—yes
Showers—yes
Laundromat—yes
Boat ramp—yes
Pool—yes
Restaurant—a few nearby on the highway
Cabins—yes, on site
Motels—nearby on highway
Convenience stores—nearby on highway

Upriver from the highway bridge, the river narrows in some places to as little as 15 yards wide. Semisubmerged tree limbs also begin encroaching from the riverbanks. Low overhead branches are another consideration. Nevertheless, if you haven't already used your camera, have it ready. The water depth remains nine to 15 feet deep, but the current doesn't abate. There is a hairpin turn in an enchanting pool about a mile and a half past the highway bridge. But this pool is too deep for anchoring—between 20 and 40 feet deep. The "end of the line" is another half-mile up. The berm from the barge canal blocks our access to the rest of the enchanting Withlacoochee River. A spillway and a restricted boating area are off to our RDB. Water flowing out of Lake Rousseau is channeled onto this fast-moving spillway.

Returning to the Gulf of Mexico, north-south navigation in between the Withlacoochee and Crystal rivers is most interesting.

Workboats on the Withlacoochee River

There are two east-west industrial channels that must be *crossed*. The northernmost channel is the unfinished Cross Florida Barge Canal and the southernmost channel is the Florida Power Crystal River Nuclear Power Plant Channel. Coal barges occasionally use the Power Plant Channel. The Power Plant Channel has a controlling depth of 20 feet, and the Cross Florida Barge Canal has a controlling depth of 11 feet. HAZARD *The sides of both of these industrial channels are strewn with spoil islands.* In many places these spoil islands make a near-impregnable north-south barrier. This area is "spoil bank" city. There is a thicker and longer row of spoil islands on the south side of Barge Canal Channel. And there is a thicker and longer row of spoil islands on the north side of the Power Plant Channel. You need to study the northern part NOAA chart 11409 very carefully.

HAZARD *There are some tricky north-south shortcuts through these spoil islands.* Carl, at Riverside Marina, is the best one to ask if you are inclined to take a north-south shortcut. The first southbound shortcut deviates from the Withlacoochee Channel near aid "R18A." A near south heading should allow you to slice between a couple of spoil islands of the Barge Canal Channel and remain in no less than seven feet at MLW. But crossing the spoil islands of that Power Plant Channel is more perplexing. We found a "cross-the-channel" gap with seven to 15 feet, MLW, just west of lighted aids "G39 and R40" of the Power Plant Channel and near way point 28.56.222N/82.48.100W.

Crystal River and Kings Bay

Crystal River—or the headwaters, Kings Bay—is created by Florida's second largest system of natural springs. On a daily basis, more than 30 springs pump out about 3 million cubic yards of water. As the name implies, the waters really are almost crystal clear. Without doubt, this is the largest font of clear water along Florida's Big Bend. The water temperature is 72 degrees year around. Crystal River is one place that especially capitalizes on that "manatee industry." From October until March each year, Crystal River may be the home to the largest herd in Florida of wintering manatees. Each January, Crystal River hosts the Florida Manatee Festival. At certain times of the year, folks can swim with, but not touch, the manatees. Crystal River is also home to one of Florida's better-known pre-Columbian archaeological sites. Visitors can view the remains of ancient Indian mounds and burial grounds.

The Crystal River Channel is about five miles long, and then it's another five miles in the Crystal River to Kings Bay. There are two large marinas and a few smaller boating facilities in this area. Of the three recreational channels in this chapter, the Crystal River Channel and River is the easiest one to negotiate. From out in the Gulf of Mexico, position yourself off "G1 and R2" in 12 feet at MLW near way point 28.54.703N/82.44.920W Navigation aid "G1" is the only lighted marker for the Crystal River Channel. We encountered MLW depths in the channel ranging from six to eight feet. But once again the *U.S. Coast Pilot* states considerably less water at a four-foot controlling depth to aid "R24." And NOAA stated a five and a half-foot controlling depth. At "G5 and R6," the channel makes a pronounced dogleg to the starboard. The shallowest stretch of this channel is between "G13 and R14" and "G19 and R20." We were getting readings as shallow as five-to-six feet at MLW. After "G21 and R22," the water deepens back to eight feet, and then back to 14 feet at "R24."

A pretty beach can be seen on the LDB near the mouth of the Crystal River. The Fort Island Public Boat Ramp is south of this beach. The boat ramp has a floating dock and a ramp for shallow-draft boats. Nearby, there is also another nice beach with a bathhouse on the Gulf of Mexico—Fort Island Gulf Beach.

Back on the Crystal River, after aid "G25," the channel numbering system restarts at "G1," but there will still be no more lighted navigation aids. The land on the LDB is actually an island—Pine Island. We observed a couple of wild boars rooting along the beaches of Pine Island. We encountered ten-to-eighteen feet water depths MLW in the remainder of the channel of the Crystal River, although the US Coast Pilot stated only a three foot controlling depth. The last pair of daymarks (i.e., after the "second G1") are "G29 & R30." Both the river and the channel are very wide all of the way to Kings Bay. This river has an open airy feeling in contrast to many other rivers along the Big Bend.

There is a small bay about three miles from the river's mouth on the RDB. A boat ramp with a 30-foot floating aluminum dock, a USCG Auxiliary flotilla building, and the St. Martin's Marsh Aquatic Preserve Nature/ Visitor's Center are in this small bay. The Salt River diverges from the Crystal River about a quarter mile upstream from the visitor's center on the opposite shore (the LDB of Crystal River). After taking a right turn into the Salt River, the numbers on the navigation aids start decreasing, so I guess we are going back out to sea on the Salt River and Pine Island is now on our RDB. Beware, there is an overhead power line over the Salt River! Both the *U.S. Coast Pilot* and the NOAA charts indicate that this power line has 47 feet of overhead clearance. In February 2002, cruising guide guru Claiborne Young got wind of, and then ran down, a potentially calamitous situation involving this power line. The stated 47-foot-high cable had been knocked down and was soon subsequently replaced by a much lower (temporary?) cable. Shortly thereafter, an unknowing sailboat with a 32-foot mast caught the lower replacement cable. The sailboat sustained damage to the radio, antenna, and mast, but luckily, nobody aboard was fried. If you are close to the "uncertain" height limit, please contact Twin Rivers Marina and obtain their latest local knowledge.

The Twin Rivers Marina is just inside the Salt River, before this first bridge, only a quarter mile from the Crystal River Channel. You'll find this nice facility on the south side of the Salt River. A blue high-and-dry storage facility signals this marina. This professionally maintained marina houses a well-integrated medley of boats—from commercial shrimpers to sportfishermen to trawlers to small run-abouts to a few sailboats. They have a modest-sized working boatyard, a 35-ton opened travel lift, a forklift, about 52 wet slips, and many 40-footers in this marina.

Twin Rivers Marina (352) 795-3552

Approach depth—6 feet
Dockside depth—6 feet
Accepts transients—limited
Fixed wooden docks—yes
Dockside power connections—30 amp
Dockside water connections—water
Showers—yes
Gasoline—yes

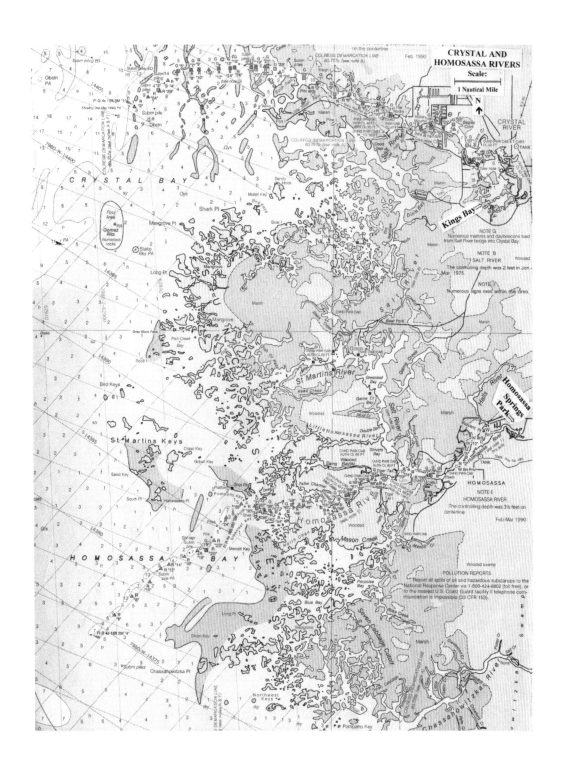

Diesel—yes

Mechanical repairs—yes

Below-waterline repairs—yes, with 35-ton
  open-ended travel lift

Boat ramp—private

Ship's store/variety store—yes

Restaurant—no but sandwiches available in store

In the Salt River, stay close to the Twin Rivers Marina side of the channel; it's shallow on the opposite side. HAZARD *The first low bridge (i.e., with about 11 feet of clearance) over Salt River is about a half-mile past the Crystal River turnoff.* A small commercial shrimp-boat docking facility, the Shrimp Landing Fresh Seafood docks, is on the south side of this bridge over the Salt River. The Citrus County Academy of Environmental Science sits at the north end of this bridge. I was hoping to park at the Environmental Science's dock and pay them a cordial information-exchanging visit, but I ran aground trying to reach their dock and had to back off that idea.

There is about a ten-mile-long shortcut to the Homosassa River through the Salt River. I understand that this route is very shallow. Getting constantly beaten up by four-plus-foot seas "outside," I was most tempted to take this calm water shortcut to the Homosassa River. The NOAA chart indicated that the Salt River controlling depth was two feet in 1975. I would be making this potential trip around the high-tide time. But making a dicey trip at high tide can be bad news, too. High tide is the worse time to run aground and get stuck. We asked a few marina folks in Crystal River, and they all invariably tried to dissuade me from taking this calm-water route. After the dread of facing another day in the pounding

Gulf in my little boat, and some gnawing in my stomach, I decided to listen to the local knowledge and forewent taking this inland Salt River shortcut route to the Homosassa River. I guess I'll really never know if I could have made it to the Homosassa via the Salt River. And later, by car, I was able to make an estimate of a low overhead bridge along this route. There was barely an estimated six feet of overhead clearance at MHW. If you have a dinghy or a canoe, you may wish to try it, then let me know what that Salt River trip is like. In nearby Ozello, there is also a concrete boat ramp for shallow-draft and airboats, picnic tables, and the Old Port Cove Restaurant.

Back on Crystal River, the Fort Island Fishing Pier is in a nice park on the LDB, about a quarter mile upstream from the Salt River. But transient boats can't dock here because of the shallow rocks nearby. There is a boat ramp area in a small creek upriver from the pier. This nice park area has two concrete boat ramps, three small piers, and three 25-foot-long floating docks. Beyond Salt River, the Crystal River Channel holds six to 16 feet at MLW depths. The Crystal River Archaeological State Park, (352) 795-3817, is north of "G19" on the RDB. Pre-Columbian Indians lived here between 500 B.C. and 900 A.D., well before the Apalachee. This area has a tasteful small museum and outdoor trails leading to Indian burial grounds.

Attractive homes and private docks grace much of the shoreline of Crystal River and Kings Bay. After "G29 and R30," look for Pete's Pier toward the east. Pete's Pier has a large high-and-dry facility in the big blue building. They also have about 100 slips, most covered, and this facility can accommodate several 60-footers.

Pete's Pier (at Kings Bay Marina) (352) 795-3302

Approach depth—6 feet
Dockside depth—4 feet
Accepts transients—yes
Fixed wooden docks—yes
Dockside power connections—30 and 50 amp
Dockside water connections—yes
Waste pump-out—yes
Showers—yes
Laundromat—nearby
Gasoline—yes
Diesel—yes
Mechanical repairs—yes
Below-waterline repairs—yes, limited to about
   26 feet and a forklift
Boat ramp—yes

Variety store—yes
Restaurants—in dinghy distance

The embayment to the northeast of Pete's Pier heads toward the center of the town. If you wish to head in this direction, you will need to pass the small island with a house on the LDB (or to your starboard side). HAZARD *There is shallow water and low overhead power lines to the southeast of this island.* Pass the second, and even smaller, island also like the LDB.

Ashore, and in the center of the town of Crystal River, there are three waterfront restaurants, a few motels, and other commercial facilities near the head of this embayment. From west to east, the two westernmost floating docks belong to a complex housing the Crystal Lodge

Pete's Pier, Crystal River

Dive Center, Caribbean Cravings on the Water Restaurant, and a Best Western motel. There is also a private boat ramp located here. The third small (dinghy-sized) floating wooden dock, in about three to four feet of water, belongs to Crackers Bar and Grill, (352) 795-3999. But this nice restaurant threatens to "tow away" boats who try to tie up to their dock for the night. Dockside Ice Cream Shoppe Marina sits east of Crackers. Dockside Ice Cream Shoppe has a small private marina with about a dozen slips capable of accommodating 30-footers. This facility also has a public boat ramp. Charlie's Fish House Restaurant and Seafood Market is east of Dockside Ice Cream. This restaurant has no boat dock. Ashore and in the center of Crystal River, there is a service station and a convenience store. Off shore, the water depth shallows in between Crackers and Dockside Ice Cream. If you travel between these two establishments, you need to arc out away from the shore.

> **Dockside Ice Cream Shoppe Marina**
> **(352) 563-2730**
>
> **Approach depth—less than 3 feet**
> **Accepts transients—no (private marina)**
> **Fixed wooden docks—yes**
> **Dockside power connections—30 amp**
> **Dockside water connections—yes**
> **Boat ramp—yes**
> **Dive shop—yes, on site**
> **Gift shop—yes**
> **Restaurant—several nearby%er**

There is also a Boat/U.S. towboat operation out of Crystal River, and the first commercial towboat we've seen since Carrabelle. SeaTow boat-towing services has a large operation based in Clearwater. This SeaTow fleet, (727) 593-3555, also has boats that operate as far north as Crystal River. The next SeaTow operation to the northwest is west of Apalachicola and operates out of Port St. Joe, Florida, (850) 227-4049.

Kings Bay, at the head of Crystal River, is like a pleasant freshwater lake with a few lovely islands thrown in the mix. Much of Kings Bay is uniform, at about five to six feet deep at MLW with a mud bottom, sometimes covered with sea grass. Buzzard Island is the largest island in Kings Bay. The wreck of the *Palace II* sits near the northeast corner of the island. But there are several restricted boating areas in the small Crystal River National Wildlife Refuge. From November 15 to March 31, boats are not allowed within about 200 yards on the northwest and northeast sides of Buzzard Island. The south side of Buzzard Island is also off-limits to boats during this time. And there are other areas restricted to boaters (e.g., north of Warden Key and north of Sunset Shores). During November 15 to March 31, all of Kings Bay south of Buzzard Island—that is not already restricted—is designed as an "idle speed" waterway. All other portions of Kings By are designated as "slow speed." Only on the Crystal River boating channel, and in between the buoys, are boats allowed to travel up to 25 miles per hour. Besides the many restricted boating areas in Kings Bay, there is grass, hydrilla, and a floating moss that can foul in your propeller. Overhead power lines may also cross the waters in certain areas. The *U.S. Coast Pilot* indicates that no power lines should have less than 32 feet of vertical clearance. The Port Hotel and Marina is near the southeast corner of Kings Bay. This facility is more of a dive center than a marina. Nearly all the dock space is occupied by pontoon dive boats.

Port Hotel and Marina (352) 795-7234

Approach depth—3-4 feet
Floating wooden docks—yes
Swimming pool—yes
Boat ramp—private
Dive shop—yes
Tiki bar—yes

If your boat's draft or height won't permit you to take that ten-mile Salt River canoe-or-dinghy route between Crystal River and the Homosassa River, there is another semi-off-shore alternative between the Crystal River Channel's "G1" and the Homosassa River Channel's "R4." This route is about 12 miles long and is in between both channel sea buoys (i.e., Crystal River Channel "G1" and Homosassa River Channel "R4"). But you still

can't have a real deep-draft vessel for this route. Taking this course, you'd be leaving a few islands, obstructions, and foul areas to the seaward direction, and not all of these seaward obstructions are shown on our section of NOAA chart presented for this area. Southbound, and from Crystal River Channel's "G1," you'd start out by heading about 202 degrees for about 5.4 miles, passing the submerged Gomez Rock on your port side and heading for a fixed quadrapod in the water at way point 28.49.987N/82.46.018W. During our first leg of this route, we had no problem and encountered four- to eight-foot depths at MLW. But after that quadrapod, during the second 6.3-mile leg, and on a supposed heading of 170 degrees, we ran into much shallower water west of the St. Martins Keys. After

The wreck of the *Palace II* in Kings Bay

our trip through this questionable area, I talked to the folks at Pete's Pier. They said that I should have been able to find a "four-foot-deep trench" and that "shrimp boats run this route all the time." We weren't able to find this comfortably deep trench. If you decide to attempt this route, talk to the folks at Pete's Pier first, try to ascertain their best advice, and obtain their sketch of this charted route.

Note: In my little boat, I made it through this gap with no problems. But I honestly didn't find enough comfortable water depth in the second leg of this route to recommend this as a route for bigger boats at MLW. In any event, whatever route you chose, you need to work your way to Homosassa Channel's "R4" at way point 28.43.588N/82.45.925W.

The Homosassa River, Homosassa, and Chassahowitzka Bay

In the Seminole tongue, Homosassa either means "place of peppers" or "place of whiskey." The modern-day settlement of Homosassa began in 1846 when David Yulee, an entrepreneur and Florida's first senator, built a sugar mill and started a plantation. Besides building this fascinating sugar mill, Yulee helped build Florida's first state-crossing railroad. After it had been operating about 13 years, the mill was supplying Confederate troops with sugar, syrup, and molasses. So, in 1864, Union naval forces attacked and burned Yulee's mansion, which also warehoused ammunition and supplies for Confederate soldiers. But the Blue troops missed the sugar mill, because it was farther inland. Nevertheless, the mill was soon abandoned. Today, one can still visit the ruins of Yulee's sugar mill.

The Homosassa River has at least two very quite distinct and varied characteristics. The lower part of this river is rustic, at times vivid, and challenging to navigate. The upper part of the Homosassa is a 180-degree opposite—with posh houses, manicured lawns, many restaurants (some for fine dining and some with a very local flavor), and an easy navigational channel. There are also many boating facilities on the Homosassa River. As far as the number of boating accommodations and options go, this area rivals Carrabelle (which was nearly 200 miles ago). Homosassa hosts an annual arts, crafts, andseafood festival in mid-November. Like Crystal River, the Homosassa River is also home to a thriving population of wintering manatees.

It is more than a ten-mile run from lighted navigation aid "R4" to the developed area on the Homosassa River. Our way point off Homosassa lighted "R4" in the Homosassa Channel is 28.43.588N/82.45.925W, in eight feet at MLW. The initial heading after "R4" is about 55 degrees. Water depths in this channel ranged from six to 12 feet at MLW, with eight feet being most common for about the five miles between navigation aids "R4" and "R28." The *U.S. Coast Pilot* indicated a controlling depth of only three and a half feet. At "R12," this channel takes a pronounced bend to starboard. Just after the first green mark, "G19," the Homosassa Channel doglegs to port. At the second lighted navigation aid, "R26," the channel makes another dogleg to starboard. HAZARD *The shallowest parts of this channel are in between "R28" and "R32."* A few spots in the channel have as little as four to seven feet of water depth at MLW. But there are also many navigation aids in this part of the channel—a signal for us to properly heed all of these channel aids closely. After "R32," the water depths are between four and eight

Small island on the Homosassa River

feet at MLW. The actual Homosassa River mouth is quite narrow, and the daymarks will often be paired and tightly spaced through this tricky part—where the Gulf channel transforms to a river channel. The Sunset Island private docks are in a small embayment on the RDB, about a half-mile into the river. After "G45," the channel depths increase to five to 12 feet at MLW. The worst of any shallow sections are now behind us. Comfortably deep readings hold all the way to and past "R72."

The tight turns on the Homosassa Channel are quite a contrast from the Crystal River Channel, less than ten miles away. Flooding and ebbing tidal currents can also be strong on the narrow Homosassa River—adding another navigational concern. The Homosassa's banks are uneven and sometimes hard to distinguish. HAZARD *There are many choke points*

in the channel. You need to especially follow the channel navigation aids. If you cheat any of these markers, there's a good chance your hull will be introduced to some unfriendly submerged rock outcroppings. This is probably more true in areas with tightly spaced navigation aids. This is one river where even the shortest lapse of that "red, right, return" rule could be very costly for the captain. Many small, fast, planing-hull boats also zip up and down the Homosassa River Channel, adding another edge to navigating on this river. When we traversed this river, none of these many fast planing-hull boats practiced any wake etiquette. There may also be some floating weeds in this tight river, with the potential to foul propellers. A few crab pots are also seen on the river, but the watermen have sense enough to lay them outside the channel. There are also many small rocky islands all over this river. Some of these islands support nothing more than a lone palm tree. Yet, the bigger ones might support a small house. Your undivided attention is needed on the lowest five miles of the Homosassa River.

The Homosassa is perhaps the most unusual river on Florida's Big Bend. It shares few similarities with any of the other rivers. The development on the Homosassa River is an odd amalgamation. There may be a nice home in one bend, a ramshackle dwelling off the next bend, followed by a little cabin on an island in the river.

An overhead power line crosses the river between "R58A" and "G59. HAZARD *The NOAA chart stated that the clearance of that power line is 55 feet and the* U.S. Coast Pilot *stated that the clearance was at least 45 feet.*

The Salt River, the shallow-draft route back to Crystal River, enters the Homosassa in between "R70" and "R72" on the RDB. Upriver from the Salt River, the tidal current on the Homosassa abates significantly, and some of that Homosassa "unusualness" fades away. "G81" is the last navigation aid for a while—if you stay in the channel in between "G81" and the next aid, "R2." Like in the Crystal River, the channel-numbering scheme restarts at a second "R2." You will find the water to be deep, contrary to the *U.S. Coast Pilot's* statement that the controlling depth is only three feet in between aids "G81" and "G5."

After slightly more than six miles of an unusual, river navigation experience, we arrived at the shrimp docks, marinas, restaurants, and the like. Cedar Key Fish and Oyster Company

Island with a rustic house on the Homosassa River

and Hampton's Fish House are shrimp docks off the LDB side. After Hampton's, the Riverhaven Marina will be spied on our RDB. Riverhaven Marina is primarily a large high-and-dry facility, but this marina has three wet slips for transient boaters and a ship's store. KC Crumps Fine Dining Restaurant and Kibbie's Dockside Tiki Bar are just upriver on this RDB side. KC Crumps/Kibbie's Dockside has about 20 very small slips, but they do have about 100 feet of side-tie docking. MacRae's is across the river on the LDB. MacRae's has about 20 slips and can accommodate a few 40- and 50-footers. The Homosassa Riverside Resort is just upriver from MacRae's and is also on the LDB. The Homosassa Riverside Resort is likely to be the most first-class and inclusive operation on the Homosassa River. Besides the marina, this facility has a restaurant, two taverns, motel rooms, a pool, tennis courts, and a dive shop. Recently, some questions have been flagged about transient availability at the resort in Claiborne Young's comprehensive electronic newsletter, the *Salty Southeast*. There may not be transient space available during nights when the resort is heavily preoccupied with its core business (i.e., resort rooms starting at $75 per night). The small island with the red-striped miniature lighthouse, upriver from the Homosassa Riverside Resort, is teeming with live monkeys. Not surprisingly, it's called Monkey Island.

Monkey Island, Homosassa River

Riverhaven Marina (352) 628-5545
www.riverhavenmarinacom

Dockside depth—4 feet
Accepts transients—limited (3 slips and a 32-
    foot dock length, and not always)
Floating wooden docks—yes, 32-feet long
Dockside power connections—30 amp (a long
    power cord may be needed)
Dockside water connections—yes
Showers—yes
Gasoline—yes
Mechanical repairs—yes
Below-waterline repairs—yes, limited to 36 feet
    with forklift
Boat ramp—yes
Ship's store—yes
Restaurant—next door

KC Crumps/Kibbie's Dockside Tiki Bar
(352) 628-1500

Dockside depth—3-4 feet
Accepts transients—yes (if staying for dinner)
Fixed wooden docks—yes
Dockside power connections—none
Restaurant—yes, fine dining and a tiki bar

MacRae's (352) 628-2602

Dockside depth—3 feet
Accepts transients—limited (advance notice
    appreciated)
Fixed wooden docks—yes
Dockside power connections—20 amp
Dockside water connections—yes
Gasoline—yes
Boat ramp—no but one nearby
Bait-and-tackle shop—yes
Restaurant—nearby
Tiki bar—yes
Motel—on site

Homosassa Riverside Resort (352) 628-0622
www.homosassariverside.com

Dockside depth—8 feet
Accepts transients—yes
Fixed wooden docks—yes
Dockside power connections—limited, 15 amp
Dockside water connections—yes
Showers—yes
Laundromat—yes
Swimming pool—yes
Gasoline—yes
Boat ramp—yes
Variety store—yes
Restaurant—on site, Charlie Brown's Crab
    House
Tavern—two (on site—the Yardarm and the
    Monkey Bar)
Motel—on site

The newer development on the Homosassa River appears to be on the RDB, while the older part of Homosassa appears to be on the LDB. The Homosassa public boat ramp is in between MacRae's and the Homosassa Riverside Resort. Close to the Riverside Resort, and in nearby Homosassa (i.e., on the LDB side), there is a convenience food store, a dive shop, a post office, a very small library, and Gulf Coast Marine Services. The Yulee Sugar Mill Ruins are slightly less than one mile down the road from Homosassa Riverside Resort. In the early 1800s this location was great for a sugar mill because of Florida's fertile, moist soil and mild climate. And slaves were used in the labor-intensive task of cane harvesting. Today, you can see the remnants of the mill's boiler and the steam engine that was used to run the gears that ground up the cane. This open-air site is free and worth visiting. The Old Mill Tavern and another restaurant are adjacent to these ruins.

When going back up the Homosassa River, and upriver from the Homosassa Riverside Resort, it is highly advisable not to deviate from the channel. There are crab pots lining both sides of the channel. Water depth in the channel decreases to about four to six feet at MLW. The aid-to-navigation numbering system restarts with another "G1" after the Riverside Resort. The channel veers hard and makes a near-hairpin turn toward the LDB in the vicinity of navigation aids "R2," "G3," and "R4." The Magic Manatee Marina is on the RDB, past aid "G5." Their ship's store has a very good array of marine supplies. The Magic Manatee has about four 80-foot docks. The Last Resort, (352) 628-7117, is next to and upriver from the Magic Manatee Marina. The courtly Last Resort has three small fixed wooden docks and a boat ramp. They rent cottages and pontoon boats, and a transient boat could tie up if a room was also rented.

Magic Manatee Marina (352) 628-7334

Dockside depth—6 feet
Accepts transients—limited to space available
Fixed wooden docks—yes
Dockside water connections—yes
Gasoline—yes

New development and island on the Homosassa River

Yulee Sugar Mill Ruins, Homosassa

Mechanical repairs—yes
Below-waterline repairs—yes, limited to 32 feet
   with forklift
Ship's store—yes
Restaurants—three within a mile
Resort hotel—nearby

Upriver from the Magic Manatee, and all the way to the state park, the channel water depths range from four to eight feet, MLW. A handful of small inexpensive boating facilities and docks, short on amenities but having a bit of local color, are upriver from the Magic Manatee. The Sea Grass Pub and Grill is the largest of these. The Sea Grass is at the north end of a wide embayment. To enter the Sea Grass, leave navigation aid "G7" well to your port side. HAZARD *There are submerged rocks southwest of "G7."*

The Sea Grass has about 28 slips, and they may be able to accommodate a 40-footer. On the opposite shore (the LDB), there are a few narrow canals. These canals house several covered boat slips, developments, a boat ramp, and even another tavern—the Manatee Pub.

Sea Grass Pub and Grill (352) 628-3595

Dockside depth—3 feet
Accepts transients—yes
Fixed wooden docks—yes
Gasoline—yes
Boat ramp—yes
Dive shop—nearbyRestaurant and pub—yes

Beyond "R8," there are reports of submerged rocks in the river. Pay close attention

Homosassa River near Homosassa Springs Wildlife Park

to the channel. The last navigation aid is "R10." The river has a very manicured residential feel, and it's a world away from ten miles downstream. The Halls River enters the Homosassa about a half-mile upstream from the Sea Grass Pub. There is another small restaurant with docks on the Halls River's RDB, just before the bridge. The often-packed Marguerita Grill, (352) 628-1336, has a few floating wooden docks with slips in about four feet at MLW. HAZ-ARD *There is a low bridge (i.e., with less than six feet of overhead clearance, MHW) over the Halls River.* The River's Inn Bar and Grill and Nature's Resort Marina are on the other side of this low bridge, but we couldn't reach them by boat because of the low clearance.

Nature's Resort Marina (352) 628-9544

Dockside depth—1-2 feet
Fixed wooden docks—yes
Gasoline—yes
Showers—yes
Laundromat—yes
Swimming pool—yes
Boat ramp—yes

Camp store—yes
Snack bar—yes
Tavern—yes
Cottage rentals—yes
Trailer park—yes

The Homosassa River becomes almost crystal clear upstream from the Halls River as you near Homosassa Springs Wildlife Park. This park has about one mile of nature trails, with areas for encountering many creatures from birds to a hippopotamus. The park also has an education center, a gift shop, and a sandwich bar. On the Homosassa River, the state park has a pavilion but no place to dock a boat. There is also a boating-restricted area near the springs on the RDB.

Back on the Gulf of Mexico, Chassahowitzka Bay, Chassahowitzka Point, and Chassahowitzka River are in a northeast direction from navigation aid "CW." "CW" is located off way point 28.39.440N/ 82. 44.225W in eight feet at MLW. A steel frame and a lighted navigation aid sit atop a quadrapod platform. The light is supposedly 16 feet high. Chassahowitzka National Wildlife Refuge comprises almost 50 square miles of shallow bays, swamps, and salt marshes in this area. Chassahowitzka Bay and Chassahowitzka River are too shallow for displacement-hull boats. This bay is most suitable for shallow-draft boats and airboats. The *U.S. Coast Pilot* indicates a controlling depth from one and a half to two feet. If you are able to venture up the Chassahowitzka River, BEWARE OF THE LOW OVERHEAD POWER LINE (i.e., about 20 feet high) near Chassahowitzka Springs. Chassahowitzka River Campground, (352) 382-2200; a camp store; a concrete boat ramp; and a picnic pavilion are up the Chassahowitzka River near Chassahowitzka Springs. Two lodges are also within boating or walking distance from Chassahowitzka Springs.

The Seminole name Chassahowitzka translates roughly to "hanging pumpkins." The notorious gangster and racketeer Al Capone once hung out along the Chassahowitzka River during the 1930s. The Crystal River Nuclear Power Plant can still be spied as far away as Chassahowitzka Bay. This great shoreside landmark can be seen, in normal conditions, from out in the Gulf of Mexico in a swath that is over 40 nautical miles long—from Cedar Key to Chassahowitzka Bay.

The Hudson Region, from Bayport to Anclote Key

Even though there are nine channels in this 25-mile section of the Florida Gulf Coast, only one of those channels, the Pithlachascotee (locals refer to it as the Cotee) River, was navigable for a deep-draft vessel at low tide in late 2001. But there are plans to dredge a couple more of those channels deeper in 2002. There is also a broken and irregular series of shallows, St. Martins Reef, extending out between about four and eight miles from the coast. St. Martins Reef extends north-south about twenty-five miles, starting from near Chassahowitzka Bay in the north to near Anclote Key in the south. Aside from St. Martins Reef, there are many other shallow areas, and some areas inside St. Martins Reef contain rocks. Some of these dangerous areas are marked with unofficial navigation aids. Please study NOAA chart 11409 very carefully and avoid any shallow parts of St. Martins Reef

Weeki Wachee River

Pithlachascotee River Channel and bridge, New Port Richey

as well as the shallow areas inside of St. Martins Reef.

Hudson and Hernando Beach are two fair-sized Gulf Coastal developments laced with canals. Both have substantial commercial shrimping fleets competing with residential development along their many canals. Port Richey and New Port Richey are fair-sized towns along the Pithlachascotee River. Gulf Harbors is another coastal residential canal development that is actually a part of New Port Richey. Aripeka, a small fishing village with hardly any commercial facilities, may not be accessible to many displacement-hull boats even at mid-tide. The Weeki Wachee River is slightly deeper, and this narrow river leads to a curious residential development along the confines of that waterway. We'll end this chapter, and the southern end of this book, near Anclote Key and where the Gulf Coast Intracoastal Waterway restarts.

Backyards on the Weeki Wachee River

Bayport and the Weeki Wachee River

Bayport was once a small, albeit thriving, port for about 30 years. In the 1850s, cotton was exported from Hernando County through Bayport. During the Civil War, and in the early stages of the Union blockade of the South, small Bayport was overlooked because the Union navy focused on bigger ports. But the Union wasn't fooled for too long, and they eventually put an end to Bayport's blockade-running. Shortly after the Civil War, Bayport exported lumber and agricultural products. But by 1885, the railroad reached nearby Brooksville, and Bayport's days as a commercial shipping center were permanently over. Today all that's left of Bayport is this beautiful park and boat-ramp area. The interesting and somewhat far-out Weeki Wachee River extends beyond the Bayport park and boat ramp.

Today, there is not much room for a large or mid-sized vessel in the Bayport-Weeki Wachee area. But if you have a small vessel, you may wish to consider exploring here. It's definitely unique. Off Beacon Rock, at way point 28.32.765N/82.42.244W, there are water depths of seven to nine feet at MLW. This way point is between unlighted navigation aids "G1" and "R2." HAZARD *There are many hazards in this area (e.g., stakes, platforms, rock piles, etc.).* No less than four danger posts in the water marked submerged rocks. With all of the nearby obstructions in the water, this way point definitely does NOT have a 180-degree safe-semicircle of approach. This is a daylight approach with good visibility only.

After safely arriving at "G1 and R2," this channel, starting near Beacon Rock, is fairly easy and straightforward. From "G1 and R2,"

start out on a heading of about of 120 degrees. This wide (i.e., about 40 yards wide) channel has four to seven feet at MLW to navigation aid "8." A strange-looking thing on a peach-colored pole, "8" has a light atop. In spite of not being depicted on the NOAA charts, this well-marked wide channel continues to have sufficient navigation aids past "8," and we encountered no less than four feet at MLW. However, the *U.S. Coast Pilot* indicates a controlling depth of only two feet. Nearly all of the navigation aids are paired. At navigation aids "G13 and R14," the still well-marked channel finally narrows and shallows to about three to five feet at MLW. There are a few spots in the channel that might be slightly shallower, while there are other places, especially past the fishing pier, where the water is deeper than six feet at MLW.

A long (about 200 feet) fixed wooden fishing pier and picnic pavilions appear on the RDB, past navigation aids "R24 and G25." The Bayport boat ramps are in the canal on the RDB just past the fishing pier. Water depths in this 50-foot-wide canal are about three to four feet at MLW. The two ramps are on the RDB of the canal. The area has three no-less-than-20-feet-long floating aluminum docks, ample parking, covered picnic pavilions, restrooms, and a telephone in a very beautiful picnic area. There is another public boat ramp nearby at the head of Jenkins Creek, which is recommended for boats no larger than 16 feet. Jenkins Creek is south of Bayport and has a single ramp, a floating wooden dock, and a fishing pier.

After the last navigation aids, "G43 and R44," there is a fork in the river. The wider fork, on the RDB, is the mouth of the shoal-strewn Mud River. The narrower Weeki Wachee River—the more navigable route—takes a turn on the LDB side. The Weeki Wachee River continues to be between three and five feet deep at MLW but soon narrows to about 20 to 30 yards wide. This river has also become very clear. As you enter a residential canal area, the water depths increase to five to seven feet at MLW. Concrete sea walls line this highly manicured waterway, with more tight twists and turns than a snake over a bed of coals. A few "square" residential lots literally have water on three sides. But it's still pretty. I've never been there but I imagine this is what boating through Venice, Italy, must be like, except with a Florida twist. There are diving boards, tree swings, and sliding boards everywhere. A kid slipping down a sliding board could land on my boat! I felt like I was boating in someone's swimming pool. Although you'll see a few bigger boats at some of the docks, we'd recommend a maximum boat length of about 30 feet for comfortably negotiating the many turns on the Weeki Wachee River. And it's an idle-speed waterway.

Children directing boat traffic on the Weeki Wachee River

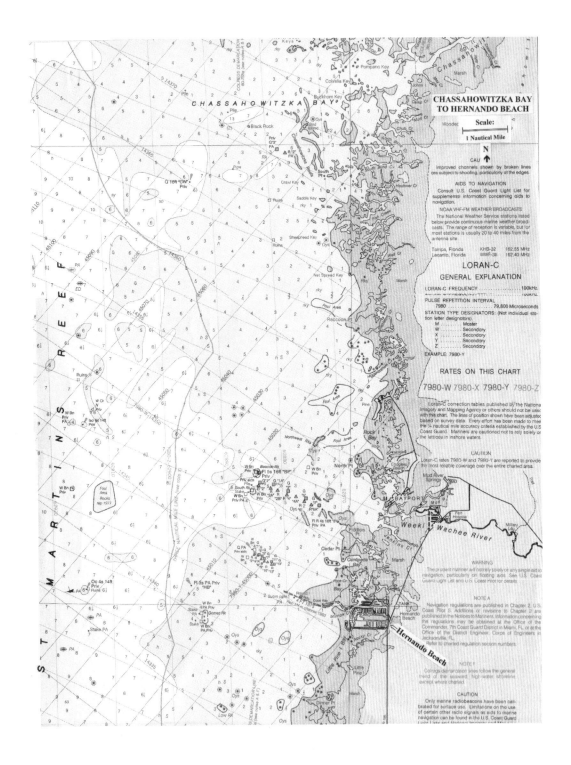

HAZARD *About a nine- to ten-foot-clearance bridge at MHW straddles this most unusual waterway about a mile past the Mud River junction.* The Upper Deck Restaurant is on the RDB just past this bridge. This restaurant has about three boat slips for less than 30-footers on a fixed wooden dock with no utilities. On the road nearby, there is another restaurant— the Riverplace Restaurant. There is a nice wide sandy beach on the LDB in Roger's Park. Besides a beach, Roger's Park has a boat ramp with an 80-foot wooden dock, covered picnic pavilions, and bathhouses. The Weeki Wachee Marina is in a creek entering from the LDB side of the Weeki Wachee River with about four feet at MLW. This marina has canoe and johnboat rentals, as well as about 100 feet of dockage. The Seminole name Weeki Wachee means something like "small spring."

Weeki Wachee Marina (352) 596-2852

Approach depth—3-4 feet
Fixed wooden docks—yes
Gasoline—yes
Ship's store—yes
Restaurant—two nearby

Hernando Beach

Hernando Beach has no fewer than a half-dozen major boating facilities. The largest shrimp fleet since the one found in Carrabelle can be found here. I was told that vacationers started coming to Hernando Beach in the 1940s. The northern sections of this "resort area" were first developed, and the southern

Working boatyard in Hernando Beach

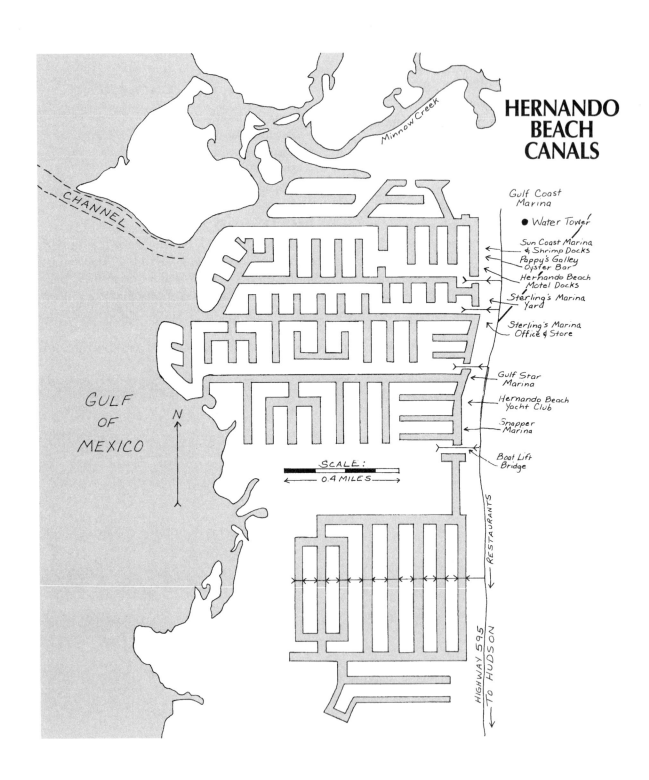

HERNANDO BEACH CANALS

Minnow Creek

CHANNEL

GULF
OF
MEXICO

N

SCALE:
0.4 MILES

Gulf Coast Marina

● Water Tower

Sun Coast Marina & Shrimp Docks
Pappy's Galley Oyster Bar
Hernando Beach Motel Docks
Sterling's Marina Yard
Sterling's Marina Office & Store

Gulf Star Marina
Hernando Beach Yacht Club
Snapper Marina
Boat Lift Bridge

RESTAURANTS

HIGHWAY 595
TO HUDSON

sections followed; some southern parts are much newer. Subsequently, the many canals were dug into the limestone to accommodate the influx of recreational boats. Despite a refined residential facade along the canals, there is a blue-collar heart to Hernando Beach, with all the shrimpers and working recreational boatyards. The shrimpers got squeezed into one area, primarily at the head of the main northern canal.

The working-boat tradition doesn't die easily, nor should it. For a channel to be maintained by the Corps of Engineers, there must be some complicated formula whereby the commercial interests (i.e., shrimpers) have to have a 51 percent financial savings stake. So if the shrimpers disappear, or even dwindle to a smaller fleet, the recreational boats will not receive the benefit of having this channel maintained and dredged by the Corps of Engineers. Just before dusk, the channel may be loaded with shrimp boats departing for their night of work. They'll need to be back before 3:00 A.M. if they are returning with bait shrimp, or before 5:00 A.M. if they are returning with "fresh daily" restaurant shrimp. Some fair-sized Hernando Beach shrimp boats draw about four feet of water. I was told that four-foot-draft shrimpers have no problem with the Hernando Beach channel depth most of the time. I question this. I was also told that the biggest shrimpers, drawing as much as six feet, must go in and out with the tide.

Shrimp fleet in Hernando Beach

At some of the local working boatyards in Hernando Beach, you'll also see many large sailboats hauled out that have six feet of draft. Much of the channel is deeper than four feet. But there are a few isolated rocks that protrude to within four feet from the surface in certain places, especially in some of the Hernando Beach canals. There are plans to improve this tricky channel to dredge it to seven feet deep, MLW, and 80 feet wide. And this will likely be a difficult channel to dredge. The channel is long, the dredge spoil must be moved a far distance, and much of that spoil material is rock. You only want the challenge of negotiating a Hernando Beach channel once a day. Channel navigation aids go all of the way up to "R110." That's a heck of a lot of navigation aids, but you'll be thankful that each one is located where it is. Furthermore, there is no beach in Hernando Beach.

Like Beacon Rock off the Weeki Wachee Channel, there are several danger areas at the seaward end of the Hernando Beach Channel. HAZARD *Several platforms mark rocks in this area.* One of the larger platforms is the Bill Watts Rack, marking submerged rocks. The Bill Watts Rack, named after a former local Coast Guard Auxiliary commander, has a light atop. Our way point for this area is closer to the channel and right off unlighted markers "G1 and R2." Beside the light at the Bill Watts Rack, we observed very few lighted aids in this heavily used channel. Be especially careful. Like the earlier channel in this chapter, this way point does not have a 180-degree safe-semicircle of approach due to all of the nearby obstructions in the water. Pete, at Snapper Marina, indicated that the safest approach, avoiding most submerged rocks, is to approach the outside of this channel from a more northerly direction (i.e., leave the many

outside-of-the-channel structures to your south or treat them like distant red navigation aids). This is also an approach only recommended during good visibility conditions.

Way point 28.31.088N/82.42.359W is in between "G1 and R2," inside of the Bill Watts Rack, and is in five to six feet at MLW. If you are making a run between the Hernando Beach Channel and points to the south (e.g., the Aripeka Light), it's highly recommended that you pass outside of the Hernando Beach white flashing "turn light." NOAA chart 11409 depicts a few of these channel turn lights. Turn lights are navigation aids slightly seaward of the primary channel entrance, and they usually forewarn of underwater seaward obstructions on one side or the other, before reaching the main body of the channel. In this instance, the "HB" turn light signals possible underwater obstructions south of the Hernando Beach Channel entry. If you don't pass this aid on the northwest side, you could run afoul of Gomez Rocks, on the southeast side of this aid. There are some stakes around Gomez Rocks. This "HB" turn-light aid is located near way point 28.30.880N/ 82.44.091W in about seven feet at MLW.

Once in the Hernando Beach Channel, a rock spoil bank is soon found on the RDB (i.e., the north) side. Approaching the shore, these rock spoil islands become progressively bigger, and some even support small trees. Most of this part of the channel has depths of seven to ten feet at MLW, with typical water depths of eight to nine feet. The *U.S. Coast Pilot* indicates that this channel had a controlling depth of four feet in 1992, and that, in 1999, there was a large submerged rock in the middle of the channel at about 28.30.00N/82.40.30W. The Hernando Beach Channel is only about 40 to 50 feet wide for nearly its entire length. There are many more navigation aids than shown on NOAA chart 11409. Our very first lighted navigation aid in this channel is "R36" (not shown on the NOAA chart). After "R38" the channel shallows slightly to about six to seven feet and then shallows further to about five to six feet at MLW near "G43." The channel narrows a bit in the vicinity of "R50," "R52," and "R54." HAZARD *There are also submerged protruding rocks at the edge of the red side (i.e., LDB) of the channel near these navigation aids.* "R50" and "R72" are our second and third lighted navigation aids in this over-three-mile-long channel.

At "R80 and G81," the "artery channels" start converging in five feet at MLW. Near here, there are many canals and it's easy to become confused. After the dicey Hernando Beach outer channel, there are no less than four major artery canals, which feed the many smaller canals. At least the canals near the north end of Hernando Beach are wide. Most of the canals are chock-full of residential development and small private docks. But surprisingly, there are about three fairly large working yards, a dry-storage boat facility for smaller boats, and a sizable shrimp fleet based in Hernando Beach. All of the commercial-boating facilities are at the head of one artery canal or another and are right off the main north-south highway that passes east of Hernando Beach. The southernmost artery canal has to be one of the most confounding water routes in the entire Big Bend. The NOAA chart doesn't depict this route, or the channel, well. So we'll offer you a route sketch derived from a U.S. Geological Survey (USGS) map. But please be mindful that we were unable to present water depths or other features useful to the mariner from USGS maps.

Northern Canal

The northern canal shoots off from the old original creek, Minnow Creek. This canal is as deep or deeper than that main channel leading to the Gulf of Mexico. HAZARD *However, there are a few submerged rocks in this wide canal.* These obstructions are often marked with orange and white "danger" daymarks. You are on the main artery leading to the Sun Coast Marina and Shrimp Docks and the Gulf Coast Marina, if you are able to line up the canal with the white water tank. This helpful navigational water tower has a red-and-white checkerboard band and a powerful, quick-flashing, white light atop. We were able to spy this great Hernando Beach landmark from as far north as Chassahowitzka Bay and as far south as the Hudson channels.

The Hernando Beach Public Dock, with a very ample parking area, is beneath the water tank at the head of this canal. Three boat ramps and two small floating docks are also in this area. There is also a forklift bay and three more small docks immediately north of this area that belong to Gulf Coast Marina. This marina is primarily a dry-storage facility. The Gulf Coast Marina ship's store carries a good variety of basic boating supplies. The shrimp docks are in the side canal running to the south of the public dock. Sun Coast Marina and Shrimp Docks is the largest shrimp dock, and it is located past about seven smaller private shrimp docks. Pappy's Galley and Oyster Bar, (352) 597-2227, is connected to Sun Coast Marina. The Hernando Beach Motel and Condos dock sits at the end of this spur canal. The motel and condo complex has about ten floating wooden docks, generally not bigger than 25 feet, with no electrical service. This facility will accept transient boaters if the crew takes a room in the motel. An Exxon station and a convenience store are also nearby. We were told that there may be some submerged rocks at the head of this canal near the Hernando Beach Motel and Condos dock.

Gulf Coast Marina (352) 596-1212

Gasoline—sold to high-and-dry customers
Mechanical repairs—yes
Below-waterline repairs—yes, limited to 25-ton forklift
Boat ramp—nearby
Ship's store—yes
Restaurant—one within walking distance

Sun Coast Marina and Shrimp Docks (352) 597-2300

Approach depth—no less than 4 feet
Accepts transients—very limited
Floating and fixed wooden docks—yes
Dockside power connections—15 amp
Dockside water connections—yes
Gasoline—yes
Diesel—yes
Boat ramp—nearby
Ship's store—yes (supplies primarily cater to shrimpers)
Restaurant—nearby

Hernando Beach Motel and Condos (352) 596-2527

Approach depth—no less than 4 feet
Accepts transients—yes, if taking a motel room
Floating wooden docks—yes
Dockside water connections—yes
Swimming pool—yes
Restaurant—nearby
Motel—yes

Middle Canals

Back near the head of the canals, and in the vicinity of "G87 and R88," the middle canal diverges from the main canal to the east, south of the Hernando Beach Club. This middle canal has many branch canals, and most of the shore in all these branch canals is residential. But the main spur of this middle canal leads to a few commercial establishments. Sterling's Marina's wet slips and yacht yard are the main attraction at the head of this canal. Sterling's has about 35 slips and is limited to about 35-footers. Sterling's office and ship's store are across the street and actually off the next canal to the south. Sportsman Fisherman's Landing Marina, (352) 597-3900, is a small facility located north of Sterling's on a spur canal off the primary middle canal. The local U.S. Coast Guard Auxiliary flotilla has a building across the street.

Sterling's Marina (352) 596-4010

Approach depth—6 feet
Dockside depth—6 feet
Accepts transients—limited
Floating wooden docks—yes
Dockside power connections—15 amp
Dockside water connections—yes
Waste pump-out—yes
Gasoline—yes
Diesel—yes
Mechanical repairs—yes
Below-waterline repairs—yes, with 25-ton opened travel lift
Ship's store—yes
Restaurant—four within walking distance

Southern Canal

The southern canal houses three more

Landmark water tower in Hernando Beach

commercial-boating facilities, and the head of this canal is closest to the array of restaurants along the highway in Hernando Beach. Be careful. Without a doubt, this is the trickiest of all the Hernando Beach canals. At "R80 and G81," initially head south and past the middle canal (i.e., near aids "G87 and R88"). The channel aids marking this route run from "R80" to "R110" (and the channel runs well past "R110"). There is one hairpin turn, another five 90-degree turns, and a couple of 45-degree turns along this harrowing narrow route. This course is not for the fainthearted! After following the channel in a southerly direction, hug the shoreline west of Hernando Beach. The water depths in this southern canal range from four to ten feet deep at MLW, with five- to six-foot depths being most common.

Gulf Star Marina, the Hernando Beach Yacht Club, and Snapper Marina can be found at the head of this southern canal. Gulf Star Marina has about 40 slips and can accommodate about a 55-footer. A Boat/U.S. towboat also parks here. This facility has a 32-ton and a 50-ton open-ended travel lift and a sizable working boatyard. The marina staff can work on your boat, you can work on your boat, or the marina will allow both you and their staff to work on your boat (i.e., after you foul up a do-it-yourself job, the marina staff is more than willing to step in and bail you out). A fair portion of their boatyard is across the highway. The next facility to the south is the Hernando Beach Yacht Club. This private club has only about 11 slips, but they can accommodate a 42-footer. Snapper Marina is the southernmost facility at the end of this canal. This marina has about 32 slips, can accommodate about a 40-footer, and offers Boat/U.S. discounts. This facility also has a large high-and-dry storage building and a boatyard.

The management staff at Snapper Marina is most knowledgeable about the many vignettes relating to the historical past and the present channel-dredging and development situations around Hernando Beach.

Gulf Star Marina (352) 596-5079

Dockside depth—6 feet
Accepts transients—yes
Fixed wooden docks—yes
Dockside power connections—15 amp
Dockside water connections—yes
Showers—yes
Gasoline—yes
Mechanical repairs—yes
Below-waterline repairs—yes with 50-ton
  opened-ended travel lift and a forklift
Ship's store—yes
Restaurant—four within walking distance

Hernando Beach Yacht Club (352) 596-4830

Dockside depth—6 feet
Accepts transients—limited
Floating wooden docks—yes
Dockside power connections—20 amp
Dockside water connections—yes
Restaurant—four within walking distance

Snapper Marina (352) 596-2952

Dockside depth—6 feet
Accepts transients—yes
Floating wooden docks—yes
Dockside power connections—20 amp
Dockside water connections—yes
Gasoline—yes
Diesel—yes
Mechanical repairs—yes
Below-waterline repairs—yes with 25-ton
  open-ended forklift

Ship's store—yes, limited

Restaurant—four within walking distance

There are no less than four restaurants within about a mile south of Snapper Marina (and a tad farther away from the Hernando Beach Yacht Club and Gulf Star Marina). B. J. Gators Restaurant, Hernando Beach Seafood and Steak House, Captain Brad's Seafood and Crab House, and Two Crabs Restaurant are south and down the road. But it's not a nice walk. There is no shoulder or sidewalk along the road, the grass may be tall, and there is just enough traffic on the highway to keep you from walking on the road. In October 2002, I couldn't state anything positive about my meal at Hernando Beach Seafood and Steak House, but I had previously heard that B. J. Gators Restaurant was quite nice. The other two restaurants were closed when I visited.

There is also a motel, a VFW, an ice-cream shop, and many real-estate offices along this road. If you are willing to travel even farther south down the road, there are two more restaurants—the Hernando Beach Deli and Restaurant and the Bare Bones Fish and Steak House. It strikes me that real estate, in the form of canal development, rules in Hernando Beach. And the boaters are fettered to the whims of the convoluted canal designs.

Aripeka

Aripeka is a small fishing village named after a Seminole Indian chief. Our way point, near the Aripeka turn light, is 28.27.401N/ 82.44.634W. From this way point, we headed east to another nearby way point between "G1" and "R2," in about seven feet at MLW. This way point is 28.27.401N/ 82.44.490W.

Hammock Creek Channel, Aripeka

After entering the channel, head about 110 degrees. Many red, and a few green, navigation aids mark this channel. And there are many more navigation aids than are depicted on NOAA chart 11409. We found four to nine feet of water at MLW, with five-foot depths being most common. The second green mark, "G7," is paired with "R16" (an unusual pair?). At "G13 and R18" (another offbeat pair), the channel makes a slight dogleg to starboard and the water depth shallows to about three to four feet at MLW. The channel depth maintains three to four feet, MLW, to navigation aids "R30 and G31" and gradually shallows by another foot near "R32." After "R32," the channel redeepens to between three and four feet, MLW, all the way to "R40 and G41." HAZARD *After "R40 and G41," the channel shallows to about two to three feet at MLW and makes a few doglegs.* The entrance to Hammock Creek starts near "R50," and the last navigation aid, "R54," soon follows.

After you arrive in Hammock Creek, on the RDB side, you'll find a few houses with docks. On the LDB side, before the bridge, there is a small bait-and-variety store that sells ice and beer and has a phone. There is also a 25-foot floating wooden dock and a narrow concrete boat ramp nearby. An emergency anchorage might be off in the bayou on the LDB, in the event you can find enough anchoring depth. The main part of Aripeka village has a small post office about a half-mile south of the bridge.

Hudson

Unlike Hernando Beach, there are three separate channels (not canals) leading into the Hudson area. Sea Pines is the northernmost channel. Leisure Beach is the southernmost channel. And the Main Hudson Channel is between these two. After all three channels break the shoreline, they become canals with their own (many) branch canals. And that middle channel, the Main Hudson Channel, has a few major arteries.

Sea Pines Channel

Sea Pines is primarily an area of narrow residential canals. There are no commercial facilities, no places to dock, or even a place to anchor in this narrow set of canals. The first navigation aid to the Sea Pines Channel is on a quadrapod and labeled "G1." It is positioned near way point 28.23.177N/82.44.890W in about five to six feet at MLW. This channel is as straight as an arrow, on a heading of about 100 degrees, and water depths hold to about five to six feet MLW. There are many navigation aids (once again, many more than depicted on the NOAA chart), but none after "G1" are lighted. The channel is narrow, only about 15 yards wide. At the first red mark, "R10," the channel shallows a tad to about four feet, MLW, but then deepens back to five feet afterward. HAZARD *Partially submerged rocks start appearing at the channel edge on the green side at about "G15" and "G17."* "R30 and G31" are the last navigation aids, near the area where the Sea Pines Channel becomes a canal. In the mangrove-lined canal, the water depth increases by a foot to about five to six feet at MLW.

In the Sea Pine Canal, many of the residential docks have private property signs that say Keep Out. Along with many nice, large, manicured homes and lawns, there are more than a few manicured Doberman pinschers that will be barking at your boat as you pass by. A few people were peekabooing my boat and I behind the protective cage of their fenced-in, large, private,

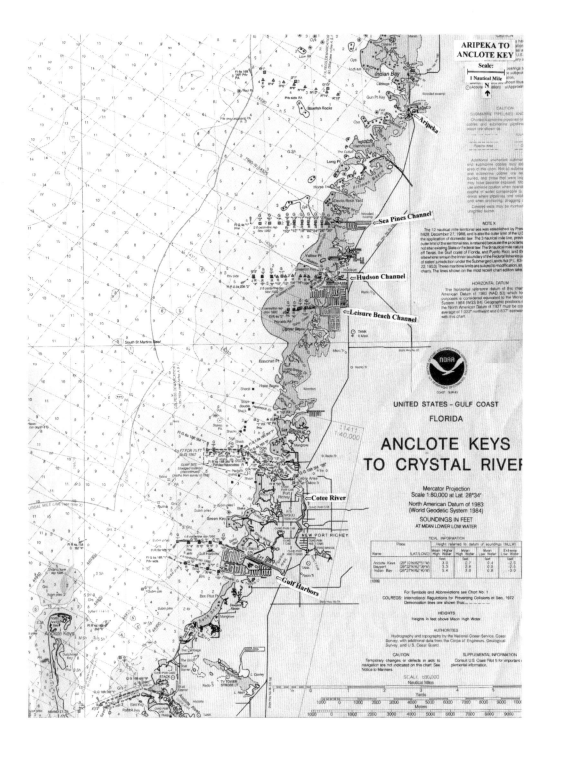

ARIPEKA TO
ANCLOTE KEY

Scale:

1 Nautical Mile

N

UNITED STATES – GULF COAST

FLORIDA

ANCLOTE KEYS
TO CRYSTAL RIVER

Mercator Projection
Scale 1:80,000 at Lat. 28°34′

North American Datum of 1983
(World Geodetic System 1984)

SOUNDINGS IN FEET
AT MEAN LOWER LOW WATER

For Symbols and Abbreviations see Chart No. 1

COLREGS: International Regulations for Preventing Collisions at Sea, 1972
Demarcation lines are shown thus.

HEIGHTS
Heights in feet above Mean High Water.

AUTHORITIES
Hydrography and topography by the National Ocean Service, Coast
Survey, with additional data from the Corps of Engineers, Geological
Survey, and U.S. Coast Guard.

CAUTION
Temporary changes or defects in aids to
navigation are not indicated on this chart. See
Notice to Mariners.

SUPPLEMENTAL INFORMATION
Consult U.S. Coast Pilot 5 for important supplemental information.

SCALE 1:80,000
Nautical Miles

Yards

Meters

swimming pools. You won't find any shrimpers or workboats in Sea Pines. There was almost no room to even turn my small boat around at the head of the channel. And a few of those manicured mean-looking Dobermans were getting uncomfortably close when I needed to rock my boat back and forth a few times just to turn around near the head of the narrow channel.

Main Hudson Channel

The Main Hudson Channel is the primary channel servicing the local commercial businesses. There are two bona-fide marinas, a good ship's store, and access to much of Hudson via this main channel. There are also many offshoot canals stemming from this main channel. Three large Gulf Island white condominium buildings are perched on a point of land south of the Main Hudson Channel. The Hudson Channel sea buoy is actually a tripod with a lighted aid labeled "R2." "R2" is near way point 28.21.798N/82.45.023W, in about five to six feet at MLW. There are no more lighted navigation aids in this channel. The heading in this straight channel is 105 degrees. The channel is also fairly narrow, about 15 yards wide. This is the most heavily used channel in Hudson, and the *U.S. Coast Pilot* indicates a controlling depth of only two feet MLW. In the summer of 2002, dredging, which should deepen this channel to seven feet deep at MLW and lengthen it to 50 feet wide, is supposed to start.

We encountered four to six feet of water at MLW most of the way in, which is more depth than stated by the *U.S. Coast Pilot*. But Bob at Skeleton Key Marina stated that there are some places in the Main Hudson Channel that are barely two feet deep at MLW. He indicated that the shallowest places in this channel are between "R16A and R18" and near "G23." Although, when we passed nearby—even factoring in low tide—we experienced slightly deeper water. If you have a question concerning your boat's ability to negotiate the Main Hudson Channel, we recommend that you first contact the friendly folks at Skeleton Key Marina over the VHF radio. At "R20," the channel takes a slight dogleg to port. After "R22 and G23," there is a junction in the channel. The line of green can buoys off to port lead to Hudson Creek and the basin harboring Port Hudson Marina. On this route, you pass very close to the point of land. Port Hudson Marina has a large boatyard and a sizable covered shed for boat repairs. This marina has about 50 slips and can accommodate about a 40-footer. They also have hundreds of feet of concrete sea wall acceptable for side tying. Port Hudson Marina also offers Boat/U.S. discounts. The Dockside Restaurant, on the Port Hudson Marina premise, should be open soon.

Port Hudson Marina (727) 869-1840
www.porthudson.com

Approach depth—2-3 feet
Dockside depth—8 feet
Accepts transients—yes
Floating wooden and concrete docks—yes
Concrete sea walls for side tying—yes
Fixed wooden dock and a sea wall—yes
Dockside power connections—limited 15 amp
Dockside water connections—yes
Showers—yes
Gasoline—yes
Mechanical repairs—yes
Below-waterline repairs—yes, up to 30 feet
   with two forklifts
Boat ramp—yes

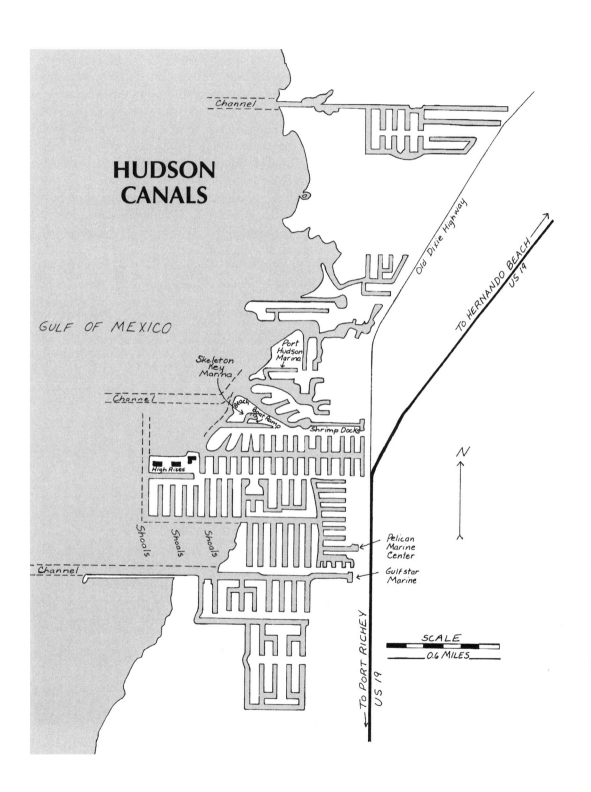

Ship's store—yes, limited
Restaurant—under construction

Back near the head of the channel, near "R24," you could continue east in a major artery canal sometimes known as Sponge Crawl Creek. Leave the public beach to your starboard. In the Sponge Crawl Creek Canal on the LDB, you'll find the Dockside Motel and another small, commercial, shrimp-boat facility, the Sea Turtle Marina. Near the head of this canal, you'll find more shrimp-boat docks. Canal development in Hudson appears to be a bit more mature than in other residential canal areas—and this is nice. The "protect your waterfront property with Doberman pinschers" attitude has probably come and gone by now. If canals are worth exploring any-where, the canals in Hudson get top billing. There are a couple of convenience stores, an Italian restaurant, and a French restaurant not far from the head of this canal. You could also walk slightly less than a mile from Skeleton Key Marina to reach this area by foot.

Near navigation aid "R24," if you turn toward your starboard side and leave the public beach on your port side, the channel-numbering system begins anew with another "G1." Between "G1" and "R6 and G7" we found water depths of six to eight feet at MLW. Continuing south past "G7" will lead to more Hudson canals. A sharp left turn at "G7" will lead to another canal that, in turn, leads to Skeleton Key Marina and the Hudson boat-launch area. This canal has depths of about four to six feet at MLW. The Hudson public

Hudson public boat-ramp area

boat-ramp area, in a nice little basin, has three sets of floating wooden docks, about eight slips, and a restroom facility. These are about the nicest set of municipal docks I've seen anywhere on the Big Bend. And you can tie up gratis for up to 18 hours once within any ten-day period. There is even about 50 feet of side-tie area in these docks. These are the docks I dream about finding every day at dusk. (Boy, I wish I had known about this place last night. It's only too bad that it's well before noon on this day, and it much behooves me to do more work, so I can be done and in the protected ICW waters in another two days—Hurricane Michelle is also barely two days away from making a potentially nasty strike somewhere in Florida.) Besides a marina in the immediate vicinity,

there is a nice public beach, a boardwalk, a wooden fishing pier, three covered picnic pavilions, bathrooms, and two restaurants—the Inn on the Gulf and Sam's Restaurant. The Inn on the Gulf also has a motel. Skeleton Key Marina has about 25 slips, can accommodate a 42-footer, and also has an uncovered high-and-dry storage facility. This well-managed marina also operates a sailing school.

Skeleton Key Marina (727) 868-3411

Approach depth—2-3 feet
Dockside depth—10-12 feet
Accepts transients—limited, based on availability
Floating wooden docks—yes
Dockside power connections—twin 30 amp
Dockside water connections—yes
Showers—yes

Skeleton Key Marina, Hudson

Gasoline—yes
Mechanical repairs—nearby contractor
Below-waterline repairs—limited to about
    15,000 pounds and two forklifts
Boat ramp—nearby
Ship's store—yes, limited
Restaurant—three within walking distance
Motels—two nearby

Back on the Main Hudson Channel, at aid "R16A," we turned south and out of any channel. We were aiming for a spot in the water just off the point of land to the east. Along this route, we encountered no less than three to seven feet at MLW, with most depths being four and five feet. In Hernando Beach, Hudson, and Gulf Harbors, we encountered these deeper trenches very close to the shoreline. Most times, except in the fluky canals of Hernando Beach, there were no official channels or aids in these shoreside channels. And we surely knew that we would run aground if we navigated in many places much farther out. But close to the shoreline, and in all three of these locales, we experienced sufficiently deep enough water in these unofficial along-the-shore "channels." And it didn't hurt that we had also asked for, and obtained, some local knowledge before trying out these unofficial trench "shortcuts."

After reaching the corner of land about a half-mile south of those large white condos, turn to port (or east) and you'll gradually work your way into another canal leading to Pelican Marine Center. There are still a couple more canal turns to make, and you can follow these turns on our Hudson sketch. Please study our canal sketch for making all the proper turns to eventually reach the head of one of these branch canals and Pelican

Marine. Pelican Marine Center is a Yamaha, Johnson, and Evinrude dealer with a very well-stocked ship's store. Transient boaters can tie up at one of their four wet slips and visit their ship's store. However, boaters are not permitted to tie up overnight.

Pelican Marine Center (813) 863-5409

Approach depth—2 feet
Dockside depth—1 foot
Accepts transients—no overnighters
Fixed and floating wooden docks—yes
Mechanical repairs—certain outboard motors
Below-waterline repairs—limited to 26 feet and
    two forklifts
Ship's store—yes

Leisure Beach Channel

To enter Leisure Beach Channel, the southernmost channel in the Hudson area, position yourself at way point 28.20.890N/82.43.800W. You'll be off a tripod and "G1 and R2," in three to four feet of water at MLW. Navigation aid "R2" is lighted, but the tripod and all other aids in this channel are unlighted. Once again, there are many more navigation aids than shown on NOAA chart 11409. We found water depths to be between three and six feet at MLW, with most depths being in the three- to four-foot range. The initial heading is 100 degrees. At barely 40 feet wide, Leisure Beach Channel is even slightly narrower than some of the other channels in the Hudson area. A mangrove jetty soon materializes on the LDB and near Stake Creek Point. Soon mangrove clumps start appearing on the RDB. "R14 and G15" are the last navigation aids, in about five feet of water at MLW.

Unlike the Main Hudson Canal, with many branches, the Leisure Beach Canal has branches in only one direction—off to the south. HAZARD *There is no safe deep route between the Leisure Beach Channel and the Main Hudson Channel—including a route to Pelican Marine Center.* The Leisure Beach Canal (versus the channel) deepens to about seven to ten feet at MLW and widens significantly. The housing along the banks is a refreshing cry from those along Sea Pines Canal. There are even a few double-wide trailers parked near the water (and these folks usually don't have sleek Dobermans). Gulfstar Marine is at the head of this canal and on U.S. Route 19. Gulfstar, a Carolina Skiff dealer, has about three small floating wooden docks and were gracious enough to let me park here while I explored the nearby environs on foot.

The Pithlachascotee River, Port Richey, and New Port Richey

Believe it or not, Calusa Indians once thrived along the Pithlachascotee River. Today, a small Indian mound, Oelsner Mound, still remains on the river's edge in between American Marina and Sunset Landing Marina on the LDB. The mound was almost completely destroyed by modern development. There is a two-week-long festival held on the banks of the river every March—the Chasco Fiesta, which celebrates the Calusa and Spanish heritage of this area.

Pithlachascotee is a Seminole name meaning something like "canoes hacked out." The name

Pithlachascotee River, Port Richey

is often colloquialized to Cotee. The Cotee is the deepest river since the Withlacoochee River, about 45 nautical miles to the north. This channel also has more lighted navigation aids than any channel to the north, at least as far north as the Withlacoochee River. The Cotee River is easy to navigate, day or night. The river leads to Port Richey and then to larger New Port Richey. Port Richey is one of the earliest settled towns on the Gulf Coast of Florida. Most unfortunately, a low 12-foot-MHW-overhead-clearance bridge (according to the *U.S. Coast Pilot*) limits access to New Port Richey. If any bridge in the entire Big Bend could be raised, or made into a drawbridge, it ought to be this U.S. Route 19 bridge over the Cotee River. Downtown New Port Richey is enchanting, but it is isolated to many of us boaters because of this relatively low, fixed bridge.

Downriver, back in Port Richey, there are three marinas, but they all have certain limitations. The largest marina doesn't accept transients, another nearby marina is fairly small at present, and the third marina primarily caters to shrimp boats. Casino-gambling boat operations have also infiltrated some of the old waterfront space in Port Richey. The old Joshua's Landing Marina has been taken over by casino boats. There are also about four restaurants on the water in Port Richey. But again, one restaurant has no boat dock, another disallows overnight docking, and the third is part of that shrimp-boat facility. However, the fourth nice restaurant does allow boats to tie up overnight to their well-maintained dock after partaking in their dining room.

Back on the Gulf of Mexico, the well-marked channel into the Cotee River begins

off way point 28.17.129N/82.46.297W. There should be about six feet at MLW at this way point. You'll also notice about eight houses on stilts within a mile or so off both sides of the mouth of the Cotee River. Nearby, navigation aid "G1" is lighted, but aid "R2" is unlighted. Other lighted channel navigation aids in the Cotee River channel include "R4," "G7," "G9," "G13," "R16," "G21," "G27," "R30," and "G35." The initial heading in this well-marked channel is close to 100 degrees. This channel is also about a comfortable 25-30 yards wide. We encountered MLW depths ranging from eight to ten feet. However, the *U.S. Coast Pilot* states a controlling depth of only five feet. A pronounced dogleg to starboard is near aid "G7." Afterward, the channel continues to make a gradual curve to the right. As you leave the channel and approach the river, you'll notice some mansions on the point of land on the RDB. This restricted and exclusive community is called Sand Pebble. At "G17" the channel makes about a 90-degree turn to port. Near navigation aid "R26," there is another channel off to your starboard (or LDB) side. This short well-marked channel, beginning with navigation aids "G1 and R2," leads to American Marina. We found that this channel has five to six feet of water depth at MLW. There is a shoal off "G7," and the aids to American Marina go as far as "R14." American Marina has about 30 slips and can accommodate about a 40-footer. They are primarily an expansive high-and-dry storage facility with two buildings and have no wet slips for transient boaters. Sunset Landing Marina is after "G33" and also on the LDB side. This quaint marina also has a high-and-dry storage building and small boatyard. But they only have about 80 feet of

COTEE RIVER AND NEW PORT RICHEY

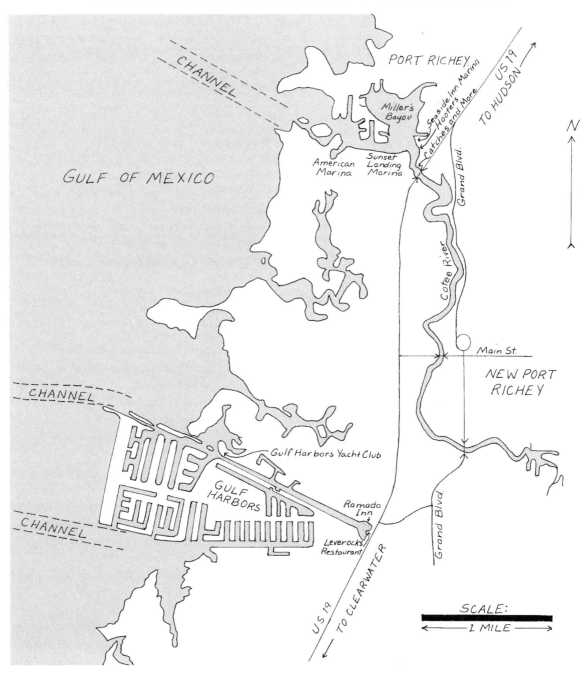

CHANNEL

PORT RICHEY

TO HUDSON

US 19

N

Miller's Bayou

Seaside Inn Marina

Hooters

Catches and More

GULF OF MEXICO

American Marina

Sunset Landing Marina

Grand Blvd.

Cotee River

Main St.

NEW PORT RICHEY

CHANNEL

Gulf Harbors Yacht Club

GULF HARBORS

Ramada Inn

Grand Blvd.

CHANNEL

Leverocks Restaurant

US 19

TO CLEARWATER

SCALE:

1 MILE

dockage. The new owner and management team have plans to construct an additional 20-25 wet slips before the end of 2002.

American Marina (727) 842-4065

Approach depth—5-6 feet
Dockside depth—3-4 feet
Accepts transients—no
Fixed wooden docks—yes
Floating aluminum docks—yes
Dockside power connections—30 amp
Dockside water connections—yes
Gasoline—yes
Mechanical repairs—yes
Below-waterline repairs—yes, 35 feet and limited
   to forklifts
Ship's store—yes, very limited
Restaurant—two nearby

Sunset Landing Marina (727) 849-5092

Approach depth—4-5 feet
Dockside depth—4-5 feet
Accepts transients—very limited at present
Fixed and floating wooden docks—yes
Gasoline—yes
Mechanical repairs—some engine work
Below-waterline repairs—limited, with a 25
   feet and forklift
Boat ramp—yes
Ship's store—yes, limited
Restaurant—nearby

The entrance to Miller's Bayou and Port Richey Waterfront Park is about a quarter mile past Sunset Landing and on the opposite (or RDB) side of the Cotee River. The Seaside Inn Marina and Hooter's Restaurant are next on the RDB. HAZARD *There is an oyster shoal in the middle of the river, and it's highly recommended that you turn on an approach for* *these two establishments after reaching "G35."* The Seaside Inn has about 20 slips and about 150 feet of side-tie docking. This facility primarily caters to the local shrimp fleet, but they do have a restaurant. Hooter's is upriver and next door. You can park at one of the three docks at Hooter's to imbibe, but they were adamant about no overnight docking.

Seaside Inn Marina (727) 846-1112

Approach depth—5 feet
Accepts transients—yes but limited to space
Fixed wooden docks—yes
Dockside power connections—limited 15 amp
Dockside water connections—yes
Restaurant—on site, and two others nearby

Hooter's Restaurant

Approach depth—5 feet
Dockside depth—2-4 feet
Accepts transients—no overnight docking
Fixed wooden and plastic docks—three docks
   at about 50 feet long
Dockside power connections—limited 15 amp
   on the plastic dock
Restaurant—on site, and two others nearby

After "R34 and G35," the channel turns to starboard. H. R. Nicks Park and the casino-boat docks are upriver from Hooter's on the RDB. Nicks Park also has a double-wide concrete boat ramp with a fixed wooden dock. Casino boats have exerted their heavy presence in Port Richey. Port Richey is a good location for these gambling boats because, after they depart the river channel, they don't need to negotiate any ICW. The Gulf of Mexico is right there, and local jurisdiction is nil. In Port Richey, there are two separate

Seaside Inn Marina, Port Richey

casino-boat operations—Sun Cruz and Stardancer Casino Cruises. Between these two operations, there are at least four casino boats plying the Cotee River. The recent history of both these casino operations is a bit sullied. Stardancer has been accused of financing its operation with embezzled money. The founder of Sun Cruz was murdered in a well-planned shooting in 2000. Joshua's Landing, a once popular marina, has been taken over as a casino-boat dock.

The Port Richey Marina, (727) 919-8954, is just beyond the casino-boat docks and near "G41." This facility has about 10 slips that are about 30 feet long, but the operation is primarily reserved for fishing charter boats. There are limited utilities on their one fixed wooden pier. We think the nicest transient docks in all Port Richey are next door to the Port Richey Marina, at Catches and More Seafood Restaurant. Catches and More Seafood Restaurant strikes us as the only place in town actively courting transient recreational boaters (i.e., until Sunset Landing Marina expands). And Catches and More is planning to lengthen their nice plastic-padded 150-foot dock by another 50 feet.

Catches and More Seafood Restaurant
(727) 849-2208

Dockside depth—3-5 feet
Accepts transients—yes, overnight free with dinner
Floating aluminum docks—yes, with nice padding
Dockside power connections—limited 30 amp
Dockside water connections—yes, limited
Restaurant—on site, and two others nearby
Motels—many nearby on the highway

Sandals Bar and Grill is across the river from Catches and More on the LDB. This restaurant has a nice pier, but it's inaccessible for parking a boat. If you can't squeeze beneath that 12-foot-MHW-clearance U.S. Route 19 highway bridge, this is the end of the line. What a shame. But if you can negotiate beneath this bridge, please continue. Or leave your big boat docked at Catches and More Restaurant, and take a dinghy ride for another two and a half miles up the Cotee River. You won't regret this trip on the enchanting Cotee River through the esplanade-like environs of New Port Richey.

Just beyond the bridge on the RDB, there is Adventure Kayak Center (rentals), (727) 848-8099, and a dive shop, followed by Cotee River Boat Storage, (727) 841-7664. After "R46," you'll be coming to a placid river park on the RDB. We think the residential development along the Cotee River shores is so much nicer than the residential dwellings found on so many of those manufactured Florida canals. This tasteful, winding river is also comfortably wide. Water depths in this part of the Cotee River range between five and 12 feet at MLW, with six to seven feet being the most common depths. There are also a few wide bends in the Cotee River that would make nice anchorages once out of the channel. The last navigation aid in the Cotee River is "R60."

A couple of overhead power lines cross the river, and the *U.S. Coast Pilot* indicates the lowest overhead power-line clearance is 38 feet. There is also another bridge, the Main Street Bridge, over the Cotee River about a mile and a half upstream from the U.S. Route 19 bridge. The *U.S. Coast Pilot* states the overhead clearance at 10 feet MHW. Sims Park, on the RDB, is just downriver from this bridge.

Pithlachascotee River, New Port Richey

In this park, there is a floating, plastic, public dock in about six feet at MLW. And there are many nearby restaurants, taverns, and a library on the east side of the Cotee River near Sims Park. There is also an amphitheater in Sims Park.

Across the river, on the LDB, the primary New Port Richey public boat ramp is just before the picturesque Main Street Bridge. This ramp has two L-shaped docks. U.S. Route 19, with its hubbub of strip malls, liquor stores, and twenty-first-century atmosphere, is about three blocks from this public ramp area. It's hard to believe, and a bit fascinating, that on one side (i.e., to the west), just past the buffer strip of the Cotee River, there is the fast-paced urban jungle along U.S. Route 19, and on the other side (to the east) of the Cotee River, barely five blocks away from U.S. Route 19, there's the quaint stretch of restaurants and taverns of "Old New Port Richey" on Grand Boulevard. New Port Richey was once a haven for early film stars in the 1920s. Silent-screen actress Gloria Swansen lived in a house on the banks of the Cotee River. Another silent-film mogul, Thomas Meighan, unsuccessfully tried to develop New Port Richey as a movie-production mecca. The plan obviously didn't work.

Another mile up the Cotee River, a third bridge, the Grand Boulevard Bridge, crosses over the Cotee River. HAZARD *This bridge only has six feet of overhead clearance, and rocks were beginning to encroach from along the shore.* We were told that there is about a four-foot tide in this part of the Cotee River.

Gulf Harbors

Gulf Harbors are the two channels about three miles south of the Cotee River Channel in the Gulf of Mexico with a New Port Richey

mailing address. The south channel and its adjoining canals contain only residential development. The longer north channel and canal extend all the way to heavily trafficked U.S. Route 19. This north channel and canal are also cloaked with residential development; however, there are also some attractions that may hold interest to the nonresidential boater. At the head of this long canal, there is a turning basin at Leverock's Seafood House; the Ramada Inn also has a restaurant. Both facilities have floating boat docks for their restaurant clientele as well as for the passing transient boater. The nice Gulf Harbors Yacht Club is also about halfway in this canal on the RDB side.

North Channel

To enter the northern Gulf Harbors channel, arrive near way point 28.14.690N/82.47. 176W. You should be off "G1 and R2." Navigation aid "R2" is a lighted aid in about five feet of water at MLW. The heading in this straight channel is 105 degrees. The channel depths range from five to seven feet at MLW, with six-foot depths being the most common. HAZARD *After "G7," a partially submerged rock ledge starts appearing on the green (i.e., north) side.* After "R10"—the last navigation aid—this channel doglegs to starboard to about 120 degrees as it gives way to the canal.

The depth in the canal is about a foot or two deeper than the channel, and the canal is about 30 to 40 yards wide. The first side canal on the LDB has a large basin that connects to three other side canals. This is about the biggest (i.e., about 100 yards by 80 yards) canal basin that we've encountered anywhere on the Big Bend. And this basin has enough swinging room to be suitable as an anchorage—

Gulf Harbors northern canal

if you like anchoring behind 30 manicured backyards. The water depths in this basin are deep, 14 to 20 feet at MLW, and perhaps a tad too deep for comfortable anchoring. If you do anchor overnight here, with potential water-borne traffic coming from as many as four directions, an anchor light is imperative!

The Gulf Harbors Yacht Club appears on the RDB about a mile into the canal. The yacht club has about 19 slips—15 to 42 feet long. The club's two floating wooden docks, which are about 60 and 80 feet long respectively, are pri-marily reserved for transients. Transient boaters from reciprocating yacht clubs receive first pri-ority, and advance notice is highly recom-mended. Each transient dock has one 30-amp electrical outlet but no water spigot. The local U.S. Coast Guard Auxiliary has a small building on the arm north of the yacht club.

Gulf Harbors Yacht Club (727) 849-4559

Approach depth—7-8 feet
Accepts transients—possibly, with advance notice

Gulf Harbors Yacht Club

Floating wooden docks—yes, two available for transients

Fixed and floating wooden docks—yes

Dockside power connections—30 amp

Dockside water connections—yes but not at transient dock

Showers—yes

Clubhouse—yes

The canal ends in a turning basin about a mile and a half past the yacht club. The turning basin borders congested U.S. Route 19, with its wide array of commercial establishments. And two facilities on U.S. 19, Leverock's Seafood House and a Ramada Inn, are situated in this turning basin. Both of these facilities have floating wooden docks and can accommodate transient boaters. Leverock's, a local chain, has about a half-dozen restaurants and has a good longstanding reputation for serving excellent seafood entrées. Leverock's Seafood House and docks are smack at the head of the channel. Their three seaward-facing slips on the north side (i.e., on

Leverock's and Ramada Inn at the head of Gulf Harbors northern channel

your left as you approach) of their dock are reserved for transient boaters. A handful of charter boats also park at the docks at both Leverock's and the Ramada Inn. The Ramada Inn docks are north of Leverock's. The Ramada also has a restaurant and a total of about 30 slips on a dock that is a tad rickety.

Leverock's Seafood House (727) 849-8000

Dockside depth—5-6 feet
Accepts transients—yes, three slips on left,
   about 25 feet long
Floating wooden docks—yes
Dockside power connections—30 amp
Dockside water connections—yes
Restaurant—on site, and many others nearby

Ramada Inn (727) 849-8551

Dockside depth—3-4 feet
Accepts transients—yes
Floating wooden docks—yes
Dockside power connections—30 amp
Dockside water connections—yes
Swimming pool—yes
Restaurant—on site, and many others nearby
Motel—yes

South Channel

To arrive at the southern Gulf Harbors channel, position your boat near way point 28.14.179N/82.47.274W. You should be in about five to six feet of water at MLW, off lighted navigation aid "G1." Once again, the seawardmost navigation aid,"G1," is the only lighted aid in the channel. This straight channel heads about 105 degrees. The channel depths hold between five and six feet at MLW. The last navigation aids in this channel are "G9 and R10," also in six to eight feet of water at MLW. The LDB side of this canal has several side canals with residential development. The first part of the RDB side of the canal is a mangrove swamp.

Anclote Key

Three-mile-long Anclote Key is the northernmost barrier island in a chain of islands extending about 175 miles south to Cape Romano, Florida. If you have been traveling south on the Gulf of Mexico, by the time you have reached Hudson—and if you have had good visibility—you should have spied Anclote Key or at least the smokestack on the mainland across from Anclote Key, belonging to the Anclote, Florida, Power Plant. When you reach Anclote Key, you'll see an old steel light tower near the south end of this island. This 101-foot-tall tower was commissioned in 1896. The Greek sponge divers of yesteryear called this light tower their angel of mercy as they returned to Tarpon Springs.

We have two way points inside Anclote Key. At the north end of Anclote Key, inside lighted aid "R6," our way point is 28.12.611N/82.49.219W. At the south end of Anclote Key, in about 11 to 12 feet at MLW, between navigation aids unlighted "R10" and lighted "G9," our way point is 28.09.601N/82.50.033W. St. Joseph Sound and the Gulf Intracoastal Waterway (ICW) start a few yards to the south of this last way point, at unlighted navigation aids "R42 and G41." If you are heading south on the ICW toward Tampa Bay, Fort Myers, or Flamingo, we recommend *Cruising Guide to Western Florida*, by Claiborne Young.

If you have been sailing from north to south, once you reach Anclote Key you are back in the protected Intracoastal Waterway!

Well done! And there will be protected waters from Anclote Key all the way to Fort Myers—another 150 miles down the road. On this part of the ICW, if southbound, the navigation-aid numbers will be descending (e.g., "R42," "R40," "R38," etc.). And all of those red ICW navigation aids will always be on the mainland side (i.e., to your port side while heading south along the Gulf), while those green aids will be to the seaward—or to the barrier-island—side. In any event, seeing those little yellow squares, so familiar with ICW navigation aids, should be a most welcome sight!

Apalachicola River shoreline

CHAPTER 13

The Apalachicola River, from Apalachicola to Chattahoochee, FL

This chapter covers the 106 statute (i.e., river) miles between Apalachicola, Florida, and Lake Seminole, where the Chattahoochee and Flint rivers meet to form the Apalachicola River. In terms of the volume of water flow, the Apalachicola River is Florida's largest—and the twenty-first largest river in the entire United States. The flood plain of the Apalachicola is the largest flood plain in Florida and one of the largest on the Gulf of Mexico. The Apalachicola-Chattahoochee-Flint River basin drains an area of almost 20,000 square miles.

The banks and waters of the Apalachicola River are loaded with a menagerie of swamp wildlife. At anchor, at any time of year, typical nighttime sounds include a cacophony of squawks, wails, and hoots. The only sound that I could regularly identify was the eerie bellow of a nearby hoot owl. If you can recognize the haunting nighttime animal sounds surrounding you there, anchoring on the Apalachicola River is the place for you. Twice bald eagles buzzed my boat on the lower Apalachicola River. And there are more species of amphibians and reptiles found in the Apalachicola River basin than anywhere else in the United States. To get a flavor for what's ahead, we recommend that you first visit the very well done Apalachicola National Estuarine Research Reserve (ANERR) and their nearby aquarium, (850) 653-8063.

This facility is in Apalachicola and only a few blocks southwest of the commercial shrimp docks of the Scipio Creek Commercial Marina.

Apalachicola has two Indian translations: "land of the friendly people" and "the people who live on the other side." During the British occupation in the mid-1700s, the Apalachicola and Chattahoochee rivers were an important boundary separating more promising Western Florida from pestilence-ridden Eastern Florida. Today, much of the Apalachicola and the navigable portion of the Chattahoochee River form the boundary between the Eastern time zone and the Central time zone. Beware of this, especially as you travel along the Chattahoochee River, as there will be a one-hour time difference between a marina in Georgia and a restaurant across Lake Eufaula in Alabama. The Walter George Lock on Lake Eufaula stops daily operations at 4 P.M. Eastern Standard Time—that's 3 P.M. Central Standard Time. Slightly more than half of the border between Alabama and Georgia is formed by the Chattahoochee River. The Georgia Port Authority operates four ports. Two ports, Savannah and Brunswick, are on the Atlantic. But the other two, the Bainbridge and Columbus ports, are on the Apalachicola-Chattahoochee-Flint River System. The state of Alabama also has inland ports at the state docks located at Columbia, Eufaula, and Phenix

City on the Chattahoochee River. These Chattahoochee-Flint River inland ports are terminals for such products as fertilizer, ammonium nitrate, asphalt, steel, lime, sand, gravel, and agricultural products.

Between 1828 and 1928, as many as 200 stern- or side-wheeled steamboats worked the Apalachicola River. In the 1830s, there may have been as many as 150 steamboats plying the river at the same time. And during their heyday, there may have been more than 200 steamboat landings between Apalachicola, Florida, and Columbus, Georgia. Steamboats were still using this waterway as late as the 1920s. Cotton, timber, and seafood dominated commerce on these rivers. We have heard stories that during the era of Prohibition, bootleg liquor was sometimes trans-ported on boats from as far away as Havana, Cuba, to Phenix City, Alabama.

Fort Gadsden

Fort Gadsden, a national historic site, is on the LDB of the Apalachicola River at mile 19.8. The first fort was built by the British during the War of 1812. The British used the fort as a recruiting post for Indians and former slaves who wanted to fight against the Americans. In 1814, the British abandoned the fort. By 1816, the fort was manned by Seminole Indians, runaway slaves, and other fugitives from justice. Runaway slaves had been finding their way to this no man's land of north Florida for about 140 years prior. Hence, the fort was also known as the Negro Fort. Its leader was a man named Garcon,

Boat landing at Fort Gadsden, Apalachicola River

who was either a mulatto or a black man. Garcon and his men were intent on either harassing American supply lines or extorting tolls from American shipping, while allowing the "friendly" British ships safe passage through this section of the river. In July 1816, American colonel Duncan Clinch and two gunboats arrived near the fort, intent on putting this extortion scheme out of business. Fortuitously for Clinch, the fifth shot from his gunboat hit the fort's powder magazine. This lucky round, and the immediate explosion, blew the fort to smithereens. Only 33 of the 300-320 people inside the fort at the time of the massive explosion survived. And only three were uninjured. Tragically, a large number of Seminole women and children were also taking refuge in this fort at the time of the tremendous blast. Nearly all were instantly killed. Garcon and a Seminole chief were two of the few who survived the explosion. But soon afterward, they were put to death—burned at the stake, after the Americans purposely handed them over to rival Indians.

In 1818, during the first Seminole war, Gen. Andrew Jackson sailed down the Apalachicola River with the intent of destroying Seminole villages. Impressed by the strategic location of the flattened fort, he ordered another fort built in spite of Spanish protests. Jackson named the new site after the lieutenant in charge of the fort's construction, James Gadsden. After Spain ceded Florida to the Americans in 1821, the fort was no longer needed. Gadsden went on to greater fame—the Gadsden Purchase of southern New Mexico and Arizona in 1853. Confederate troops briefly reoccupied the old fort between 1862 and 1863.

Navigational Nuances

Water Levels

The controlling depth of the Apalachicola River from the Gulf ICW to Lake Seminole is supposed to be seven feet. The water depths can be significantly higher. But at times of low water, in certain places the depths can be even lower. It was lower in some of the areas when we did our exploration. If you are heading up the Apalachicola River, Capt. Charles Creamer, at Scipio Creek Marina in Apalachicola, is a reliable source of information on water levels and river conditions. If you are heading downriver, the helpful lock tenders at the Jim Woodruff Lock and Dam, (850) 663-4692, are also excellent ones to ask. Beyond Lake Seminole, and all the way to Columbus, Georgia, the channel is supposed to be nine feet deep and 100 feet wide.

If the water level is low, water is occasionally systematically released during "higher-water navigation windows." Extra water is released from the Woodruff Dam on Lake Seminole, raising the level of the Apalachicola River for short-term navigational purposes. These higher-water windows normally last for about ten days. Generally, in times of normal flow, a high-water window might occur every month or so. But in 2000, because of perilously low water levels, the higher-water windows were more infrequent. There were only two barge windows from April to December in 2000. The spring of 2001 was a wet one, and lake and river water levels remained naturally high. Hence, there was no need for higher-water navigation windows during the first part of 2001.

Several interests conflict when creating barge windows. There is much political wrangling over this issue. There are well-meaning folks who think the Chattahoochee and Apalachicola river water levels should not be manipulated in the very least. Furthermore, water levels do have to be drained from each dam farther up the river—oftentimes from at least the large West Point Reservoir and many times from all the way to Lake Lanier outside of Atlanta. The sprawling Atlanta metropolitan area consumes a very significant amount of water that would otherwise normally flow into the Apalachicola River. At the other side of this spectrum, many commercial, navigational, and recreational interests think the river should be responsibly managed for commercial- and recreational-vessel traffic. Dr. John Davis, of Dothan, Alabama, makes an interesting case for no controlled navigation windows on the Apalachicola River. He recommends only a few minor and relatively inexpensive adjustments that are much less expensive than dredging. Perhaps, his most astounding idea is to redirect some of the water that started "unnaturally" flowing into the Chipola River in 1882 back into the Apalachicola River. This could be done by constructing a partial diversion dam near the Chipola Cutoff. Stay tuned.

In the 106 miles below the Jim Woodruff Lock and Dam, the Apalachicola River drops by more than 50 feet (or an average of more than six inches per mile). This creates a swift current for those 106 miles—and the swiftest navigable section south of Columbus, Georgia. The strongest downstream current peaks—in the neighborhood of four knots—between Apalachicola River miles 30 and 50. The Apalachicola River has more current than any of the other Gulf-flowing rivers. Upriver from mile 50, the downstream current on the Apalachicola

River abates by at least a knot. Bob, a lock tender at Woodruff Lock and Dam, indicated that in times of high runoff, and very near the dam, the Apalachicola River current can reach as high as four to five knots (in an area where I was experiencing only three adverse knots of current). The lowest six miles of the Apalachicola River, below the fork with the Jackson River, has a tidal affect along with the downstream current. In this lowest six-mile section, when the tide is rising up the river, the flooding tidal current is almost unnoticeable. The rising current is neutralized by the downhill Apalachicola river flow.

Beware, if you are going upstream in this current. The entire Apalachicola River is a remote area with very limited fuel availability. Your fuel supply may be taxed more than initially anticipated. Mine was. Furthermore, we found no recreational-boating facilities selling diesel fuel between Apalachicola and Eufaula, Alabama. Obviously, the towboats have to buy their diesel from somewhere. There are a few river towns with nearby service stations that sell diesel fuel (e.g., in Chattahoochee, Florida, and in Bainbridge, Georgia). Marinas with haul-out capabilities (i.e., travel lifts or marine railroads) are virtually nonexistent. I was told that some big boats that park as far as 200 miles up these rivers must travel all the way down to Apalachicola, Florida, for a haul out.

During times of low water, we found the depths to be most dicey between river mile 35 and mile 44. If you can make it through this nine-mile stretch on the Apalachicola River, I'd say you're home free with the water depths farther up the Apalachicola, Flint, or Chattahoochee—and all the way to either Bainbridge or Columbus, Georgia. We also noticed that after heavy rainfalls, there was much less debris found floating down the Apalachicola River than what is typically found on other rivers after a heavy rainfall.

Overhead Clearances

The Corps of Engineers pegs bridge clearance in these rivers to a level called the Bridge Reference Elevation for Navigation or BRENC for short. Only the two most downriver bridges on the Apalachicola River do not use this BRENC water-pegging level. The water level beneath those two lowest bridges, the Gorrie Bridge and the Apalachicola Northern Railroad, is more a function of the tide (i.e., high, low, or in-between tide). But the other twenty bridges on the Apalachicola-Chattahoochee-Flint River System are pegged to the BRENC level. By definition, the BRENC level "is that water stage which on average is exceeded only twice annu-

ally and whose duration is less than five days." So a seagoing salt can think of BRENC somewhat like mean high water. Yes, the water level does occasionally exceed BRENC (or MHW) levels, but when it does, it's the result of unusual meteorological circumstances.

The lowest fixed bridge on the Apalachicola River is at mile 100—the Interstate 10 bridge—at 37 feet above BRENC. When we made our trip, we were experiencing water considerably lower than the BRENC level—sometimes by more than 10 feet, especially on the upper Apalachicola River. In the spring time, you may be close to, or occasionally even above, the BRENC level. The Apalachicola Northern Railroad Bridge at mile 4.5 has been open every time that we checked it. It just may remain more often open than closed. The following table presents the bridges and overhead obstacles on the Apalachicola River.

BRIDGE NAME	TYPE	VERTICAL CLEARANCE (FEET)	APPROX RIVER MILE
John Gorrie Memorial Bridge (U.S. Route 98)	Fixed	65.0	0
Apalachicola Northern Railroad Bridge	Swing	11.0*	4.5
Overhead Transmission Lines	Cable	66.0	20.2
Calhoun Bridge, Blountstown (state route 20)	Fixed	48.9	79.4
Overhead Transmission Lines	Cable	50.0	79.4
Interstate 10 Bridge	**Fixed**	**37.1**	100.0
Twin Overhead Transmission Lines	Cable	56.0	103.1
CSX Railroad Bridge	Swing	19.0	104.9
Overhead Transmission Lines	Cable	46.0	105.5
U.S. Route 90 Bridge	Fixed	38.1**	105.7
Jim Woodruff Lock and Dam	**Lock**		106.3

* The *U.S. Coast Pilot* and NOAA chart 11401 indicates 11 feet of overhead clearance. The U.S. Army Corps of Engineers, Mobile District, states 13 feet of overhead clearance.

** Information on Corps of Engineers aerial photographs states 38 feet of vertical clearance. However, interpolating from the water-line mark, the bridge clearance appears to be much greater, with 54 to 55 feet of vertical clearance beneath this bridge.

Along the lower Apalachicola River, we occasionally observed water-level stakes near the shore. We believe these stakes depict the present water level in relation to the BRENC. When we made this trip, the water level on these measuring stakes was consistently about two feet *below* the zero mark on the lower Apalachicola River. That made sense. We were traveling at a time of low water. Hence, we likely had at least an extra two feet of overhead clearance beneath the bridges on the lower Apalachicola River. The high-water hash mark on these stakes went up as high as nine feet. As we went farther up the Apalachicola, I think the difference between the BRENC and the actual river level became even greater. The Interstate Route 10 Bridge at river mile 100 had a stated BRENC clearance of 37.1 feet. I can't say with certainty, but I have gone beneath a few bridges, and I'd say my clearance beneath that particular bridge was at least ten feet more than that BRENC-stated clearance (i.e., I guess, over 47 feet of overhead clearance).

Navigation Aids

The Apalachicola, Flint, and Chattahoochee rivers are the only rivers maintained for navigation by the Corps of Engineers for any significant distance from the Gulf of Mexico in the Big Bend. The Mobile, Alabama, district of the Corps maintains these rivers. Navigation aids on these rivers are reasonably good. But when it comes to reading buoys and daymarks, there are some nuances. Like navigational aids in tidal waters, floating nun or can buoys—and green, square or red, triangular daymarks—are positioned near the channel's edge. But some daymarks have a slightly different meaning than that green square or red triangular daymark. A diamond daymark indicates that the deepest water can be found by steering *for* that particular diamond daymark,

whether it be green or red. For this reason, more often than not, you'll see these diamond daymarks on the outside of bends. These diamond marks are usually slightly bigger and more eye-catching. Diamond daymarks are aiming points, like range marks, for their side of the river. Generally, you steer toward a diamond mark and then adjust your course when you sight the next navigational aid on the river. A diamond daymark may have four diamonds nested within the larger diamond placard, or it may have four even smaller diamonds at each corner of the diamond placard. In any event, on the Apalachicola-Chattahoochee-Flint River System, you can almost always spy the next navigation aid—a diamond, square, or triangular daymark or a floating buoy.

The Apalachicola River also has white mileage placards posted on trees—oftentimes on the same trees that support navigational daymarks. Generally, these mileage indices are at intervals not exceeding one mile. The mileage numbers are listed to the nearest tenth of a mile upstream from the John Gorrie Bridge. The 65-foot vertical-clearance Gorrie Bridge crosses the river in the heart of Apalachicola at river mile zero. Floating can and nun buoys are NOT numbered, as they are on many of our tidal rivers. And sometimes, these buoys get knocked out of place on the Apalachicola-Chattahoochee-Flint River System. We noted a handful of obviously misplaced floating aids (e.g., a green can only a few feet away from the LDB or a red nun only a few feet away RDB). Knowing that some floating aids may be out of place, you should use common-sense cues when assessing them. If you notice that a buoy appears out of place, it most likely *is* out of place. These buoys are designed slightly different than round-bottom tidal-coastal buoys.

These river buoys have a fin to help them maintain their linear position in the strong unidirectional current below the waterline.

Outside of the Channel

Anchorages

In the Apalachicola River, as well as any river, it's more than highly advisable to get out of the channel, especially when anchoring overnight. If not, you could get run over by another boat or a towboat, although there is not nearly as much towboat traffic on the Apalachicola as there is on other inland rivers. Radio traffic for the towboats operating on the Apalachicola-Chattahoochee-Flint Rivers is often heard on VHF channel 14. Side creeks, if they are wide enough—and those that don't have too little or too much water depth—are good anchorages.

Surprisingly, there are more than a few very deep side creeks that are too uncomfortably deep for anchoring. Being out of the current is a very important aspect of a good anchorage in this particular river. Besides, it's less strain on your ground tackle. It is also good to be out of the current because floating debris (e.g., large tree parts) can occasionally come barreling down with the current. The overall ambiance of an anchorage is another consideration (e.g., being surrounded by cypress or tupelo trees with Spanish moss has to enhance a potential anchoring gunk hole).

The St. Marks River contains one of the first good anchorages on the Apalachicola. There are many other anchorages along the river. If you wish to anchor in another deep-water creek, try Owl Creek. The shore of Owl Creek is laden with cypress knees and beautiful cypress trees. This fairly wide creek is navigable for a few miles, and the water depths range between 16 to 25 feet within a mile from the Apalachicola River. Between river miles 43 and 46, there are no less than four anchorages on the Apalachicola River. Two of them, in my opinion, are outstanding—two of the best three on the entire river. It's only too bad they all have to be so close together. The third-best anchorage on the entire Apalachicola River is in a basin at mile 43.1 on the LDB. There is another fair anchorage on the LDB in a bulge off mile 44.8. At mile 45.2 on the RDB, there is a spacious arm with a wide entry near the Iola boat ramp. There are no less than two great spots at which to anchor out of the Apalachicola's current in this big arm. There is about 15 feet of water depth across nearly the entire width of that arm. An anchorage area is on the RDB of that arm, and about 50 feet from the shore, with about 15 feet of water depth. In my opinion, the nicest anchorage on the entire Apala-chicola River is farther up this same arm, close to the head of the arm, and slightly past the Iola ramp. This anchorage is 360-degree-protected by tall trees, has plenty of swinging room, and is situated in eight to 11 feet of water depth. It's just gorgeous—and there is even a nearby receptacle at the boat ramp to discharge your trash. Another anchorage is found at mile 49.8 on the RDB. There is another very nice anchorage in a basin at mile 71.0 on the RDB. Water depths are nine feet in the entry and 11 to 16 feet in most of this large basin. Many anchored vessels could fit in here.

Jetties

Upriver from river mile 65, there are frequent series of pilings protruding into the river from either bank. On the Corps of Engineers aerial photographs, these areas are often labeled as Dikes. I think of a dike as something that holds water back or possibly channels the water flow. I think of a jetty as something that protects a shoreline or an inlet from erosion. I was later told that these structures were built to stabilize the shoreline. So despite the corps label, we'll refer to these "dikes" as jetties. They are most often around bends or just upstream from bends where the shoreline could get eroded.

Each jetty area has between three and nine rows of pilings extending perpendicular to the shoreline. You sure as heck would not wish to smack into these pilings at night—while operating a boat too close to the shore. And if you remained near the center of the river, you'd likely miss the rows of pilings. A jetty area with three rows of pilings would have two embayments of calm water, while a jetty area with nine rows of pilings would have eight embayments of protected water between the rows of pilings (i.e., x number of rows of pilings = x-1 embayments). We even noticed several camp houses (e.g., trailers on pontoons) moored inside some of these jetty embayments. So we poked our boat into about a half-dozen of these wider, protected embayments. We

Floating camp house on the Apalachicola River

were out of the current and potential river traffic. And, to my pleasant surprise, I found comfortable anchoring depths in every one explored (e.g., from seven to eight feet to 11 to 20 feet in each embayment explored). Obviously, we only explored the wider embayments—and the ones with more anchoring room. Nevertheless, many of these areas make acceptable anchorages, and this is in an area of the upper Apalachicola River where out-of-the-channel anchorages are much more limited.

Going Upriver

Slightly less than six miles out of Apalachicola, the Jackson River and the ICW head to the northwest on the RDB side of the Apalachicola River. This route heads to shallow Lake Wimico and then on to Panama City. The narrower Apalachicola River heads north and then makes a hairpin turn at the Pinhook on the LDB side. But before we make that right hairpin turn at the Pinhook, we'll address two small marinas tucked on the RDB of the Apalachicola River, slightly downriver from the Pinhook. The Bay City Lodge and the Breakaway Marina and Motel primarily cater to local fishermen. The entrances to both of these facilities are quite obscure and not visible from the Apalachicola River. They are in almost hidden channels about 15 to 20 feet wide, and the water depths approaching these channels are approximately four feet. To get to the Bay City Lodge, from "G13" head 215 degrees to find the facility's westernmost entrance. There is a second, eastern entrance about 50 yards downriver, but a low bridge about 70 yards into that eastern entrance limits some boats. The two entry channels connect, and the land between them is an island. Bay City Lodge has about 30 covered slips and can accommodate up to 28- to 30-

footers. To arrive at Breakaway Marina and Motel, head 235 degrees from "G15." The entrance is also signaled by a Chevron sign on the riverbank. This marina has a few shallow-draft 30- to 40-footers (e.g., houseboats) and about 50 covered slips.

Bay City Lodge (850) 653-9294

Approach depth—3 feet
Accepts transients—very limited
Fixed wooden docks—yes
Dockside power connections—limited
Dockside water connections—yes
Gasoline—yes
Mechanical repairs—yes
Boat ramp—yes
Ship's store—limited
Restaurant—on site
Motel—yes

Breakaway Marina and Motel (850) 653-8897
www.BreakawayMarina.com

Approach depth—3 feet
Accepts transients—yes
Fixed wooden docks—yes
Dockside power connections—30 amp
Dockside water connections—yes
Showers—yes
Gasoline—yes
Mechanical repairs—limited to certain outboards
Boat ramp—yes
Ship's store—yes
Restaurant—on site
Motel—yes

There are many wide and inviting sandy river beaches on the Apalachicola. One of the first is on the RDB about a third of a mile upriver from Breakaway Marina. We've heard that many of these beaches make good stops,

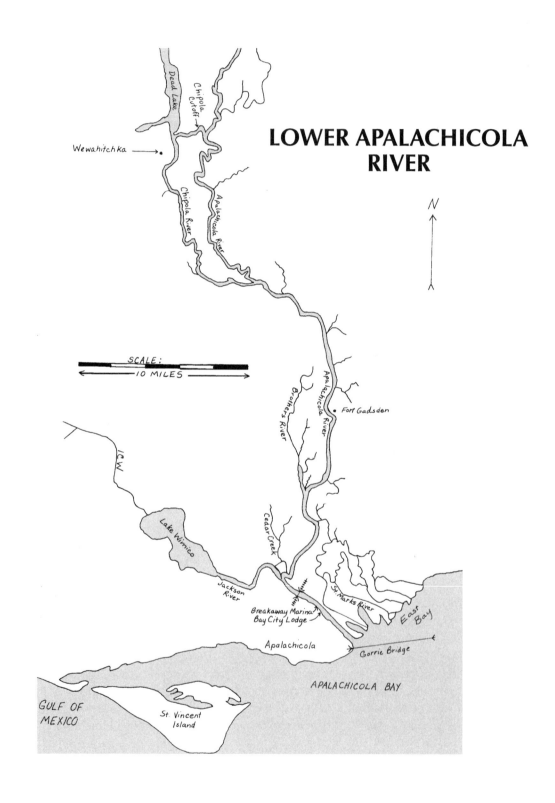

LOWER APALACHICOLA RIVER

N

Dead Lake

Chipola Cutoff

Wewahitchka →

Chipola River

Apalachicola River

SCALE:
10 MILES

Brothers River

Apalachicola River

• Fort Gadsden

ICW

Lake Wimico

Cedar Creek

Jackson River

St. Marks River

Breakaway Marina
Bay City Lodge

Apalachicola

East Bay

Gorrie Bridge

APALACHICOLA BAY

GULF OF
MEXICO

St. Vincent
Island

UPPER APALACHICOLA RIVER

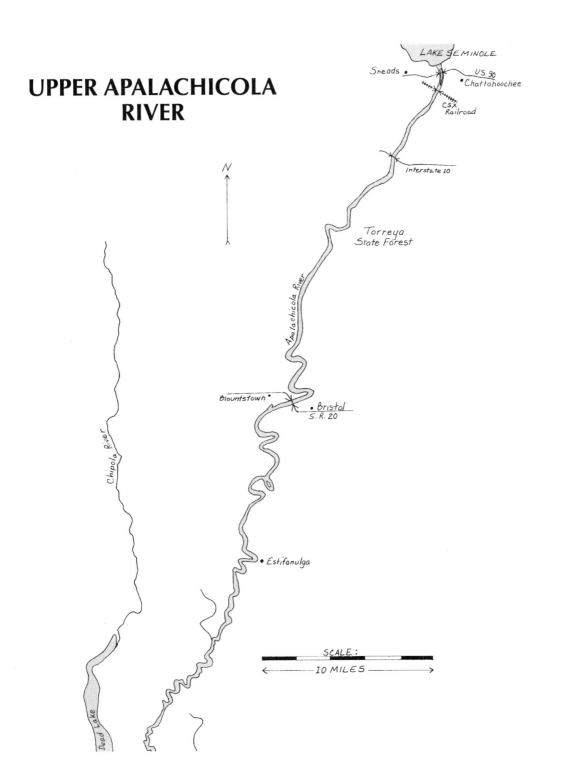

LAKE SEMINOLE

Sneads •

US 90

• Chattahoochee

CSX
Railroad

Interstate 10

Torreya
State Forest

N

Apalachicola River

Chipola River

Blountstown •

• Bristol
S.R. 20

• Estifanulga

Dead Lake

SCALE:

← 10 MILES →

The following table presents some other possible stopovers (e.g., anchorages, beaches, interesting historic sites, and two nearby towns) on the Apalachicola River. And you may also use these features to gauge your progress up (or down) the river.

FEATURE	MILEAGE	SIDE	COMMENTS
Bridge	0.0	center	John Gorrie Memorial Bridge, Apalachicola
Marina	3.5	RDB	Bay City Lodge
Marina	3.8	RDB	Breakaway Marina and Motel
Beach	4.1	RDB	Nice wide beach
Beach	5.3	LDB	Small beach
Anchorage	off 6.1	RDB	In Cedar Creek, off the Saul Creek loop
Anchorage	10.2	LDB	Anywhere in the St. Marks River
Anchorage	off 12.0	RDB LDB	In Little Brothers Slough, off the of Brothers River
Site	19.8	LDB	Fort Gadsden
Anchorage	21.3	LDB	At south end of Brickyard Island, in 10 feet of water depth
Anchorage	22.2	LDB	Within a mile up Owl Creek, in 16 to 25 feet of water depth
Anchorage	23.9	LDB	In Brushy Creek, on RDB side of creek, in 9- to 15-foot water depths
Anchorage	43.1	LDB	In large basin, water deepens to ten to 13 feet, after 8- to 9-foot entry
Anchorage	44.8	LDB	In a bulge, 10-15 feet of water depth in entry and anchorage
Anchorages	45.2	RDB	In Iola arm, deep across entry and in anchorages (The head of arm is protected by tall trees.) Best anchorages on entire river!
Anchorage	49.8	RDB	In narrow creek, 8-15 feet deep, 60 yards up the creek
Beaches	62.5-63.3	RDB& LDB	Nice beaches on both sides of river
Anchorage	71.0	RDB	In large arm, very nice, 9-16 feet of water depth
Beaches	73.8-76.5	RDB& LDB	There are three beaches in this stretch.
Town	77.4	RDB	Best access to Blountstown from boat ramp
Anchorage	78.3	RDB	In narrow arm, 5- 6-foot depth at entry, no good access to Blountstown
Dock/Town	105.6	LDB	Only public dock on river, 110 feet of floating dock, and only access to Chattahoochee, Florida
Lock	106.3	RDB	Jim Woodruff Lock and Dam, Lake Seminole

even for overnighting, if you have a shallow enough draft vessel to nose your bow onto the beach. We overnighted once on one of these beaches and had no problems. Surprisingly, even though my bow was sitting on the beach, there was four feet of water off the stern. If you do this, please tie at least one long bowline (or an anchor line) to a secure place on the beach. If you don't, and the water level rises overnight, you'll be floating away.

The LDB side of the open-swing bridge for the Apalachicola Northern Railroad had 20-foot water depths. We believe that this railroad bridge remains open most of the time. We've heard of boaters missing the Pinhook turn on the Apalachicola River and finding themselves in Lake Wimico (i.e., taking the wider Jackson River route) before they figured something was amiss. Be looking for the Apalachicola Pinhook turn after a small beach near "R30" on the LDB side. If you are coming from Lake Wimico, you'd pass "R2" on the LDB before turning into the Pinhook. And this is the first of many pinhooks on the Apalachicola River.

Immediately after you turn right up the Apalachicola River in the Pinhook, the land to your RDB is an island. Circumnavigating this island is a short and haunting trip, and there are some interesting anchorages. About a quarter of a mile into the Pinhook, turn left into Saul Creek before the first green can buoy. Water depths in this route typically range from six to 20 feet, with several holes over 40 feet. Saul Creek ranges from 20 yards to 50 yards wide. About halfway out of Saul Creek, Cedar Creek branches off to the north (or to the right side). This is another deep and very beautiful creek that has great potential as a hurricane hole. Cedar Creek is much deeper than indicated on the NOAA chart and holds navigable depths for more than two miles, but there are some shallower and wide places that would be terrific for anchoring—if you like anchoring in the absolute boondocks.

The following table presents more features on the Apalachicola River that can help you gauge your progress up (or down) the river. These features include such things as bridges, power lines, river junctions, boat ramps, and jetties—places that a transiting vessel would not likely stop. Nevertheless, these features used in conjunction with the features of the earlier table can help a boater calibrate his or her location on the Apalachicola River.

FEATURE	MILEAGE	SIDE	COMMENTS
Bridge	0.0	center	John Gorrie Memorial Bridge—65 feet
Junction	0.6	RDB	Scipio Creek—and to three marinas in Apalachicola
Bridge	4.5	center	Often open
Boat Ramp	4.9	RDB	Small ramp
Junction	5.9	RDB	Jackson River, the Pinhook
Junction	6.2	RDB	Beginning of the Saul Creek loop
Junction	10.2	LDB	St. Marks River
Junction	12.0	RDB	Brothers River
Boat Ramp	14.5	LDB	Bloody Bluff Landing with an unpaved boat ramp
Power lines	20.2	center	Plenty of clearance at 66 feet, BRENC
Junction	27.9	RDB	Chipola River
Junction	41.6	RDB	Chipola Cutoff, connects with paralleling Chipola River
Boat Ramp	41.8	RDB	25-foot-wide concrete ramp, not visible from river, in a nice picnic area, up-stream from small hamlet
Boat Ramp	45.2	RDB	Double-wide concrete ramp in the Iola Landing arm
Jetty	65.5-65.7	RDB	Jetty with four sets of pilings
Ramp/Town	77.4	RDB	Neal Landing ramp is best access to Blountstown
Bridge	79.4	center	Calhoun Bridge, Blountstown
Jetty	79.0	LDB	Jetty with three sets of pilings
Boat Ramp	80.4	LDB	Bristol Landing ramp tucked in bluff in a nice park
Jetties	83.0-83.6	LDB	Nine sets of jetties (Each jetty has many pilings.)
Bluffs	84.0-84.3	LDB	High-alum bluffs
Jetties	85.6-86.0	LDB	Four sets of jetties (Each jetty has many pilings.)
Jetty	87.8	RDB	Jetty with four sets of pilings
Pipeline	87.8	center	Beneath the river (Route observed on both banks.)
Boat Ramp	88.8	RDB	Ramp tucked in narrow creek
Jetties	89.1-92.1	RDB&LDB	Eight sets of jetties (Each jetty has numerous pilings.)
Boat Ramp	94.0	RDB	Ramp in picnic area
Beach	95.4-96.0	LDB	Nice beach
Jetties	97.0-103	RDB&LDB	Six sets of jetties (Each jetty has numerous pilings.)
Boat Ramp	99.4	LDB	Narrow concrete ramp
Bridge	100.0	center	Interstate Route 10, 37 feet high when closed

FEATURE	MILEAGE	SIDE	COMMENTS
Power lines	105.4	center	Plenty of clearance at 46 feet, BRENC
Dock/Town	105.6	LDB	110 feet of dock and access to Chattahoochee, Florida
Bridge	105.7	center	U.S. Route 90—38 feet high
Lock	106.3	RDB	Jim Woodruff Lock and Dam, Lake

The St. Marks River joins the Apalachicola River past mile 10 on the Apalachicola's LDB. The St. Marks is about 60 yards wide. It is actually part of the Apalachicola River Delta. Downriver on the St. Marks, there are three routes back to Apalachicola Bay through East Bay. Like East Bay itself, there are many shallow spots in this St. Marks delta network. But water depths in the first two miles of the St. Marks range from ten to 14 feet, and there are several good places to anchor. You'll also observe about seven floating structures perched in the area where the Apalachicola joins the St. Marks River. These by-boat-access-only camp houses are for fishermen in the summer and hunters in the winter. A few of these camp houses are nothing more than small trailers on pontoons moored to the cypress trees ashore. Dr. John Davis of Dothan, Alabama, estimates that there are between 150 and 200 of these camp houses moored along the Apalachicola River and its many Florida sloughs. You won't find camp houses upstream in Georgia or Alabama because these states have stricter riverine regulations.

The Brothers River branches off the Apalachicola at mile 12 on the RDB. Like the Jackson River, the Brothers is also wider than the Apalachicola at the junction of the two rivers. The Brothers River extends northward for about seven miles, with no aids to navigation. We explored the first two miles and found the river too deep for comfortable anchoring. In many places we encountered over 20 feet of water at less than 50 feet from the shore. But we did find an acceptable anchorage in Little Brothers Slough. Little Brothers Slough starts inside Brothers River on the LDB, less than a fifth of a mile from the Apalachicola River. Cypress knees and trees cloaked in Spanish moss nearly encircle the slough beyond the mouth of this small creek. Water depths in Little Brothers Slough range between ten and 18 feet.

Fort Gadsden is at mile 19.8 on the LDB of the Apalachicola River. There is no longer a steamboat landing at the remnants of the old fort, but I was able to gently nudge my bow onto a grass thicket on the soft shore and secure a line off the bow to some old pilings—pilings from the old steamboat landing. And there was about five feet of water depth off my stern. A Mediterranean Mooring isn't likely necessary for a small vessel. Nevertheless, you could also set a stern anchor in the river. If you think you may need a stern anchor here, please read the section in chapter 17, under "Branford, Florida," on how to set a Mediterranean Mooring.

Upriver from Owl Creek, past mile 22.2, navigation aids thin out, but they are not badly needed. The Chipola River enters the Apalachicola at mile 27.9, on the Apalachicola's RDB. The wide Chipola is no deeper than ten feet across at its junction with the

Apalachicola River beach

Apalachicola River, but farther upstream, it is about 20 feet deep. The Chipola extends for about another 100 miles, well into Alabama. It reconnects with the Apalachicola, via the Chipola Cutoff, at Apalachicola River mile 41.6 on the RDB. This three-mile cutoff was dug in the 1880s by the Corps of Engineers. Its purpose was to create a shortcut for steamboats between the Apalachicola and Chipola rivers. Besides the steamboat shortcut, there were some unforeseen effects. The Apala-

chicola waters had a new route, and about 40 to 50 percent of the Apalachicola's flow streamed into the Chipola Cutoff. Where the cutoff connected to the original Chipola, the 1880s river's dynamics also changed some upstream conditions on the Chipola River. A dam on the Chipola River totally swamped the nearby cypress trees, and these soon-to-be-dying trees suggested the name Dead Lake. The local fisherman on Dead Lake don't like the talk about blocking-off the man-made

Cypress trees on Dead Lake

Boat ramp on Apalachicola River

Chipola Cutoff and returning to the pre-1880s Apalachicola River conditions because of the "new" fishing bounty found in Dead Lake.

Between the Apalachicola River and the Chipola Cutoff, there are also a handful of boat ramps on the RDB of the Chipola. The Chipola River and the Chipola Cutoff usually have between two and five knots of current. The town of Wewahitchka is about ten miles up from the lowermost Chipola River entrance on the RDB. The Wewahitchka area is renown for producing tupelo honey. This healthy honey comes from the pollen of white tupelo blooms and is excel-lent for battling allergies or diabetes because of its limited dextrose content. And tupelo honey won't ever crystallize. The town has a few restaurants, motels, banks, gas stations, a gro-cery store, and a general store. Dead Lake and the Chipola Cutoff reconnect to the Apalachicola River about three miles upstream from Wewahitchka.

HAZARD *Back on the Apalachicola River, about seven miles past the lower Chipola River entrance, near mile 35, the Apala-chicola shallows and the current begins to really pick up—flowing downhill at up to four*

Apalachicola River dock, Chattahoochee, Florida

knots. The next nine miles are the most dicey miles between Apalachicola, Florida, and Columbus, Georgia. Water depths shallowed and we experienced as little as four- to five-foot depths a few times—two to three feet below the controlling river depth of seven feet. There is one switchback after another in this section of the Apalachicola River. There are also several tall sand piles on the banks on both sides of the river between miles 35 and 37. However, these are not good places to beach a boat because these dunes slope too steeply into the river.

Knowledgeable Dr. Davis informed me that these sand piles are not natural. Prior to the Civil War, the Apalachicola River was a much straighter and deeper river in this part. During the Civil War, and starting in 1862, the Confederates blocked the river with a huge anchor chain and other obstructions, thwarting any Union boats trying to come up the river. This was just the beginning of a series of man-made alterations that extend into the twenty-first century. Not long after the Civil War, and with the Apalachicola River still gummed up, the Chipola Cutoff was constructed. From about 1890 to about 1950, the Chipola Cutoff and the Chipola River were the preferred commercial navigational routes. Besides diverting much of the original Apalachicola waters through the Chipola Cutoff, this new water route drastically altered the Apalachicola River, too. Instead of a much straighter and deeper river, the Apala-chicola developed its many switchbacks and sand deposits, and thus the river shallowed considerably. Around 1950, with certain limitations of the Chipola route (e.g., it being too narrow), the Apalachicola was again redesignated as the main channel. But since the late 1800s, much of the Apalachicola flow had been diverted into the Chipola; the Apala-chicola River required constant dredging and/or higher-water navigation windows. The sand piles that you now see are that dredged material.

We didn't have a firsthand opportunity to navigate our boat and sound the depths on the alternative Chipola River route—the route that parallels the most dicey portion of the Apalachicola River. But unlike the Apala-chicola, the Chipola River is no longer maintained by the Corps of Engineers. The corps ended maintenance on the Chipola River years ago. Nevertheless, we've heard four reliable boater accounts stating that the Chipola River and Cutoff route is the deeper alternative—with many sections being 20 feet deep. But the Chipola River, and especially the Chipola Cutoff, reportedly have some very tight turns in a very swift-flowing and channel more narrow than the Apalachicola River. The reconnecting distance is about the same at 14 miles along either river route between Apalachicola River miles 27.9 and 41.6.

Back on the Apalachicola River at mile 41.7 on the RDB, there is a small residential hamlet, consisting of many trailers, just upstream from the Chipola Cutoff. There is also a wide boat ramp in a narrow arm at George Gaskin Wayside Park at mile 41.8, also on the RDB. On both sides of the river there are a few nice beaches downstream from Estiffanulga (some locals call it Stiff and Ugly), between miles 62.5 and 63.5. The hamlet of Estiffanulga sits on a red-clay bluff about 20 to 30 feet high on the LDB side. There is no boat access to this community, and their boat ramp was in disrepair.

Around the turn of the century, the original Blountstown, Florida, was built right on the river at mile 77.4 on the RDB. In 1904, after periodic flooding, the town moved about a mile and a half to the northwest, onto higher ground. Neal Landing is all that remains of "Old Blountstown." New Blountstown still touts itself as a river town. There is a very wide, nice, concrete ramp but no dock at Neal Landing, about 100 yards downriver from the grain elevator. We anchored off this ramp and took the dinghy ashore. Blounts town has gas stations, banks, motels, a grocery store, and about a half-dozen franchise restaurants.

There is an arm on the RDB, about a mile north of the Neal Landing ramp, that is a reasonable shallow-draft anchorage. After you negotiate over a five- to six-foot part of the arm, past two old dock pilings, the water deepens to ten to 13 feet upon approaching a fork. Nevertheless, there doesn't appear to be good access to Blountstown from anywhere in this anchorage basin. The Calhoun Bridge crosses the Apalachicola River at mile 79.4. There are now twin bridges and a power line across the river. The overhead clearance is about 49 feet.

The Bristol Landing boat ramp is tucked in a

nice park on the LDB near mile 80.4. The town of Bristol, on the east side of the river, is smaller than Blountstown but closer to the river. Bristol has a few restaurants, gas stations, banks, a motel, and a hardware store. While researching in my car north of Bristol after dusk, I drove into a ditch when I missed a sharp turn in the road. I'm indebted to a young stranger named Derrick. With chains connected to his truck, Derrick pulled my muddy car out of the ditch. Afterward, he just said, "I'm Derrick, and we're [helpful] Bristol folks." There are some pretty classy folks in Bristol!

Some high bluffs—about 100 feet high—are located on the LDB about four miles upriver from Bristol. The shore is striking, but beware, there are rocks very close to this steep shore in this canyon-like topography. Torreya State Park is on the LDB on those high bluffs between miles 93 and 95. It's been said that 25 of the 28 trees mentioned in the Bible, including the rare Torrey tree, could once be found in this part of Florida near the Apalachicola River. One of the only other places where the rare Torrey tree can be found is in the Tigris and Euphrates river valleys of Iraq. And there are biblical references to Noah's Ark being constructed from Torrey wood, which is also known as gopher wood. The Torrey tree is in the yew family.

The twin spans of the Interstate 10 Bridge cross the Apalachicola River at mile 100.0. Interstate 10, the nation's southernmost cross-country interstate highway, traverses the country between Jacksonville, Florida, and Los Angeles, California. The channel beneath this bridge favors the RDB side of the river. When we went beneath the bridge, this twin span appeared much higher than the 37 feet posted on the Corps of Engineers' aerial photo book. We roughly estimate that the clearance was at least another ten to 12 feet higher. The vacated Jackson County Port Authority, with its blue warehouse, is about one-third of a mile upriver from the twin transmission lines, at mile 103.2 RDB. Although appearing to be in use, the high docks are inaccessible to recreational boaters. The CSX Railroad Bridge at mile 104.9 had a very deep channel beneath it on the RDB side (e.g., 20+-foot depths).

Unlike so many inaccessible small towns on the Apalachicola River, Chattahoochee, Florida, is accessible at a 110-foot-long floating wooden dock in the Clyde T. Hopkins Municipal Park. Chattahoochee, Florida, has the first and only public dock on the Apalachicola River since Apalachicola—105 miles downriver. This promising dock, at mile 105.6 on the LDB, was under construction when we first visited and completed by our second visit. The floating T-dock is in about seven to eight feet of water depth. There are two concrete boat ramps on opposite sides of the dock. The dock and ramps are located in a nice city park that also has covered picnic pavilions.

The Chattahoochee RV Campground and Resort is just outside the park. The campground has the typical facilities plus an exercise room and Jacuzzi. Farther up the hill, at the edge of town, there is a Hardee's restaurant, a BP gas station, and a small food mart. Farther in town, there is an auto-parts store, two motels, a city park, a drugstore, a couple of banks, an ACE Hardware, a post office, more gas stations, an IGA food store, a Laundromat, and about three restaurants. The Home Place Restaurant serves good food at reasonable prices. By many standards, the

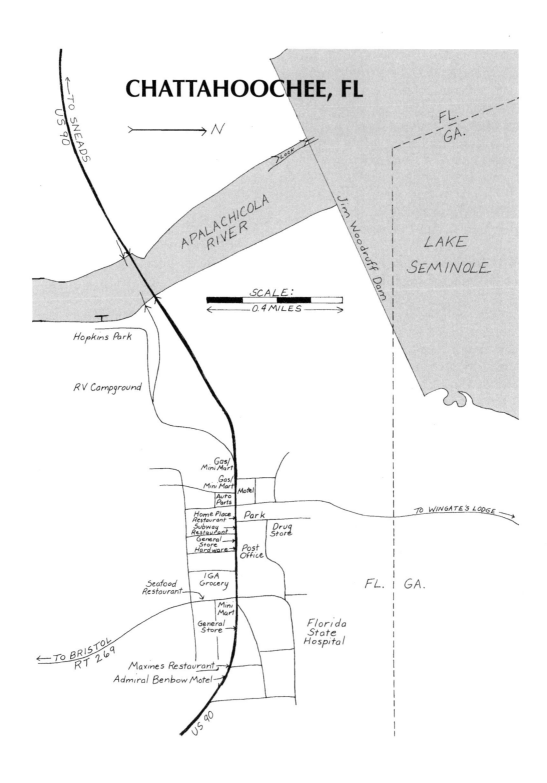

CHATTAHOOCHEE, FL

→ N

TO SNEADS

US 90

Lock

APALACHICOLA RIVER

Jim Woodruff Dam

FL. GA.

LAKE SEMINOLE

SCALE:
0.4 MILES

Hopkins Park

RV Campground

Gas/ Mini Mart

Gas/ Mini Mart

Motel

Auto Parts

Home Place Restaurant

Subway Restaurant

General Store

Hardware

Park

Drug Store

Post Office

TO WINGATE'S LODGE

Seafood Restaurant

IGA Grocery

FL. GA.

Mini Mart

General Store

Florida State Hospital

TO BRISTOL RT 269

Maxines Restaurant

Admiral Benbow Motel

US 90

town of Chattahoochee is quite modest, but after traveling 106 miles on the remote Apalachicola River, it can be a most pleasant stopover.

In January 1861, and in the early years of the Civil War, the Confederate army seized the Union arsenal in Chattahoochee. After the Civil War, this once Confederate arsenal started acquiring some very dark history. Soon the arsenal was converted to a state prison, and afterward, it was converted into an insane asylum. The prison warden made a fortune by securing lucrative prison appropriations while exhaustively working his charges. Prisoners who complained were subject to some of the worst tortures of a bygone medieval era (e.g., death by the Spanish Inquisition's water treatment or hanging by leather straps). Eventually word of the atrocities spread. Thankfully, the Chattahoochee prison closed in the early 1880s. But things weren't about to get better. For nearly 50 years (1877 to 1923), the state of Florida practiced a convict-lease system. Prisoners that would have been sent to the Chattahoochee facility had to forcibly work—usually in the turpentine industry. This was, more often than not, a death sentence. The turpentine industry remained Florida's second-largest employer as late as 1942. In the early 1900s, to insure a steady flow of free labor, corrupt local judges would often convict vagrants or African-Americans who tried to vote or homestead. In 1921, a North Dakota farm boy was convicted for vagrancy after hopping a freight train near Tallahassee. While forcibly working for a lumber company, the boy was flogged to death by his boss. The boy's persistent family and the North Dakota state legislature were finally able to put these horrid practices in the national spotlight. Not until 1923 were the days of convict

leasing and whipping bosses finally over in Florida. Today this arsenal is part of the Florida State Hospital in Chattahoochee.

Locking Through

After leaving the Chattahoochee dock, veer over to the RDB side of the river. The old U.S. Route 90 Bridge only goes about halfway across the river, while the new bridge, farther upstream, slants over the river. The Jim Woodruff Lock is just upstream on the RDB. The Woodruff Lock has a drop or lift of about 33 feet. We recommend that you make contact over the VHF 16 and then switch the radio traffic to VHF 14 for all three locks on the Apalachicola-Chattahoochee Rivers. When you make contact with the lock tender, ask him where you should tie up. If there is room, he will more than likely position you in the area of the pit where the turbulence is minimal. We generally observed that there is less turbulence in the front of the lock than in the lower or the middle portions of these locks. The lock number is (850) 663-4692.

Before entering any locking pit, all crew on deck should have donned life jackets. This is a legal requirement in any locking pit. Boat fenders should be out to protect the sides of the boat from the slimy rough concrete walls. Once in, you should find eight floating bollards inside this locking pit. All of the three locks on the Chattahoochee River have floating bollards nestled in the lock wall. Put a wrap or two of your line around a bollard from an amidship cleat. If you don't already have them, it's best to install some amidship cleats that are backed with solid metal or Delrin backing plates. Never tie up your vessel to a ladder or other immovable object in the locking pit.

Engines should be turned off because it's

difficult for the exhaust fumes to be dissipated in a locking chamber. Any movement aboard the deck should be limited to that which is essential. Always enter and leave the locking pit at a no-wake speed. I have found that lock tenders are generally the most knowledgeable and helpful folks on their portion of the river. They are undoubtedly great reservoirs of local knowledge. If you treat them respectfully, and if they are not too busy, they'll generally answer many of your river questions.

CHAPTER 14

Lake Seminole and the Flint River to Bainbridge, GA

Lake Seminole

Between 1947 and 1957, the Jim Woodruff Lock and Dam was being constructed to create Lake Seminole. Lake Seminole covers about 60 square miles and has 250 miles of shoreline. This lake also has many shallow places, and only the navigable channels are assured to be deep. Two main channels meet and form Lake Seminole. The Chattahoochee River Channel enters from the north-northwest and is navigable for about another 155 miles and all the way to Columbus, Georgia. The other major channel is the Flint River Channel, which comes from the northeast. The Flint River is navigable for no less than 30 miles to lovely Bainbridge, Georgia. There are two smaller arms marked by irregular navigation aids in between these two main channels. Fish Pond Drain comes from the north and is navigable for about three miles. Spring Creek comes from the north-northeast and is navigable for about ten miles. Fish Pond Drain and Spring Creek connect to each other before entering the Flint River Channel on the Flint's RDB at river mile 3.5. There are four marinas on Lake Seminole. Two are off the Chattahoochee River Channel, one is off the Flint Channel, and the fourth is in Fish Pond Drain.

Besides being the residence of tens of thousands American coots, Lake Seminole is a great bird-watching lake for other species. The bass fishing on Lake Seminole is touted to be one of the best in the country. Some folks upstream on Lake Eufaula countered that the bass fishing was just as good on their lake. Much of the lake, especially some of the arms, is surrounded in lovely pine forests. But two peculiarities of this lake make it difficult for larger boats to navigate anywhere but within those two main channels. HAZARD *Many shallow parts of the lake are clogged with water hyacinths and, especially, hydrilla.* To put it mildly, these floating aquatic plants are major nuisances to boaters. I've heard that hydrilla was inadvertently introduced to this country many years ago by someone who dumped the contents of their private aquarium in a body of fresh water. Being an introduced plant, the plant has next to no natural checks, and hydrilla has literally taken over many of our freshwater lakes and rivers throughout the country, especially Lake Seminole. As I was "exploring" some of the shoreline sections, I needed to stop about every 100 feet or so to clear hydrilla from my outboard propeller. I experienced hydrilla on other freshwater bodies of water (e.g., the upper Potomac River), but I've never seen it as physically choking as it is in Lake Seminole. During my third day on this lake, I needed to shut down my engine about 40 times in the space of less than three hours to clear hydrilla from my prop. This was maddening. I was told that the worse time for hydrilla is during the late fall months. The hydrilla breaks off from its millions of moorings and it floats down the

Snags on Lake Seminole

rivers, eventually accumulating in this lake. Since not much hydrilla can pass through the Jim Woodruff Lock and Dam, it collects and gathers on Lake Seminole during these late fall months.

Aside from the floating, aquatic, vegetative nuisances, there is another, even more threatening, second scourge to boaters, often lurking just beneath the surface of Lake Seminole. When the lake was dammed, unfortunately many old trees weren't cut and harvested. What an economic shame—and what a present danger to boaters. Thousands of dead trees can be seen standing in the shallow waters of the lake. HAZARD *Worse than the visible remnants are those tree remains that can't be seen, lying just beneath the surface of the water.* The tough fiberglass hull of my boat found a few of those lurking stumps while I was exploring some outside-of-the-channel areas. This is a beautiful lake, full of bass, but unless you're bass fishing in a small boat, please stay in the major channels. Some shallow parts of Lake Seminole are worse than others. In my opinion, Spring Creek has the worst stump fields. With all of the just-below-the-water-line stumps, I think the recreational utility of the lake is seriously compromised, except for bass fishing from a small boat. Water-skiing would be extremely dangerous with all of those submerged stumps and snags.

Water hyacinths, Lake Seminole

LAKE SEMINOLE

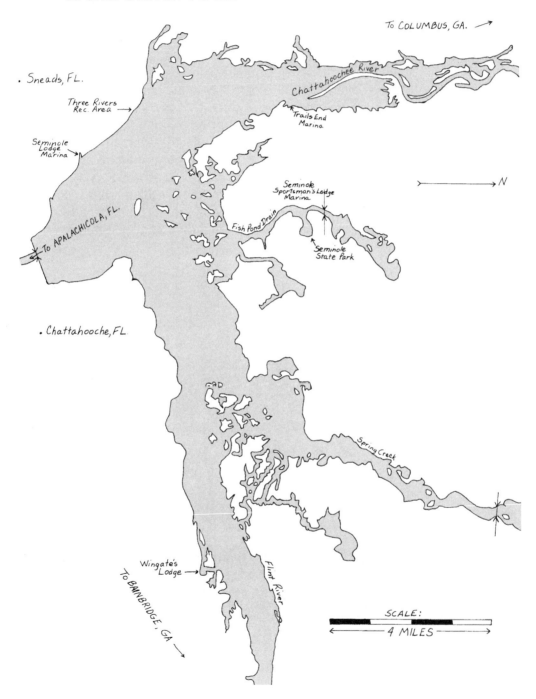

To COLUMBUS, GA.

. Sneads, FL.

Three Rivers
Rec. Area

Seminole
Lodge
Marina

Chattahoochee River

Trails End
Marina

N

To APALACHICOLA, FL.

Seminole
Sportsman's Lodge
Marina

Fish Pond Drain

Seminole
State Park

. Chattahooche, FL.

Spring Creek

Wingate's
Lodge

Flint River

To BAINBRIDGE, GA

SCALE:
4 MILES

Sailing would also be most difficult, because of the limited luxury to tack back and forth outside of any narrow stump-free channel. Sometimes there are signs on the lake stating Danger Snags. That's one heck of an understatement.

Anchoring in any man-made lake also has the potential to be problematic. An anchor could easily become fouled in an old stump or any other obstructions that would not normally be found on a natural lake bed. A trip line (i.e., a second line not designed to be under tension) attached somewhere to the crown of an anchor may be helpful in retrieving a snagged anchor. If your anchor should become fouled on the bottom, oftentimes pulling an anchor from a

second point (e.g., near the crown of the anchor instead of the end of the shank) will free the anchor from the bottom. The only time a trip line should ever be under load (i.e., strained) is when retrieving that anchor.

The Chattahoochee River Channel

Seminole Lodge Marina and Trails End Marina are situated off the Chattahoochee River Channel. The Chattahoochee River Channel has fewer stump fields than any of the three other channels. The following table presents some of the major features for the first 15 miles of the Chattahoochee River Channel in Lake Seminole.

Seminole Lodge Marina is best approached

FEATURE	MILEAGE	SIDE	COMMENTS
Lock	0.0	RDB	Jim Woodruff Lock and Dam, Lake Seminole
Coast Guard	0.2	LDB	Buoy tending station
Junction	0.6	LDB	Flint River Channel to the north (Take this route for the Fish Pond Drain and the Spring Creek channels.)
Marina	1.9	RDB	Seminole Lodge Marina, Motel, and Campground
Park/Ramp	2.0	RDB	Sneads Landing Recreation Area
Park/Ramp	4.1	RDB	Three Rivers Recreation Area (campground, picnic area, small dock)
Boat Ramp	4.3	RDB	Three miles off main channel, small ramp, no dock
Marina	8.2	LDB	Trails End Marina and Campground
Park/Ramp	8.3	LDB	Fairchilds Park is three miles off channel through sloughs
Boat Ramp	9.1	RDB	Two miles off channel through sloughs, small ramp, no dock
Park/Ramp	14.2	RDB	Off channel to Parramore Landing

from mile 1.9 and then head west toward the RDB. Nevertheless, when we approached this marina, we often found ourselves in serious patches of hydrilla and often had to kill the motor to clear it from the propeller. Seminole Lodge does have a line of stakes (blazed red from one direction and painted white on the other side) leading to their entrance. Monte Anderson at Seminole Lodge says passing on the north side of these stakes is best, whether coming in or going out. Seminole Lodge Marina has about 20 slips in a small, protected channel and can generally accommodate boats up to about 40 feet in length.

Seminole Lodge Marina, Motel, and Campground (850) 593-6886

Approach depth—8 feet
Dockside depth—4 feet
Accepts transients—yes
Floating and fixed wooden docks—yes
Dockside power connections—20 amp
Dockside water connections—yes
Showers—yes
Gasoline—yes
Mechanical repairs—nearby contractor
Boat ramp—yes
Variety store—limited
Restaurant—in town (Sneads, Florida, is two
    miles away.)
Motel—yes

Nearby Sneads, Florida, has two restaurants, a hardware store, a grocery store, and a post office. In the early 1830s Dr. John Gorrie, the inventor of modern refrigeration, lived in Sneads. The Sneads Landing Recreation Area is just upriver from Seminole Lodge Marina, on the RDB. This pleasant and shaded park has covered picnic pavilions, restrooms, a swim-

ming area, and twin concrete boat ramps with fixed wooden piers. Three Rivers Recreational Area, (850) 593-6565, and two more boats ramps are also on the RDB about one mile upriver from the Sneads Landing Recreation Area. However, a dense mat—or I should say thick covering—of hydrilla physically obstructed my boat's ability to visit this facility. Had I tried to forge into this hydrilla, I might have been stuck for days. I later visited Sneads Landing Recreation Area by car. In 1992, a new two-and-a-half-mile-long channel in the Chattahoochee was dredged, starting near mile 3.7. This straighter channel favors the LDB shore, and the navigation aids mark this newer channel. The curvy older channel favors the RDB side, and its navigation aids have long been removed. Both channels reconnect near mile 6.1 near the LDB side.

Trails End Marina is situated off a small canal on the LDB near mile 8.2. This narrow channel is about 40 feet wide but was choked with water hyacinths. Nevertheless, water hyacinths are not nearly as nasty as hydrilla. Flowering water hyacinths tend to float more atop the water, and because of this, there is less likelihood that they will become entangled in your propeller. In their two dozen slips, Trails End Marina can only accommodate about 20-footers, but we noted two 50-foot houseboats moored in their marina basin.

Trails End Marina and Campground
(229) 861-2060
www.trailsendmarina.com

Approach depth—2-5 feet
Accepts transients—yes
Fixed wooden docks—yes
Dockside power connections—limited 15 amp
Dockside water connections—yes

Showers—yes

Gasoline—yes

Mechanical repairs—limited to certain engines

Boat ramp—yes

Variety store—limited

Snack bar with hot sandwiches—yes

Motel—yes

The entrance to Parramore Landing, at mile 14.2 on the RDB, is wide and fairly deep (e.g., about six to eight feet deep). Parramore Landing has a boat ramp and a couple of wooden piers. There has been no restaurant here for years. Nevertheless, there is a small campground, a bait store, restrooms, picnic tables, trash receptacles, and about a half-dozen small boat slips for campground clientele. The hydrilla starts thinning out after mile 16 on the Chattahoochee River Channel. If you don't plan to travel east or on other parts of Lake Seminole, and you are continuing north toward Columbus, Georgia, you can skip right to the next chapter.

Fish Pond Drain Channel

To enter the Fish Pond Drain or the Spring Creek channels, branch off the Chattahoochee River Channel at mile 0.6 on the LDB. This route is also the Main Flint River Channel. After about three miles on the Flint River Channel, the Fish Pond Drain and Spring Creek channels branch off again, this time on the RDB side near Flint River Channel and mile number 3.1. HAZARD *There are several stump fields near the mouth of the Fish Pond Drain Channel.* The Fish Pond Drain Channel heads north near the RDB side of this channel. Spring Creek heads northeast (we really couldn't identify the LDB shore because there was too much surface water and stumps

were everywhere). The stumps and snags in the Fish Pond Drain Channel start thinning out about a mile to the north.

There is another junction about a mile from the junction with the Flint River Channel on the LDB of Fish Pond Drain. This channel leads two miles to Cypress Pond. Cypress Pond has a small boating facility with a half-dozen small (i.e., about 20 feet) covered slips and two boat ramps for small boats. The Cummings Access ramp is about two miles up the creek from the junction channel with Spring Creek on the RDB. There is a fairly long dock with trash receptacles in the Cummings Access ramp parking area. And Fish Pond Drain starts becoming a pleasant little creek. Water depths range from 14 to 25 feet and there is a fair amount of residential development and boats located in Fish Pond Drain. Upriver from Cummings Access, there appear to be many places in the Drain that look like reasonable anchorages for both small and large boats.

Seminole Sportsman's Lodge, Marina, and Campground is situated about another mile up Fish Pond Drain and very close to the main channel on the RDB. This facility has about 40 covered slips and can generally accommodate boats under 40 feet long. HAZARD *A low-clearance highway bridge and a fence cross Fish Pond Drain about a half-mile upstream from this marina.*

Seminole Sportsman's Lodge, Marina, and Campground (229) 861-3862

Approach depth—4-6 feet

Accepts transients—yes

Fixed wooden docks—yes

Dockside power connections—limited 15 and 30 amp

Dockside water connections—yes

Showers—yes

Gasoline—yes

Boat ramp—yes

Variety store—very limited

Snack bar—yes

Motel and campground—yes

Seminole State Park, (229) 861-3137, sits nearly across from Seminole Sportsman's Lodge, Marina, and Campground. This park surrounds a beautiful basin. Picnic areas with pavilions, a swimming beach, a miniature golf course, and a campground are all nestled in a stand of many tall longleaf pine trees. HAZARD *A partially submerged island is in the mouth of the channel leading to the park basin.* Passing on the south side of the island is best. The water is deeper there than on the north side but still only four to five feet deep. If you can get past this shallow mouth, and more hydrilla, there is much deeper water in the protected basin. The depths in the basin are spotty, but they can be as deep as 15 feet. There is also a triple boat ramp, four short piers, and a few other piers in lovely Seminole State Park. In addition to tent and trailer camping, this park has cottages.

Spring Creek Channel

The Spring Creek Channel branches off the Fish Pond Drain Channel about a mile north of the Flint River Channel. This channel generally heads north-northeast for more than ten miles to shallow Decatur Lake. HAZARD *I thought the worst and the greatest number of stump fields anywhere on Lake Seminole were in Spring Creek.* This creek, though long and relatively wide, has a tricky and narrow stump-free boating channel. There was no place to relax the guard and just enjoy boating in Spring Creek.

Stump and snag hazards are lurking everywhere, making the creek a minefield. About two miles into Spring Creek, there is a boat ramp (and a small dock and restroom facilities) at Sealey Point Park on the RDB. The channel to the Spring Creek Park boat ramp is about five miles farther, on the RDB. The Spring Creek Park access area has a paved ramp with a dock. Lulu's, a small restaurant, is also nearby, but it was closed when we visited. About seven miles past the Spring Creek Park access area channel, there is another concrete boat ramp, along with two short piers and plenty of parking space, on the LDB of Spring Creek.

About six miles up on the LDB side of Spring Creek, there is a narrow two-and-a-half-mile-long channel leading back to the Flint River Channel. This winding side channel is shallow and may be clogged with hydrilla. It was when we visited. Water depths in this side channel ranged from four to ten feet, with five-foot depths being the most common. The channel is about 40 feet wide. HAZARD *The hydrilla extending out from banks makes the navigable section of this channel even narrower.* About twenty pairs of stakes mark the twists and turns in this channel. You'd be returning in this channel if you were coming from the Flint River Channel to Spring Creek.

The Flint River Channel

The Chattahoochee River Channel is undoubtedly the longer boating thoroughfare off Lake Seminole. However, more water volume and shoreline of Lake Seminole belongs to the Flint River Channel. The following table presents some of the more important features in the first 15 miles of Flint River Channel in Lake Seminole.

FEATURE	MILEAGE	SIDE	COMMENTS
Lock	0.0	RDB	Jim Woodruff Lock and Dam, Lake Seminole
Junction	0.6	RDB	Chattahoochee River Channel to the north-northwest
Beach	2.4	LDB	Near Chattahoochee Municipal Park
Junction	3.1	RDB	Channel to Fish Pond Drain, Sportsman's Marina, Seminole State Park, and Spring Creek
Boat Ramp	3.2	LDB	In lovely Chattahoochee Municipal Park
Boat Ramp	4.3	LDB	Concrete ramp with small pier, camp ground nearby
Junction	10.2	RDB	Shallow side channel, shortcut to Spring Creek
Marina	10.2	LDB	Channel to Wingate's Lodge and Marina
Boat Ramp	12.7	RDB	Ten Mile Still Landing is in side channel 0.4 miles long, marked by green posts with 5-foot depths and a short dock.

Park and dock in Chattahoochee Municipal Park, Lake Seminole

One of the nicest boat ramp areas anywhere in this guide is at Flint River mile 3.2, on the LDB. This double-wide concrete ramp is in a small protected harbor nestled in a gorgeous picnic area. The picnic area has covered pavilions, bathrooms, trash receptacles, and docks. There is about five to seven feet of water depth off these docks—and the docks have boat cleats.

The channel to Jack Wingate's Lodge and Marina departs the Flint River Channel at mile 10.2 on the LDB. The entrance channel is over a mile long and arcs in a southeasterly direction. The channel is reasonably well marked with wooden posts blazed with red- or green-painted markings. The depths range from seven to 15 feet, until you reach the narrow creek. Out of the channel and into the creek, the depths shallow to five to six feet. Wingate's Campground on Bass Island is woven with canals, and fishermen can often leave their boats in the water only a few feet from their campsites. Wingate's Marina has about 50 slips and the facility houses some rather large vessels—up to 85-foot houseboats. Their on-site restaurant is one of the best in the area. Besides being a restaurant, the restaurant hall is a museum adorned with Jack Wingate's colorful collections. In his restaurant, there are about 2,000 artifacts, including Spanish silver coins, Dutch pipes dating back to 1680, old guns, and arrowheads. Retired Jack Wingate is quite accomplished. Besides the lunker fishing lodge, Jack runs a summertime fishing camp for young boys.

Wingate's Lodge and Marina (229) 246-0658

Approach depth—4-5 feet
Accepts transients—yes
Fixed and floating wooden docks—yes
Dockside power connections—15 amp

Dockside water connections—yes
Waste pump-out—yes
Showers—yes, on nearby Bass Island
Laundromat—yes, on nearby Bass Island
Gasoline—yes
Mechanical repairs—on call
Boat ramps—yes
Ship's store—yes
Restaurant—on site
Motel, lodge, and campground—yes

Although the wide Flint River arm of Lake Seminole appears fairly straight upriver from Wingate's, the Flint River Channel snakes back and forth from one side of the wide lake to the other. HAZARD *Taking any shortcut will most likely land you in a partially submerged stump field.*

The Flint River

While the Chattahoochee River originates north of Atlanta, the Flint River begins its journey slightly south of Atlanta, near Hartsfield Atlanta International Airport. From its origins, the Flint River makes about a 350-mile trip to Lake Seminole and joins the Chattahoochee to form the Apalachicola River. The Flint River is aptly named, because much flint was found along the banks, especially near Bainbridge, Georgia. The U.S. Corps of Engineers maintains a navigable section of the Flint for about 30 miles downriver from Bainbridge, Georgia. The lower Flint River has some current, but much less than the Apalachicola River. The Flint drops less than three feet in the 30 miles to Bainbridge, at an average of only slightly more than one inch per mile (versus an average drop of nearly six inches per mile on the Apalachicola River). Bainbridge receives a fair amount of barge traffic—carrying fertilizers, asphalt, and steel.

Wingate's Lodge, Lake Seminole

Depths in the Flint River Channel usually range from ten to 27 feet. Mileage-indicator posts on the river, on average, occur about every half-mile. Stump fields decrease once out of the environs of Lake Seminole, and this gradual transition occurs somewhere between miles 14 and 16. After Faceville Landing, Lake Seminole looks more like the Flint River. The Flint River has a few tight bends, and unlike the downriver "lake," visibility can be obstructed in these bends. Be careful, there are many high-speed, small, planing-hull boats flying around blind bends.

The following table presents some observations found on a Flint River cruise to Bainbridge.

The Faceville Landing area, at mile 16.4 on the LDB, is in a welcoming little cove near the mouth of Sanborn Creek. The cove has a boat ramp, a small pier, picnic pavilions, and trash receptacles and is perhaps the nicest gunk hole on the Flint River. About 80 yards beyond

FEATURE	MILEAGE	SIDE	COMMENTS
Lock	0.0	RDB	Jim Woodruff Lock and Dam, Lake Seminole
Boat Ramp	16.4	LDB	Faceville Landing (concrete ramp, park,pier, ample parking)
Anchorage	16.4	LDB	Faceville Landing, 9-12 feet deep, plenty of swinging room
Anchorage	16.6	LBD	Dry Creek in 8 to 12 feet of water, more secluded than Faceville
Boat Ramp	20.7	LDB	Horseshoe Bend Park, in narrow canal, 5-foot water depth
Boat Ramp	20.8	RDB	Hales Landing, a wider and deeper channel, at 6 to 7 feet deep
Anchorage	23.4	LDB	In Fourmile Creek, with 8 to 11 feet of water depth
Beach	24.3-24.8	RDB	Beach
Power lines	24.7	center	With no less than 60 feet of over-head clearance
Site	26.1	RDB	High pier and a small tank farm
Site	26.6	RDB	Industrial site, commercial docks, and white water tower
Ramp/Basin	27.5	LDB	Bainbridge boat basin, park, ramp, 4-6 feet in channel
Bridge	27.7	center	U.S. Route 84 Bypass, twin span
Bridge	28.0	center	Georgia Southwestern Railroad
Boat Ramp	28.1	LDB	Cheney-Griffin Park triple concrete boat ramp, pavilions
Boardwalk	28.2	LDB	Flint River Seafood Restaurant and 150-yard boardwalk
Bridge	28.4	center	U.S. Route 27
Power lines	28.5	center	Not depicted on Corps of Engineers aerial photographs
Bridge	28.7	center	Georgia Southwestern Railroad

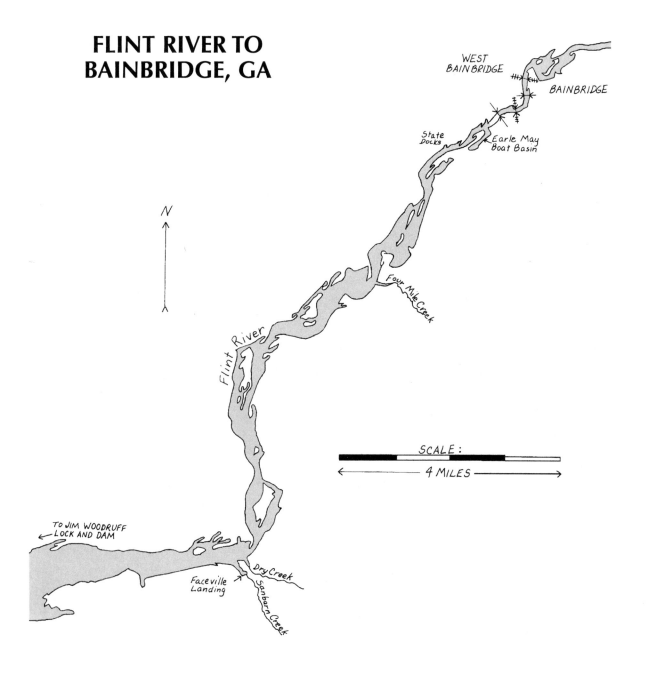

FLINT RIVER TO
BAINBRIDGE, GA

N

WEST
BAINBRIDGE

BAINBRIDGE

State
Docks

Earle May
Boat Basin

Flint River

Four Mile Creek

SCALE:

4 MILES

To JIM WOODRUFF
LOCK AND DAM

Dry Creek

Faceville
Landing

Sanborn Creek

the boat ramp, we found nine to 12 feet of water depth. There is also plenty of swing room in this most pleasant cove. If you wish to anchor in a more secluded environment, the next cove, at the mouth of Dry Creek—about one-fifth of a mile upriver and also on the LDB—fills this bill nicely. A third anchorage is in Fourmile Creek at mile 23.4 on the LDB. This third roomy anchorage had eight to 11 feet of water depth about 100 yards from the Flint River, and it was not choked with aquatic vegetation.

There are two more boat ramps, almost across the river from each other, near mile 20.7. The one on the LDB is in a narrow canal with only five feet of water depth. This ramp is paved and has a short pier. A wider and slightly deeper channel is in a canal across the river, on the RDB, at Hales Landing. The Hales Landing ramp is situated in a basin with more turning room. The landing has a concrete ramp and wooden dock and is situated in a pica containing a pavilion, large parking lot, trash receptacles, and a good old-fashioned

Boat ramp on the Flint River

outhouse. The water depth in the canal to Hales Landing holds about six to seven feet.

The entrance to the Earle May Boat Basin and the Sports Complex Building is on the LDB at mile 27.5. HAZARD *The narrow and shallow entry (e.g., four to six feet deep) is flanked by two white buoys and riprap jetties.* Once inside the jetties, this nice facility has four paved ramps. Floating wooden docks hold about eight small slips and there is a fixed wooden pier about 75 feet long. Only the lowermost one-sixth of this basin is open to boating. The upper five-sixths is blocked by floating booms that act as a boat barrier. There is a campground, swimming beach, and an ostrich pen near this blocked-off portion. Within a half-mile from the boat basin, there is a Super 8 Motel, two fast-food restaurants, and a convenience store that sells gasoline and diesel fuel. Within a mile walk, you'll find several banks, more restaurants, a post office, a hardware store, department stores, and a most charming city square. Bainbridge is a very manicured town with several nice parks along the river and no tall buildings.

Boat basin, Bainbridge, Georgia

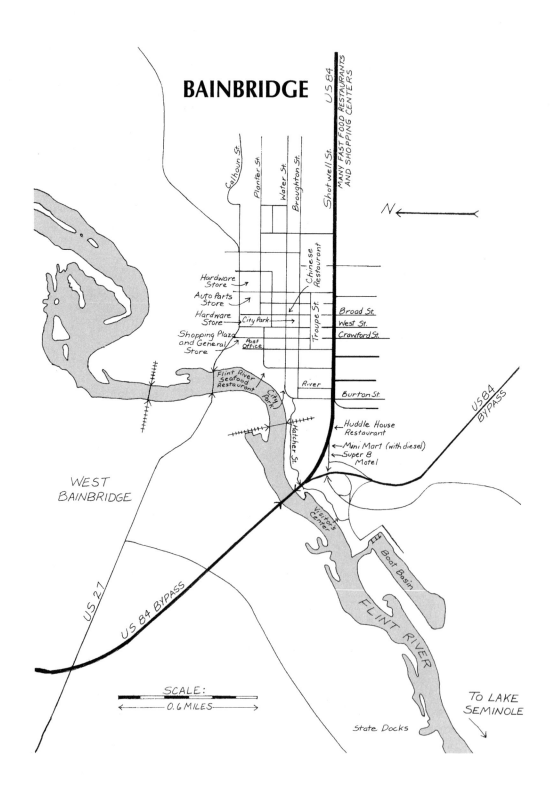

BAINBRIDGE

US 84

MANY FAST FOOD RESTAURANTS AND SHOPPING CENTERS

Calhoun St.

Planter St.

Water St.

Broughton St.

Shotwell St.

N

Chinese Restaurant

Hardware Store

Auto Parts Store

Hardware Store

Troupe St.

Broad St.

City Park

West St.

Crawford St.

Shopping Plaza and General Store

Post Office

Flint River Seafood Restaurant

City Park

River

Burton St.

US 84 BYPASS

Hatcher St.

Huddle House Restaurant

Mini Mart (with diesel)

Super 8 Motel

WEST BAINBRIDGE

Visitor's Center

Boat Basin

US 21

US 84 BYPASS

FLINT RIVER

TO LAKE SEMINOLE

SCALE:

0.6 MILES

State Docks

Ostriches in park near Earle May Boat Basin, Bainbridge, Georgia

When we went beneath it, the U.S. Route 84 Bypass appeared much higher than the 36 feet of the corps-stated BRENC clearance. About one-third of a mile beyond this bridge, and just past the railroad swing bridge, there is a quaint city park on the LDB. This park is only three blocks away from downtown Bainbridge. This Cheney-Griffin Park has tennis courts, covered picnic pavilions, restrooms, trash receptacles, and three concrete boat ramps. The three boat ramps have short perpendicular piers (i.e., less than 20 feet long with no cleats). We measured between four and seven feet of water depth off the end of these three stubby piers. The Flint River Seafood Restaurant sits just upriver from the park along a 150-yard boardwalk. The restaurant is open seasonally. Shotwell Street (i.e., U.S. Route 84), heading east out of town, has a library, motels, shopping centers, and just about every fast-food franchise imaginable. Bainbridge hosts their annual Riverside Artsfest along the banks of the Flint River the first weekend of each May.

Railroad swing bridge, Bainbridge, Georgia

The following table depicts overhead obstructions on Flint River around Bainbridge, Georgia.

BRIDGE NAME	TYPE	VERTICAL CLEARANCE (FEET)	APPROX RIVER MILE
Power lines	Cable	63.0-77.0	24.7
U.S. Route 84 twin span bypass	Fixed	36.2	27.7
Georgia Southwestern Railroad	Swing	14.9	28.0
U.S. Route 27	Fixed	35.6	28.4
Power lines	Cable	unknown	28.5
Georgia Southwestern Railroad	Swing	18.8	28.7

There is a fair amount of history surrounding Bainbridge, Georgia. Our ruthless conquistador acquaintance Hernando De Soto passed through present-day Bainbridge in March 1540. After departing from his winter encampment near present-day Tallahassee, he crossed the Ochlockonee River the next day. Two days later, he arrived in Bainbridge and built a large raft to ferry his army across the Flint River. After De Soto's army crossed the Flint, they headed north to the Carolinas. During the Spanish colonization period, the *camino real* (or the royal road) ran through Bainbridge and connected the two most important cities in Spanish America—St. Augustine and Pensacola. Around 1817, Andrew Jackson, along with the Georgia militia, wreaked havoc on the nearby Creek and Seminole Indians. The troops stayed near present-day Wingate's Lodge, at a place called Fort Scott. Soon Jackson and his men attacked a Creek Indian village near Bainbridge, and the first Seminole war was underway. Bainbridge is now the county seat of Decatur County, Georgia. The county was named for U.S. naval hero Stephen Decatur. Decatur's heroics were exercised in Tripoli and later during the War of 1812.

Sunset on the lower Chattahoochee River

CHAPTER 15

The Chattahoochee River, from Lake Seminole to Lake Eufaula

Three-quarters of the Apalachicola River's fresh-water contribution to the Gulf starts upriver from the Woodruff Lock and Dam and Lake Seminole. From the mountains of north Georgia, north of Atlanta, the Chattahoochee River has flowed about 430 miles before reaching Lake Seminole. But near Atlanta, the Chattahoochee River is merely an afterthought spanned by the short interstate highway bridges. Only the lowest 155 miles of the Chattahoochee River are navigable and maintained by the U.S. Army Corps of Engineers. Two more locks and dams are upriver from the Jim Woodruff Lock and Dam. On the Chattahoochee, upriver from Columbus, Georgia, there are many more dams, but none have locks. If you are coming from the Gulf of Mexico by boat, Columbus, Georgia—about another 140 miles upstream—is the end of the line. A nine-foot channel should be maintained all the way to Columbus, Georgia.

But before arriving in Columbus, there are 1) more than 30 miles of beautiful Lake Eufaula; 2) about 50 miles above Lake Eufaula; and 3) about 60 enchanting miles of the Chattahoochee River between Lake Seminole and Lake Eufaula. Those 60 miles below Lake Eufaula are addressed in this chapter. There are no marinas and very few navigational buoys on this narrow stretch of the Chattahoochee (or "Hooch" for short) River. The Indian name Chattahoochee roughly means something like "marked by stones." In more recent years, coun-

try singer/songwriter Alan Jackson made the Chattahoochee famous with the lyrics, "Way down yonder on the Chattahoochee . . . never knew how much that muddy water meant to me. . . . I learned a lot about living and a little about love." Likewise, the Atlanta Rhythm Section lavishes an ode to the area: "Dreamy Alabama on the Chattahoochee River . . . from Eufaula . . . to Apalachicola Bay."

The Chattahoochee River has weaker current than the swift Apalachicola River, but the current varies from one part of the river to the next. There are sections with almost no current and sections with almost three knots of current. The expression "still waters run deep"—or at least the converse of that statement: "shallow waters run faster"—can easily be applied to this section of the Chattahoochee River. The deeper sections (i.e., around 20 feet deep) have very little current, and some of the shallower segments (i.e., less than 11 feet) have a noticeable current. About ten miles before the George Andrews Lock and Dam, the current begins picking up. And about five miles before the Walter F. George Dam, the current again picks up to about three knots. A generalization may be that the closer you get to any dam going upstream, there is a greater likelihood of experiencing a stronger current. And there could also be other things going on (e.g., the dam may be releasing more or less water than usual).

Lower Chattahoochee River

Between the Jim Woodruff and George Andrews dams, the Chattahoochee generally drops eight feet in 47 miles, or about two inches per mile (versus an average drop of about six inches per mile on the Apalachicola River). Water depths upriver from the Andrews Dam are sometimes as deep as 30-40 feet for about ten to 15 miles upstream from the dam. The current just upriver from the Andrews Dam slackens by as much as about three-quarters of a knot. Between the Andrews and Walter F. George dams, the river generally drops about 12 feet in 28 miles (or about five inches per mile).

Near mile 25.5, we cross the 31st parallel. Check your GPS! Between 1795 and 1819, this line of 31°N latitude, running from the Chattahoochee River to the Mississippi River, separated the United States from Spanish Florida. In 1795, the United States and Spain diplomatically agreed on this boundary. This was the first diplomatic acquisition for our newly formed country. Today, the 31st parallel forms the boundary between Florida and Alabama and, farther west, parts of the boundary between Louisiana and Mississippi.

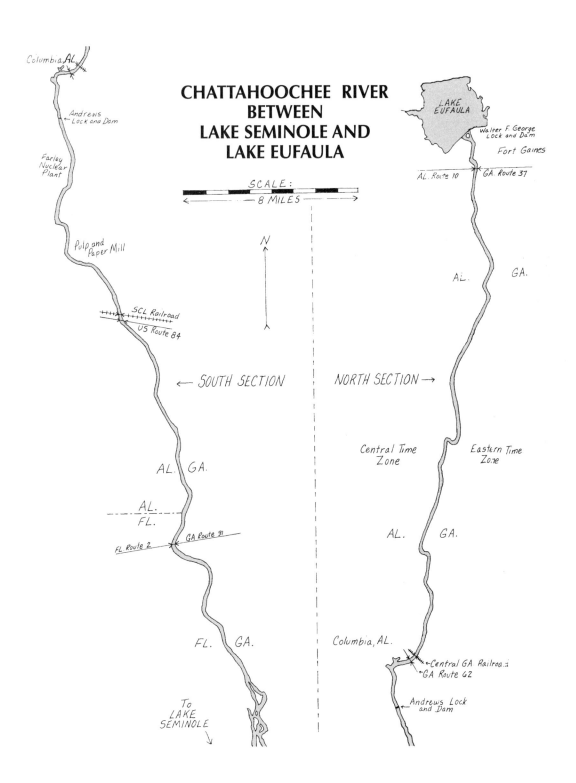

CHATTAHOOCHEE RIVER
BETWEEN
LAKE SEMINOLE AND
LAKE EUFAULA

SCALE:

— 8 MILES —

N

Columbia, AL.

Andrews
Lock and Dam

Farley
Nuclear
Plant

Pulp and
Paper Mill

SCL Railroad
US Route 84

← SOUTH SECTION

NORTH SECTION →

AL. GA.

AL.
FL.

FL Route 2   GA Route 91

FL. GA.

To
LAKE
SEMINOLE

LAKE
EUFAULA

Walter F. George
Lock and Dam

Fort Gaines

AL. Route 10   GA. Route 37

AL.   GA.

Central Time
Zone

Eastern Time
Zone

AL.   GA.

Columbia, AL.

Central GA Railroad
GA Route 62

Andrews Lock
and Dam

The following table presents some of the more noticeable features found on this part of the Chattahoochee River.

FEATURE	MILEAGE	SIDE	COMMENTS
Lock	0.0	RDB	Jim Woodruff Lock and Dam, Lake Seminole
Boat Ramp	14.2	RDB	Off channel in Parramore Landing
Boat Ramp	15.7	LDB	Off 5-foot-deep channel to Desser Landing, short dock, paved ramp, trash receptacles, much tree overhang
Boat Ramp	17.5	RDB	Off 5- to 7-feet-deep channel to Buena Vista Landing; marked by stakes, paved short pier, trash receptacles; very shaded
Boat Ramp	23.8	RDB	Neals Landing in a picnic area, concrete ramp, no dock, trash receptacles, and bathroom
Bridge	23.9	center	Herman Talmadge Highway (Georgia Rt. 91, Florida Rt. 2)
Border	25.5	RDB	Florida-Alabama Border
Boat Ramp	31.1	LDB	Small concrete ramp
Site	33.6	LDB	Residential development, houses, docks, and small boats
Bridge	35.4	center	U.S. Route 84
Bridge	35.5	center	Seaboard Coastline Railroad
Site	37.0	LDB	Industrial docks and water tower
Boat Ramp	37.1	RDB	Gordon Landing, wide ramp, protected by riprap
Site	39.5	LDB	Georgia Pacific paper mill
Site	44.1	RDB	Industrial dock—Farley Nuclear Power Plant
Boat Ramp	46.5	LDB	Wide concrete ramp, no dock, ample parking area
Lock	46.7	LDB	George W. Andrews Lock and Dam
Power lines	46.9	center	Stated at 61.6 feet of overhead clearance
Boat Ramp	47.8	RDB	Omusee Creek, 5-7 feet of water depth, no dock, park area
Power lines	47.9	center	Stated at 55.0 feet of overhead clearance
Anchorage	48.2	RDB	Fair-sized protected basin, 7- to 10-foot depths, swinging room
Boat Ramp	48.2	RDB	Concrete single ramp, trash receptacles, limited parking
Bridge	48.9	center	Georgia Route 62, near Columbia, Alabama, on the RDB
Site	49.1	RDB	Alabama State and grain elevator dock in Columbia, Alabama
Bridge	49.2	center	Central Georgia Railroad Boat Ramp

FEATURE	MILEAGE	SIDE	COMMENTS
Boat Ramp	50.8	LDB	Off obscured channel to Coheelee Creek Park, no dock
Boat Ramp	56.0	LDB	Odom Creek, right on Chattahoochee, paved ramp, no dock
Boat Ramp	58.6	RDB	Abbie Creek, 5 feet deep, tucked 50 yards past creek mouth
Beaches	59.9-60.1	RDB&LDB	Two beaches in double horseshoe-bend area
Bridge	73.4	center	Georgia Route 37, perhaps much more clearance than stated
Anchorage	73.6	LDB	An OK anchorage in bulge behind sand bar in 8- to 9-foot depth
Boat Ramp	73.6	RDB	Twin concrete, no dock, trash receptacles
Power lines	74.6	center	Stated at 56.0 feet of overhead clearance
Lock	75.1	LDB	Walter F. George Lock and Dam, Lake Eufaula

Initial radio contact with the Andrews Lock should be made on VHF channel 16 and then traffic should be switched to radio VHF channel 14. Like any lock or drawbridge, it's highly advisable to make initial VHF radio contact. This early radio contact proved to be a good idea, because the upper lock gate was open and the lower gate was closed. By the time I arrived, 15 minutes later, the lock tender had already let the water out and reversed the lock gates (i.e., the lower gate was now opened and the upper gate was closed). Hence, I didn't have to wait. At certain times, the lock tenders on the Chattahoochee River aren't very busy, and sometimes I think they just enjoy conversations with recreational boaters. All three tenders at the locks on this river wanted to jaw over the radio a bit. The Andrews Lock has eight floating bollards (four on each side). Unlike the other two locks on the Chattahoochee, the Andrews Lock does not hold back a wide lake on the high end. In normal conditions, the George Andrews Lock has a drop or lift of about 25 feet. The Andrews Lock operates 24 hours a day and their number is (912) 723-3482. George W. Andrews, after whom the lock is named, served as an Alabama congressman from 1944 to 1971.

Anchoring options on this part of the Chattahoochee are not as frequent or as good as those on the Apalachicola, or even the Flint, River. Although the current isn't nearly as strong as on the Apalachicola River, in many places the river is narrow and the banks are steep. The steep banks, especially north of the Andrews Dam, have a peculiar and somewhat pretty flair with the striking and odd-looking erosion patterns on some of the rocky ledges.

About the only decent anchorage between Lake Seminole and Lake Eufaula is in a reasonably sized basin at mile 48.2 on the RDB. The basin has about seven to ten feet of water depth and is surrounded by tall trees. There is also a concrete boat ramp, with trash receptacles but no dock, in this nice basin. It's about a mile-and-a-half hike from this boat ramp and picnic-area basin to the center of Columbia, Alabama.

Columbia has an IGA grocery store, a hardware store, a post office, a bank, a pharmacy, two auto-parts stores, three restaurants, and three convenience store/service stations. The Columbia Alabama State Docks are slightly upriver on the RDB, in between the highway bridge and the railroad bridge.

There is another narrow but marginal anchorage about a mile and a half below the Walter F. George Dam, in a small bulge in the river on the LDB side. This anchorage is about two-tenths of a mile upstream from the Georgia Route 37 Bridge. A submerged sand bar extends into the river from a beach on the LDB near mile 73.7 and upriver from this anchorage area. A red buoy is near the tip of this sand bar. If you are heading into this anchorage from the south, pass that red buoy and that sand bar about 40 yards off your port side. If you arrive late in the afternoon, and after the Walter F. George Dam has ceased its daily operations, this is likely to be the best place to "wait until tomorrow." This anchorage has about eight to nine feet of water depth. There is also a double-wide concrete boat ramp across the Chattahoochee River from the anchorage on the RDB. This Franklin Landing ramp area has trash receptacles and ample parking but no dock. Fort Gaines,

Boat ramp on the lower Chattahoochee River

Georgia, is less than a half-mile on the other, LDB, side of the river and over the bridge. Fort Gaines has one convenience store/gas station, one bank, a grocery store, a hardware store, an auto-parts store, a pharmacy, a post office, a library, and two restaurants.

Fort Gaines, one of the oldest towns in Georgia, was established as a frontier post in 1816. Before the first bridge was constructed in 1817, a log ferry transported settlers across the river. There were several Chattahoochee River floods before the dam was built. In 1888, a flood wiped out the village of Abbeville on the Alabama banks. The present bridge over this Chattahoochee gorge is the fourth bridge built.

The Walter F. George Lock is by far the tallest one on these rivers at a normal height of 88 feet. It's also the second-tallest lock east of the Mississippi River. And the locking pit fills up, or drops, extremely fast (i.e., that 88-foot raising and lowering range is covered within minutes). You could do some damage to your boat in this particular locking pit if you are not constantly fending your boat off the slimy concrete walls of the pit as you rapidly ascend or descend. Unlike the other two locks on this river system, the Walter F. George Lock only operates from 8:00 A.M. until 4:00 P.M., Eastern Standard Time (and that is 7:00 A.M. until 3:00 P.M. Central Standard Time).

The following table presents the overhead obstructions and vertical-clearance information for this chapter.

We'd estimate that beneath the Herman Talmadge Highway we experienced no less than three extra feet than what is shown on the above table. There were height-clearance markings beneath the U.S. Route 84 Bridge, and again, we extrapolated the overhead clearance to be 45-46 feet—about ten feet more than what's shown on Corps of Engineers information. The Georgia Route 62

BRIDGE NAME	TYPE	VERTICAL CLEARANCE (FEET)	APPROX RIVER MILE
Jim Woodruff Lock and Dam	**Lock**		0.0
Herman Talmadge Highway (Georgia Route 91)	Fixed	36.0	23.9
U.S. Route 84	Fixed	34.6	35.4
Seaboard Coastline Railroad	Fixed	35.1	35.5
George W. Andrews Dam	**Lock**		46.7
Power lines	Cable	61.6	46.9
Power lines	Cable	55.0	47.9
Georgia Route 62	Fixed	37.7	48.9
Central Georgia Railroad	Fixed	27.1	49.2
Georgia Route 3	Fixed	39.5	73.4
Power lines	Cable	56.0	74.6
Walter F. George Dam	Lock		75.1

Bridge is listed at 37.7 feet, but again, we estimated we had considerably more clearance. The Georgia Route 37 Bridge indicates a 39.5-foot clearance above BRENC. There was a height-clearance measuring stick beneath this one, and we interpolated between 70 and 75 feet of overhead clearance—quite a difference from that 39.5 feet.

CHAPTER 16

Lake Eufaula to Columbus, GA

Okay, is it Lake George or Lake Eufaula? Many road maps and atlases call it Lake George. Fishing maps invariably call it Lake Eufaula. After the construction of the dam, the Corps of Engineers named the lake the Walter F. George Reservoir. Many folks in Georgia refer to it as Lake George, and a few even call it Lake Chattahoochee. Many folks in Alabama, and the Alabama legislature, refer to it as Lake Eufaula and pronounce it *you-fal-uh*. There are more people, and there is more development and usage, coming from that Alabama side. So for this book, we'll choose Alabama's designation of Lake Eufaula. If we want to be politically correct (which I seldom am), I guess we can say that the Walter F. George Dam, constructed in 1963 on the Chattahoochee River, created Lake Eufaula. The lake has hundreds of miles of shoreline and swallows between 28 and 80 miles of the Chattahoochee River—and that depends on where you draw the line between river and lake. That line can be loosely drawn in many places. But we will end our coverage of Lake Eufaula about 35 miles from the dam, near Chattahoochee River mile 110. This is also about where those floating buoys diminish and where the shoreside daymarks predominate. Also, this way we can offer you two relatively large-scaled sketches of the lake—one of lower and another of upper Lake Eufaula. But be mindful, fishing regulations define the waters of Lake Eufaula/Lake George well upriver from Chattahoochee River mile 110.

Our second section of this chapter will address the "last" navigable 45 miles of the Chattahoochee River between Lake Eufaula and Columbus, Georgia. Beyond Lake Eufaula, the channel is supposed to be maintained to nine feet deep and 100 feet wide. We feel that multi-faceted Columbus—the end of the line for navigation—merits another entire section of this chapter. Between Columbus, Georgia, and the Walter F. George Dam, the Chattahoochee River averages a drop of less than one inch per mile.

The Central Georgia Railroad Bridge and the U.S. Route 82 Bridge cross Lake Eufaula between Georgetown, Georgia, and Eufaula, Alabama. The other four bridges cross the Chattahoochee River upriver from Lake Eufaula. In Lake Eufaula, there are many other bridges and overhead power lines over the many creeks feeding into the main body of the lake. There is no good official information on these other overhead clearances. In the text, we usually made an estimate of these off-the-channel clearances. But the lake level can fluctuate by ten feet. HAZARD *If you enter a creek off Lake Eufaula, please don't fail to look up and make your own overhead-clearance assessment before proceeding beneath an off-the-channel power line or bridge.*

Lake Eufaula

Beyond the towering Walter F. George Dam, Lake Eufaula has about 70 square miles and over 400 miles of shoreline. This long lake is between one and a half and three miles wide for its lowest 12 miles. It narrows slightly for the next 17 miles—to between one and one and a

BRIDGE NAME	TYPE	VERTICAL CLEARANCE (FEET)	APPROX RIVER MILE
Walter F. George Dam	Lock		75.1
Central Georgia Railroad	Fixed	33.8	94.2
Power lines	Cable	65.0	94.7
U.S. Route 82	Fixed	48.1	94.8
Alabama Route 208	Fixed	35.6	116.7
Georgia Southwestern Railroad	Lift*	19.2 (closed) 54.2 (open)	117.1
Power lines	Cable	47.8	117.2
Power lines	Cable	68.0	128.9
Power lines	Cable	51.2	138.3
General Eddy Highway	Fixed	36.2	141.0
Fourth Street, Columbus, Georgia	Fixed	56.8	155.4
Railroad Bridge	Fixed	not stated	156.0
Dillingham Street Arch Bridge, Historic District	Fixed	not stated	156.1

* If closed, the bridge tender needs eight hours of advance notice for an opening. Phone the Georgia Southwestern Railroad Company in Richland, Georgia at (800) 741-0812 between 8:00 a.m. and 5:00 p.m.

half miles wide. The Walter F. George Lock doesn't operate 24 hours a day. Their number is (912) 768-2032. Walter F. George, after whom the lock and dam were named, was a Georgia senator from 1922 to 1957.

HAZARD *The water level on Lake Eufaula can vary up to ten feet.* The lake level was unusually low when we visited, and we were told this level was likely to drop another five feet. This anticipated lowering was to occur within weeks, as a barge window was forecasted in order to raise the water level on the Apalachicola River. Some power-plant generators (e.g., high-dollar cargo) were to be transported from Apalachicola to the Farley Nuclear Power Plant on the Chattahoochee River. Not far beyond the dam, as expected,

there are some water-depth readings of well over 50 feet.

Like Lake Seminole, the bass fishing in Lake Eufaula is outstanding. Unlike the previous segment between Lake Seminole and Lake Eufaula, there is no scarcity of anchorages on this lake. Just tuck your boat into one of the scores of creeks, small or large, off Lake Eufaula, being mindful of partially submerged snags and the water depth.

There are stump fields and snags on Lake Eufaula, but they are not nearly as bad as those on Lake Seminole. *But beware, on Lake Eufaula stumps and snags can often be found near the entrances to many of the side creeks.* Many times square white and orange placards mark a snag on this lake. And these helpful

Lakepoint Marina, Lake Eufaula

U.S. Route 82 Bridge over Lake Eufaula

Bridges over the Chattahoochee River, Columbus, Georgia

aids are much more prevalent than those few found on Lake Seminole. There are also many shallow patches near the middle of the lake and slightly outside of the Chattahoochee River Channel. Near the mouth of Pataula Creek and again in Cowikee Creek, we saw a great blue heron standing on the water only a few only yards from our boat. And both times my vessel was in over 20 feet of water! Actually those herons weren't standing on the water—they were perched in ankle-deep water on shoals uncomfortably close to our deep-water route.

Buoys that mark the Chattahoochee River Channel are plentiful on the lake. These buoys are not sequentially numbered, but many floating aids have small white numbers that indicate the Chattahoochee River Channel mile. And this is a very helpful characteristic.

There are many nice boat ramps on Lake Eufaula. We identified and noted some observations on many of these ramps in a table. Almost all of the ramps on Lake Eufaula have floating docks nearby. This nice feature is absent on so many of the ramps between Apalachicola and Lake Eufaula.

Virtually all of the major side creeks on Lake Eufaula, and many of the other smaller creeks, contain scores of great anchorages. Besides anchorages and boat ramps, many creeks have park areas and variety stores. More than a few creeks also have boating facilities, lodges, campgrounds, and other services. But over most of the creeks, there are overhead power lines. Obviously, we couldn't measure their heights, but we made as many rough estimates as possible, and we might have missed noting a power line or two. HAZARD

Great blue heron in shallow water, Lake Eufaula

When entering an enchanting creek, always look up and check for overhead power lines.

Highland Park Recreation Area and Hardridge Creek Campground and Picnic Area are closest to the dam and are on the Alabama side. A convenience store/gas station is about a half-mile walk to the main highway from the Hardridge Creek boat ramp and docks.

Sandy Creek has a well-marked channel on the Georgia side of the lake. But beware of the stump field on the creek's LDB, extending well into Lake Eufaula. Also on the LDB side of Sandy Creek, a shallow spit extends between the ramp and the marina. Therefore, give the LDB shore of this creek some room. George T. Bagby State Park and Cotton Hill Park are on opposite sides of Sandy Creek, about two miles from the main channel. Cotton Hill Park has a campground, laundry, and shower, and only a boat ramp and small dock. George T. Bagby State Park has a marina with about 70 slips and houses some 30-footers. The restaurant

Boat ramp, Lake Eufaula

The following are features on a few of the larger creeks off the Lake Eufaula's main channel. We've also provided GPS way points off the Main Chattahoochee River Channel, toward the mouth of these many creeks. You can find these way points in our Lake Eufaula GPS appendix.

Name of Creek, or Facility	Channel Mile	AL or GA	Type Facility	Miles off Chan.	Side of Creek	Accommodations
East Bank Rec. Area	75.4	GA	Park/ Ramp	1.8	RDB	Floating wooden dock and ample parking in nice park area
Highland Park Rec. Area	76.0	AL	Park/Ramp	1.6	NA	Shaded rec. area, twin concrete boat ramps, piers, floating docks,beach
Hardridge Cr. Campground	76.5	AL	Park/Ramp	1.4	LDB	Nice campground, twin ramps, floating docks, convenience store/gas station nearby
Sandy Creek	78.0	GA				
Cotton Hill Park			Park/Ramp	1.8	RDB	Picnic and campground area in protected cove, concrete ramp, 5-foot depth in cove
Ramp Area			Ramp	1.9	LDB	In cove, picnic area, 5-9 feet deep
Bagby State Park/Marina			Marina, Gas	2.0	LDB	Lodge, campground, picnic area, ship's store, seasonal restaurant
Sandy Branch	79.0	GA	Ramp	1.6	RDB	Off creek in cove, paved ramp, 8-9 foot depths off dock, trash receptacles
Thomas Mill Creek	81.5	AL				7 feet deep up creek, two overhead power lines, first is lowest—at 30 feet
Thos. Mill Park			Ramp	1.5	LDB	No dock, ample parking
Wilson's Landing			Dock	1.5	RDB	Variety and limited grocery store, hot dogs
Pataula Creek	83.0	GA				
Pataula Point			Dock	2.2	LDB	Dock, 6-foot depths, café and store closed
Pataula Creek Park			Ramp	2.5	RDB	Dock, park, pavilions, picnic area
Ramp			Ramps	4.7	RDB	Docks just before bridge, trash disposal
White Oak Creek	86.0	AL				
White Oak Creek Park			Ramps	1.8	LDB	T-dock, twin ramps, trash receptacles
Mid-Lake Bait Store			Store	2.0	RDB	Past low bridge, floating wooden dock, store, nearby gas stations and restaurants
Cheneyhatchee Creek Landing	89.5	AL	Ramp/Park	1.6	LDB	Park area, floating pier, trash receptacles
Barbour Creek	90.5	AL	Ramps	2.0	LDB	Two ramps, dock, 14-foot depths nearby
Cool Branch Park	91.5	GA	Ramp/Park	0.9	RDB	Ramp, dock, in picnic area on a protected pretty cove
Chewalla Creek and Eufaula	95.0	AL				
Eufaula Yacht Club			Yacht Club	0.6	RDB	Small friendly club, ramp, pavilion, limited facilities, best access to town
Chwl. Cr. Marina			Marina	1.2	LDB	Full-service marina, diesel service
Lksd Mtr. Lodge			Dock	1.7	RDB	Floating dock near motel and restaurant
L. E. Campground			Ramp	2.0	LDB	Private and in a campground
River Bluff Park	96.0	GA	Ramps	0.3	LDB	Nice park area, 11 feet of water off dock, floating T-dock, trash receptacles
Old Creek Town Park	97.5	AL	Ramp	0.9	N/A	In picnic area with floating T-dock, 11 feet of water off dock, trash receptacles
Cowikee Creek Lakepoint Marina	101.7	AL	Marina	2.8	LDB	A first-class marina with many amenities, including fuel, ship's store and a lodge

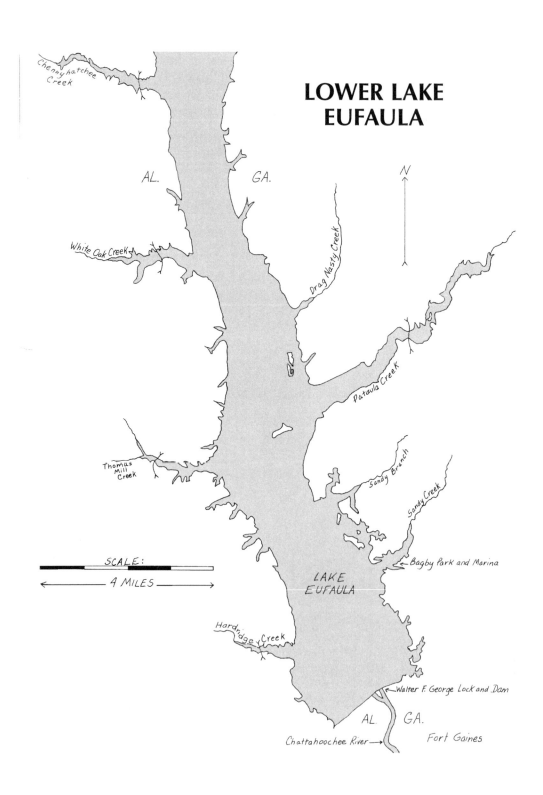

LOWER LAKE
EUFAULA

Chennyhatchee Creek

AL.   GA.

N

Drag Nasty Creek

White Oak Creek

Pataula Creek

Thomas Mill Creek

Sandy Branch

Sandy Creek

← Bagby Park and Marina

SCALE:

4 MILES

LAKE EUFAULA

Hardridge Creek

← Walter F. George Lock and Dam

AL.   GA.

Chattahoochee River →

Fort Gaines

UPPER LAKE EUFAULA

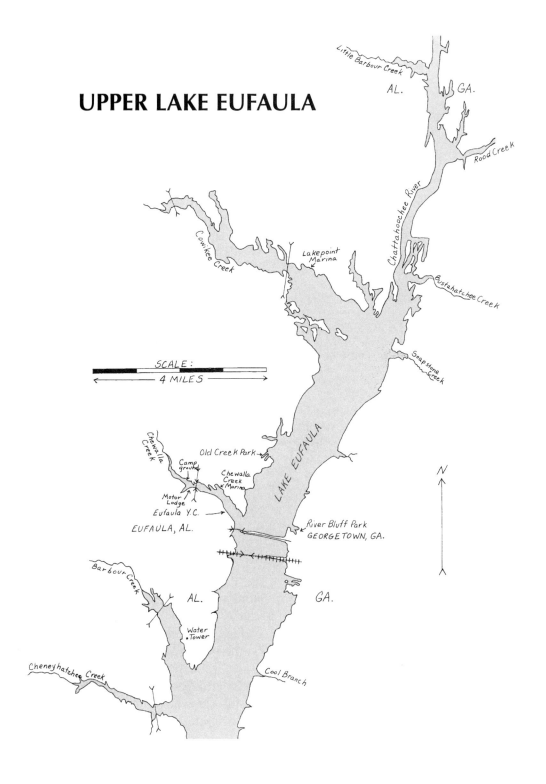

Little Barbour Creek

AL. GA.

Rood Creek

Chattahoochee River

Cowikee Creek

Lakepoint Marina

Bustahatchee Creek

SCALE:
4 MILES

Soapstone Creek

Chewalla Creek

Old Creek Park

Camp ground

Chewalla Creek Marina

Motor Lodge

Eufaula Y.C.

EUFAULA, AL.

LAKE EUFAULA

River Bluff Park
GEORGETOWN, GA.

N

Barbour Creek

AL. GA.

Water Tower

Cheneyhatchee Creek

Cool Branch

and lodge are about two miles away from the marina, but there's a telephone at the marina to call for free shuttle service.

George T. Bagby State Park
(229) 768-2571, ext. 219
www.georgebagbylodgepark.org

Approach depth—7 feet
Accepts transients—yes
Floating concrete docks—yes
Dockside power connections—30 amp
Dockside water connections—yes
Waste pump-out—yes
Showers—yes
Gasoline—yes
Boat ramp—nearby
Ship's store—limited
Restaurant—yes, distant but with a pick-up
  service
Lodge and cabins—yes

Thomas Mill Creek, on the Alabama side, has residential development with several private boat docks, covered and uncovered, along the bank. This creek is no less than seven feet deep in center. HAZARD *There are two sets of overhead power lines above the creek.* The first one is the lower one, and we estimate the clearance to be at least 30 feet high. There is a floating wooden docking leading to Wilson's Landing convenience store on the RDB, near the low highway bridge. The Thomas Mill boat ramp, with no dock, is across the creek on the LDB.

On the Georgia side, the nearly five-mile-long Pataula Creek has three sets of boat ramps but not much else. In the appendix of this book, we provided you with two GPS way points for Pataula Creek. Our first way point is

near where you'd depart from the Main Chattahoochee River Channel, and the second way point is near the mouth of the creek. HAZARD *But even if you headed from the first way point to the second way point, you could get in trouble because the Pataula Creek Channel, even out in the Lake Eufaula, snakes around between the creek entrance and the Chattahoochee River Channel.* After entering Pataula Creek, the channel continues to snake its way from the RDB to the LDB to the RDB and then back to the LDB. But this snaking avoids the many stump fields. And there are good navigation aids in Pataula Creek. There are a few nice houses and covered docks, but we could find any commercial facilities in this creek. The Pataula Shores boat ramp is just before the bridge on the RDB. This double concrete ramp has a dock.

White Oak Creek has a campground and a picnic area on the Alabama side. The RDB of White Oak Creek has private docks and homes. Beware of the overhead power lines cross the creek about one quarter of a mile from the bridge. We'd estimate the clearance beneath these lines to be no less than 40 feet. Two boat ramps, with one T-dock, are on the LDB before the bridge. There is also a restroom in the ramp area. HAZARD *The low road bridge has about ten feet of clearance.* Mid-Lake Bait Store is just beyond the bridge on the RDB side. They have a nice convenience store and a deli, but they don't sell fuel. A gas station and a couple of restaurants are within walking distance of the Mid-Lake Bait Store on the main road.

On the Alabama side, Cheneyhatchee Creek is deep, with many spots having more than 25 feet of water depth. The shore is not as developed as many of those on the other creeks on Lake Eufaula. *Beware, a high over-head power line crosses the creek.* The public boat ramp is in a picnic area on the LDB, just before the highway bridge. A floating wooden dock and toilet facilities are nearby. There are also two gas stations nearby on that highway.

Barbour Creek, also on the Alabama side, has the best-marked channel you'll encounter since being on the Flint River. Several nun and can buoys mark this channel. Just inside Barbour Creek, on the LDB, there is an indus-trial-barge repair facility. There are also sev-eral industrial parks in this area. One of those industrial parks houses Techsonic Industries—the folks who manufacture Humminbird Depthfinders and Teleflex boating instru-ments. The RDB of Barbour Creek has some scattered residential development. The chan-nel snakes back and forth across the body of Barbour Creek. Beware of running into a shal-low marshy area on the LDB, about a mile into the creek. *Beware, once again, power lines, with about 45 feet of overhead clear-ance, cross the creek about 100 yards down-stream from the highway bridge.* That great landmark—the wide, white water tower with the town name, Eufaula, blazoned on the tank (there is also another smaller white water tower in the area)—is near the point of land between Barbour Creek and Lake Eufaula.

Near Eufaula, Alabama, from about mile 91 to 95, the Chattahoochee River Channel favors the Alabama shore. There are a few hints, but not many, that there is a quaint town beyond those bluffs on this shore. The best access to Eufaula is from Chewalla Creek, upriver from the two bridges. HAZARD *The first bridge is a railroad bridge with a stated clear-ance of 33.8 feet at mile 94.2.* The second bridge, the U.S. Route 82 Bridge—with a

stated clearance of 48.1 feet—is a half-mile farther upriver. Chewalla Creek enters the lake about a fifth of a mile past the U.S. Route 82 Bridge on the RDB. Chewalla Creek has a well-marked channel, starting with a junction buoy on the Chattahoochee River Channel. Upriver from Chewalla Creek, the Chattahoochee River Channel swings over to the Georgia side of Lake Eufaula.

There are about four boating accommoda-tions in Chewalla Creek. One is a bona-fide marina and another is a small yacht club. Both the Eufaula Yacht Club and Chewalla Creek Marina are before the railroad bridge. Beyond the about nine-foot-clearance high-way bridge, there is a motel with a dock (on the RDB), and past that, there is a camp-ground with a boat ramp (on the LDB). Because of the two low-clearance bridges, the campground, the Lakeside Motor Lodge, and the Chewalla Restaurant may not be accessi-ble to vessels requiring more clearance. Most of the winding creek channel downstream from the campground has no less than nine feet of water depths. Beyond the official navi-gation aids, follow closely the line of small white and orange buoys leading up the creek.

The Eufaula Yacht Club has about 30 slips (most covered), and the largest vessel in this facility is about 25 feet long. The club also has a large picnic pavilion. Farther upstream, the Chewalla Creek Marina has 84 slips, and they can easily accommodate a 40-footer. The marina has four sets of docks, and three sets have covered slips. This is likely to be the first full-service marina (and it's a function of how you define full service) you'll encounter since Apalachicola, but they offer only limited services during the off season (i.e., the win-ter). A U.S. Coast Guard buoy-tender station is

City fountain, Eufaula, Alabama

next door to the Chewalla Creek Marina. Beyond the two bridges, the Lakeside Motor Lodge has a floating dock with about four slips and can accommodate a 40-footer side-tied on the end of their dock. HAZARD *You'd need to be able to negotiate beneath two low,*

Eufaula Yacht Club

fixed bridges that have an estimated overhead clearance as low as ten to 15 feet. The Chewalla Restaurant is next door to the motor lodge. The Lake Eufaula Campground is another quarter mile up Chewalla Creek. This campground/trailer park has a private boat ramp (with no dock), laundry, camp store, and swimming pool.

Eufaula Yacht Club

Approach depth—6-13 feet

Accepts transients—private club
Floating wooden docks—yes
Dockside power connections—15 amp
Dockside water connections—yes
Boat ramp—yes
Restaurant—several in Eufaula at fair walking distance

Chewalla Creek Marina (334) 687-5751

Approach depth—7-8 feet
Accepts transients—yes, with advance notice

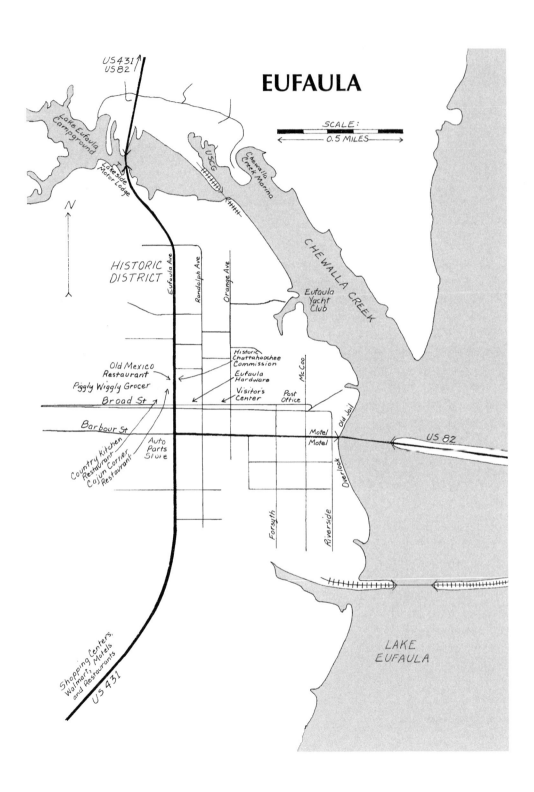

EUFAULA

SCALE:
0.5 MILES

US 431
US 82

Lake Eufaula Campground

Lakeside Motor Lodge

USCG

Chewalla Creek Marina

CHEWALLA CREEK

N

HISTORIC DISTRICT

Eufaula Ave

Randolph Ave

Orange Ave

Eufaula Yacht Club

Old Mexico Restaurant

Piggly Wiggly Grocer

Broad St

Historic Chattahoochee Commission

Eufaula Hardware

Visitor's Center

Post Office

McCoo

Barbour St

Country Kitchen Restaurant

Cajun Corner Restaurant

Auto Parts Store

Motel

Motel

Old Jail

US 82

Forsyth

Riverside

Overlook

Shopping Centers, Walmart, Motels and Restaurants

US 431

LAKE EUFAULA

Floating wooden and steel docks—yes

Dockside power connections—20 and 30 amp

Dockside water connections—yes

Waste pump-out—yes

Showers—yes

Gasoline—yes

Diesel—yes, with a mobile pump from the yard

Mechanical repairs—yes

Below-waterline repairs—yes, with 15-ton opened-ended travel lift

Boat ramp—yes

Ship's store—yes, limited

Lakeside Motor Lodge (334) 687-2477

Dockside depth—20 feet

Accepts transients—yes, if staying in motel room

Floating wooden docks—yes

Dockside power connections—limited 15 amps

Swimming pool—yes

Restaurant—next door

Creek Indians once inhabited this area and gave Eufaula its present name. In the Creek language, Eufaula means "high bluffs." White Americans arrived on the scene around 1823 and soon constructed a steamboat landing on the Chattahoochee River. By the 1850s, Eufaula became a major trading center, primarily for shipping cotton south to the Gulf of Mexico. Today, Eufaula, Alabama, is the biggest town since Apalachicola, Florida (about 200 miles to the south)—providing you didn't make that lovely 30-mile side trip to Bainbridge, Georgia, on the Flint River. Eufaula is also the county seat of Barbour County, Alabama. Eufaula has a beautiful historic district on the north end of town and boasts of over 700 buildings on the National Register of Historic Places. Most are palatial

antebellum homes. In or very near the Historic District, you can find four restaurants, a few service stations, a hardware store, a pharmacy, and a grocery store. South of the Historic District, on U.S. 431, there are many nice sit-down restaurants, about a dozen fast food-restaurants, about ten motels, gas stations, auto-parts stores, three shopping centers, and a Wal-Mart. Eufaula hosts their annual Indian Summer Arts and Crafts Festival during the second weekend of October.

Returning to Lake Eufaula, River Bluff Park, near mile 96.0, provides the closest access to Georgetown, Georgia. This channel is one of the deeper ones and is marked by white and orange no-wake buoys. This park has twin boat ramps, a floating wooden dock, ample parking, and restroom facilities. Michelle's Restaurant and four service station/convenience stores outside of Georgetown are slightly over a third of a mile from River Bluff Park. Near mile 99.5 on the Alabama side, a fishing pier and a gazebo protrude on a point of land. The Old Creek Town Park ramp is just north of this gazebo. To enter this park area, aim for the fishing pier and stay about 80 yards off the point and the pier as you work your way to the ramp area HAZARD *If you approach this area from the north, beware, there is shallow water on the northeast side of this indentation.* The ramp area is marked by a white and yellow buoy. The navigable portion of Lake Eufaula narrows north of the Old Creek Town Park. Marsh islands, which are not indicated on either the Corps of Engineers photographs or on fishing charts, start to appear on the Alabama side between Chattahoochee River Channel miles 99.0 and 101.5. Favor the higher terrain on the Georgia side, especially between miles 99.0 and 100.0.

Boat ramp, Upper Chattahoochee River

Cowikee Creek has a well-marked channel starting near mile 101.7 and heading toward Alabama. Most of the well-positioned navigation aids in this creek use daymarks instead of buoys. HAZARD *The Cowikee Creek Channel snakes back and forth several times.* Please concentrate on finding the next daymark and don't get fooled by spotting a daymark farther up this channel that is not the next one. Lakepoint Marina State Park is the largest facility on the lake, with about 200 slips on five large docks. Many 50-footers, and a few 70-footers, park in this marina. The marina is in a large, man-made, protected basin surrounded by jetty walls. This facility has every-

thing from a beach to a nearby golf course. And there is nothing second class about this operation. The grounds are immaculately maintained and all the services were most professional and friendly.

Lakepoint Marina State Park (334) 687-8011

Approach depth—9 feet
Dockside depth—8-9 feet
Accepts transients—yes
Floating concrete docks—yes
Dockside power connections—15 and 30 amp
Dockside water connections—yes
Waste pump-out—yes
Showers—yes

Laundromat—yes

Gasoline—yes

Diesel—no pump, but it can be trucked via an outside distributor

Mechanical repairs—limited, with outside contractor

Boat ramps—yes, in two separate areas

Ship's store—yes, limited

Snack bar—temporarily closed

Swimming pool—yes

Restaurant/lodge—yes, and with another boat dock

Motel, cabins, and campground—yes

Exiting Cowikee Creek, the Chattahoochee River Channel angles south toward the Georgia shore. About two and a half miles north of Cowikee Creek, on Lake Eufaula, shoreside daymarks begin to appear off the Main Chattahoochee River Channel. The lake-like impression is quickly fading, while the riverine aspects of the Chattahoochee River are becoming more pronounced.

The Upper Chattahoochee River to Columbus, GA

We only have about another 50 miles of river work before reaching Columbus, Georgia. At the north end of the lake, the Eufaula National Wildlife Refuge flanks both sides of the Chattahoochee. And there are plenty of beautiful side creeks, especially within the next 20 miles upriver. Some of these creeks are too deep to be great anchorages, and beware, others are loaded with partially submerged snags. But there are a few creeks that are great gunk holes. Exploring

Old Steamboat Wharf, Columbus, Georgia

The following are some features on the Chattahoochee River between Lake Eufaula and Columbus, Georgia.

FEATURE	MILEAGE	SIDE	COMMENTS
Boat Ramp	107.2	LDB	Rood Creek Park, two ramps, floating steel *T*-dock
Anchorage	107.2	LDB	Many choice spots in Rood Creek, water shallows up creek
Anchorage	111.1	LDB	In Grass Creek, 0.8 miles up on creek's RDB in 7-10 feet of water
Marina	112.6	LDB	Florence Marina State Park, many amenities
Anchorage	113.9	RDB	Best anchorage in Cliatt Branch is southwest of point, 8-10 foot water depths
Boat Ramp	116.0	RDB	Ramp south of Hatcheehubee Creek, 5 feet deep, park area
Anchorage	116.3	RDB	In Hatcheehubee Creek, RDB side, half-mile up, 9-11 feet deep
Bridge	116.7	center	Alabama Route 208, with 35.6 feet of clearance
Lift Bridge	117.1	center	Georgia Southwestern Railroad, 54 feet open, 19 feet closed
Power lines	117.2	center	With 47.8 feet over BRENC
Site	120.0	RDB	Mead (coated-board) Pulp and Paper Mill
Boat Ramp	120.6	RDB	In Bluff Creek, on RDB side, one-third mile up, pretty area
Anchorage	123.7	LDB	In small creek, LDB side, 8-10 feet water found 60 yards in
Anchorage	125.5	RDB	There are many options in two arms with 10-15 feet of water
Power lines	128.9	center	With 68 feet over BRENC
Boat Ramp	130.7	LDB	At River Bend Park on the river, small dock, often crowded
Marina	138.1	RDB	Uchee Creek Marina and Recreation Area
Power lines	138.3	center	With 51.2 feet over BRENC
Bridge	141.0	center	General Eddy Highway, with 36.2 feet of clearance
Site	153.1	RDB	Chattahoochee Valley Grain Elevator/Alabama State Docks
Site	155.0	center	End of dredging/turning basin
Bridge	155.4	center	Fourth Street, Columbus, Georgia, with 56.8 feet of clearance
Boat Ramp	155.9	LDB	Old Steamboat Wharf (recommended end of the line)
Bridge	156.0	center	Old Railroad Bridge
Bridge	156.1	center	Dillingham Street connecting Columbus and Phenix City
Mill Dam	156.5	center	You surely won't get this far, because of the rapids!!

many of these side creeks, I did occasionally bounce off a few submerged snags. Hull damage was minimal because I was always going at a slow speed. If you poke your nose around anywhere but in the Chattahoochee River Channel, it is highly advisable to cut your boat speed back for precisely this reason: an unforeseen encounter with a submerged snag. And a few times, even when I was in twenty feet of water, my boat and I were suddenly introduced to a submerged snag. Most of the submerged snags and stumps, although not totally soft, are well waterlogged and close to rotten.

On the Georgia side, Rood Creek is a pleasant little branch near mile 107.2. To enter this creek, follow the white and orange buoy line and then shadow the reinforced steel-retaining wall along the RDB bank to the Rood Creek Access area and ramps. The two ramps are on the RDB of the creek and are about a mile off the Main Chattahoochee

Mill Dam House, Chattahoochee River, Columbus, Georgia

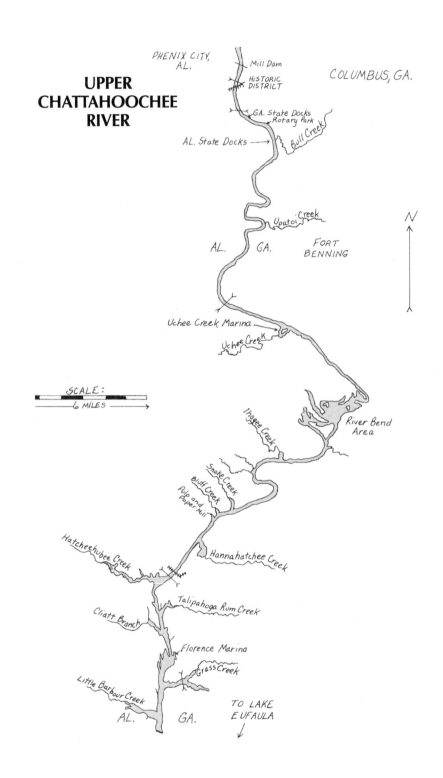

**UPPER
CHATTAHOOCHEE
RIVER**

PHENIX CITY,
AL.

COLUMBUS, GA.

Mill Dam

HISTORIC
DISTRICT

GA. State Docks
Rotary Park

AL. State Docks

Bull Creek

Upatoi Creek

AL.   GA.

FORT
BENNING

N

Uchee Creek Marina

Uchee Creek

River Bend
Area

SCALE:

6 MILES

Ihagee Creek

Snake Creek

Bluff Creek

Pulp and
Paper Mill

Hatcheehubee Creek

Hannahatchee Creek

Talipahoga Rum Creek

Cliatt Branch

Florence Marina

Grass Creek

Little Barbour Creek

AL.   GA.

TO LAKE
EUFAULA

River Channel. The area has a floating steel *T*-dock, ample parking, and trash receptacles in a very nice picnic and camping area. There are also several good anchorages in Rood Creek. But to find the shallow enough water to anchor, you need to travel a ways into this creek. Rood Creek Indian Mounds are also nearby. The 600-year-old Indian site is closed to the public, except for the guided tours leaving from Florence Marina State Park.

Little Barbour Creek, at mile 109.8 on the Alabama side, is a bit deep for anchoring, especially within the first two-thirds of a mile from the Chattahoochee River Channel. The LDB side of Little Barbour Creek is shallower than the RDB. Grass Creek, at mile 111.1 on the Georgia side, has very sporadic depths (e.g., from seven feet to 30 feet) for most of the distance to the highway bridge—about a mile

away from the Chattahoochee River Channel. The best anchorage area appears to be close to the creek's RDB, about one-seventh of a mile downsteam from the bridge.

A fixed wooden fishing pier jutting out into the Chattahoochee near mile 112.4 on the LDB signals Florence, Georgia. The opening to the Florence Marina State Park basin, near mile 112.6 on the LDB, is protected by two rock jetties. There are about six sets of docks in this protected basin, and a boat ramp is located at the southern end of the basin. Nontransient boaters, many coming from Atlanta, fill many of the slips at this marina. The state park has a campground, nature center, clubhouse, tennis courts, miniature golf course, and a swimming pool. In early December, we were fortunate enough to view the nighttime Christmas parade of boats. The many illuminated, decked-out

Florence Marina State Park, Chattahoochee River

boats made this parade outstanding. Many major improvements at the marina were taking place when we first visited. By the time of our second visit, those improvements had all been completed. This says loads about any marina. The marina remains nearly full, and usually the only space for transients is at the large fuel dock (with four slips). But there are no utilities at this fuel dock. Three grades of octane gasoline are sold.

Florence, Georgia, was initially named Liverpool, after that famous British seaport. Liverpool, Georgia, boasted a bank, newspaper, hotel, and covered bridge to Alabama in 1837. But in 1846, a disastrous flood wiped out much of Liverpool, Georgia.

Florence Marina State Park (229) 838-4244

Approach depth—8 feet
Accepts transients—limited
Floating wooden and aluminum docks—yes
Dockside power connections—20 amp
Dockside water connections—yes
Waste pump-out—yes
Showers—yes
Laundromat—yes
Gasoline—yes
Boat ramp—yes
Variety store—limited
Cottages—yes

Much of Cliatt Branch, at mile 113.9 on the Alabama side, is over 20 feet deep, except for a patch southwest of the point in the second indentation on the creek's RDB. The entrance to Talipahoga Rum Creek, at mile 114.8 on the Georgia side, has a grassy island in the middle, near the creek's mouth. There is shallow water on the south side, but deeper water

is on the north side of this grassy island. If you can get into Talipahoga Rum Creek, much of the creek has over 15 feet of water. Back on the Alabama side, there is a single concrete ramp, with a wooden T-dock, in a picnic area with ample parking on the Chattahoochee south of Hatcheehubee Creek. Hatcheehubee Creek enters the Chattahoochee at mile 116.5 from Alabama, just upstream from the marsh island that is north of the boat ramp. Hatcheehubee Creek is conveniently marked by about four daymarks. HAZARD *The two bulges on the LDB, or north side, of Hatcheehubee Creek are loaded with submerged snags, and this area is not recommended for anchoring.* The best anchorage is farther up the creek, on the RDB before the bridge, between the second green and the second red daymarks. The water depth here is nine to 11 feet. Nearby, there is also a shoreside picnic pavilion. There is a convenience store with gasoline about one mile away, north on the main road.

Beware, near Chattahoochee River mile 117, there are three overhead obstructions. The railroad lift bridge at mile 117.1 was in the lift (open) position with 54 feet of overhead clearance during our last visit. And it looked like this old rusty bridge, with broken windows in the lift house, may have corroded itself into this permanently lifted position. If the railroad bridge is permanently open, the lowest obstruction is the fixed highway bridge, at mile 116.7, with about 35.6 feet of clearance at BRENC. Hannahatchee Creek enters the Chattahoochee River Channel at mile 119.1 on the Georgia side. I wish that I had never entered this treacherous creek. HAZARD *It was difficult to find any sort of channel here. The water depths were sporadic (i.e.,*

Railroad Lift Bridge, Chattahoochee River

from three feet to 20 feet in the length of a few feet over the ground). The creek is loaded with submerged stumps and choked with aquatic vegetation.

The Mead Pulp and Paper Mill in Mahrt, Alabama, is near mile 120.0. This mill makes a couple of grades of coated paperboard. U.S. paperboard exports, shipped to markets all over world, are of the highest international quality and likely are one of the most internationally competitive of all products harvested from the pine forests of Southeastern United States. The forest-products industry creates many jobs in the Southeast—and many of those jobs are stable as long as U.S. production and exports aren't threatened.

Bluff Creek is the second creek upstream from the paper mill on the Alabama side. This pretty little creek has a twisting and somewhat narrow channel, but the channel is well marked by 11 navigation aids. There are also several helpful orange and white buoys marking some of the submerged snags in this creek. Much of the creek is seven to 16 feet deep. A reinforced river wall extends for a ways along the RDB shore of the creek. The double boat ramps and a nearby floating wooden dock are near a very nice picnic area with ample parking. This creek also has several pretty bends that look like potentially great anchorages. HAZARD *But be mindful of possible encounters with submerged snags once out of the main Bluff Creek Channel.* Nearby, there is a campground with showers and laundry. It's almost a two-mile walk to the convenience store located on the main road.

There is steep terrain for about a half-mile between miles 122.5 and 124.0 on the Georgia side. Near the end of this steep terrain section, and near mile 123.7, there is a nice anchorage in a small, unnamed creek. You can find about eight to ten feet of water about 60 yards beyond the mouth of this creek. The last decent anchorages that we were able to flag before Columbus are located near mile 125.5 on the Alabama side. There is a tributary with two arms entering the Chattahoochee River Channel from the RDB. We found no bad spots. The water depths ranged from ten to 15 feet in both arms. There are several nice places to drop the hook around here. We did not like anchoring options in Ihagee Creek, at mile 126.8 off the Alabama side. In this creek, we pounded into a submerged stump while in 15-foot depths just inside the creek's mouth.

We found that, within about seven miles downriver and upriver from the River Bend Park ramp, small-boat traffic increases significantly. Many fast, planing-hull, fishing boats were zooming all over the river. Be wary of this traffic. The River Bend Park ramp, with a small dock, is at mile 130.7 on the Georgia side. Despite the wider sections of river, and the many shallow sloughs within the three miles upriver from River Bend Park, we did not find any good anchorages. The mouth of Shell Creek, at mile 133.3 on the Georgia

side, was blocked by three orange and white Keep Out buoys.

Uchee Creek Marina is on the Alabama side near mile 138.1. Even though it's on the Alabama side, this facility is part of Fort Benning Reservation in Georgia, and it is a military facility. If someone on your boat can present proof some sort of military affiliation (e.g., army reservist, civilian working for the Department of Defense, or a defense contractor, etc.), you are more than welcome to use the facilities. The marina is in the second, or more upriver, mouth on the RDB. Uchee Creek Marina has many nice amenities, including a swimming pool, Laundromat, horse and foot trails, cabins, and picnic pavilions. I must have seen 15 almost domesticated deer milling around the marina Laundromat the evening I was there.

Uchee Creek Marina (706) 545-7238
www.benningmwr.com

Approach depth—12 feet
Dockside depth—10 feet
Accepts transients—yes (with military affiliation)
Floating wooden docks—yes
Dockside power connections—15 and 30 amp
Dockside water connections—yes
Showers—yes
Laundromat—yes
Gasoline—yes
Mechanical repairs—limited, with outside contractor
Boat ramp—yes
Variety store—yes, limited
Snack bar with hot sandwiches—yes
Lodge and campground—yes

The General Eddy Highway Bridge crosses the Chattahoochee at river mile 141.0. HAZARD

The center span has no less than 36.2 feet of overhead clearance. The Corps of Engineers aerial photograph book depicts a marina at mile 144.8 on the Georgia side. There is nothing here but a small shallow creek. In the next five miles, between miles 144.8 and 149.8, the Chattahoochee River makes four horseshoe bends. Like similar sections of the Apalachicola River (200 miles to the south), these tight horseshoe bends are usually associated with stiff river currents. We found that the current in this particular five-mile section was about one to one and half knots stronger than the current just downstream—and just upstream from this multiple horseshoe-bend section.

The Alabama State Docks serving Phenix City, Alabama, can be seen at mile 153.1 on the RDB. Columbus, Georgia's celebrated Riverwalk can be seen on the LDB near mile 153.5. Well-maintained Rotary Park, with a ramp and a dock, can be seen at mile 154.2 on the LDB. Action Marine (and my good friends

Riverwalk in Historic District, Columbus, Georgia

Chattahoochee River and Riverwalk, Columbus, Georgia

there—Wes, Bubba, and Dale) is at the head of Rotary Park on Victory Drive. The Georgia Port Authority is next, at mile 154.6 on the LDB. HAZARD *River dredging stops at mile 155.0.* We pushed it about another mile to the Old Steamboat Wharf (with a filled-in rock pier and a ramp) on the LDB, near the base of the Dillingham Street Arch Bridge. *Beware, if you go this far, give that Georgia shore plenty*

of room. Dale told me that there are several hardwood jetties and possible wrecks, dating from Civil War days, submerged close to Georgia's Chattahoochee bank between the Fourth Street Bridge and the wharf. And Wes informed me that there are even more underwater obstructions on the Alabama side, upstream from the Old Steamboat Wharf. But once you can make it to the wharf, you are in the heart of historic Columbus, Georgia. Welcome!

Columbus, Georgia

Columbus, Georgia, sits on a fall line between the Gulf Coastal plain and the rolling hills of the Piedmont region. Just like the many cities that formed along rivers flowing to the Atlantic Ocean, Columbus was formed along a Gulf of Mexico-flowing river—the Chattahoochee-Apalachicola. Just upriver from the fall line, and in the Piedmont region, a river will usually have rapids rendering it unnavigable to shipping. And this fall line phenomenon is precisely why so many great American cities (e.g., Philadelphia; Baltimore; Washington, D.C.; Richmond, etc.) developed and became inland ports. But only 60 million years earlier that same fall line was the edge of an ancient ocean (in this case, the Gulf of Mexico).

In 1639, the Spanish came close to reaching present-day Columbus. And in 1689, the Spanish built a fort somewhere downriver to keep their eyes on the British. In 1828, the Georgia legislature established Columbus as a trading town at the head of navigable waters on the Chattahoochee River. That same year, the *Fanny* was the first steamboat to arrive in Columbus. The *Fanny* was also the first steamboat on record to sink in the Chattahoochee—when it was returning downstream from this historic voyage. Besides the river commerce, cotton, ironworks, and brick-making were linchpins to the early economy of Columbus. Rich Chattahoochee River clay deposits aided in brick-making and other clay products. In the 1850s, Columbus ranked second only to Richmond, Virginia, as an industrial center in the South.

The Chattahoochee Riverwalk, with its red-bricked sidewalk and iron handrails, is 12 miles long. The walk links uptown Columbus to the Historic District then to Fort Benning—south of Columbus. The first sections of the tasteful Riverwalk were completed in 1992. Fort Benning is home to the U.S. Army Infantry School. Since World War I, the most fundamental troops in combat, those slogging and tough foot soldiers, have been receiving much of their training here. The National Infantry Museum, (706) 545-2958, on Fort Benning, is outstanding. The museum is open to the public and the admission is free.

Rotary Park has an 80-foot floating aluminum L-dock at mile 154.2 on the LDB. This park is another tasteful stop on the Riverwalk. Rotary Park has covered picnic tables, gazebos, and restrooms. Bulldog Bait and Tackle and Action Marine, (706) 322-3047, at 1330 Victory Drive, are on the fringes of this nice park. The friendly folks at Action Marine are the best source of plain old information or boating supplies on this part of the Chattahoochee River. Victory Drive, heading south, leads to many restaurants, motels, grocery stores, shopping centers, and Fort Benning.

The one-of-a-kind Port Columbus National Civil War Naval Museum, (706) 327-9798, is only about 250 yards away from Rotary Park. The spacious museum, which opened in 2001, remains open 364 days a year. (It's only closed on Christmas Day.) The remains of a 220-foot Confederate ironclad, the CSS *Jackson* and the 141-foot CSS *Chattahoochee*, are housed in this extraordinary museum. Both ships are inextricably linked to the history of the Chattahoochee River and Columbus, Georgia. The naval museum also

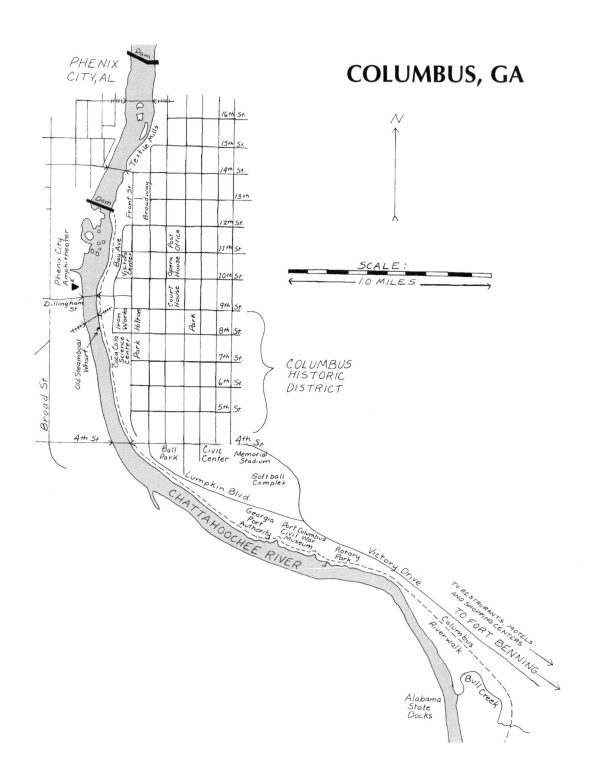

COLUMBUS, GA

PHENIX CITY, AL

Dam

N

SCALE:
1.0 MILES

16th St.
15th St.
14th St.
13th St.
12th St.
11th St.
10th St.
9th St.
8th St.
7th St.
6th St.
5th St.
4th St.

Textile Mills
Front St.
Broadway
Dam
Bay Ave.
Visitors Center
Opera House
Post Office
Court House
Park
Iron Works
Coca Cola Science Center
Park
Hilton
Phenix City Amphitheater
Dillingham St.
Old Steamboat Wharf
Broad St.

COLUMBUS HISTORIC DISTRICT

4th St
Ball Park
Civic Center
Memorial Stadium
Softball Complex

Lumpkin Blvd.

CHATTAHOOCHEE RIVER

Georgia Port Authority
Port Columbus Civil War Museum
Rotary Park
Victory Drive

TO RESTAURANTS, MOTELS AND SHOPPING CENTERS
TO FORT BENNING

Columbus Riverwalk

Bull Creek

Alabama State Docks

has displays of Civil War nautical murals, Confederate steam engines, naval mines, torpedoes, and a gift shop. You can also learn about the many successful exploits of the Confederate raider CSS *Alabama* and its last duel with USS *Kersarge* off the coast of France. If you are a naval-warfare buff, you must visit this great museum.

When Atlanta hosted the 1996 Summer Olympics, Columbus was selected as the host for the Olympic softball games. These softball fields are less than one-quarter mile from the Chattahoochee River behind the Georgia Port Authority. The South Commons is just behind the Georgia Port Authority. The area also houses Memorial Stadium—home to the minor-league Columbus RedStixx, the Columbus Civic Center, and Golden Park. Columbus also has a minor-league hockey team—the Cottonmouths.

Farther upriver, we were able to park our boat for several hours at the Old Steamboat Wharf at mile 155.9 on the LDB—right in the heart of the Historic District. The paddle-wheeler *Chattahoochee Princess* and the *Dragonfly* tour boat, (888) 464-3378, may

Port Columbus National Civil War Naval Museum

also be side tied to the Old Steamboat Wharf. The *Dragonfly* is a 42-foot trimaran and offers everything from a one-hour excursion staying near Columbus to a three-night package going all the way down to Apalachicola. The Old Steamboat Wharf is at least an 80-foot-long fixed concrete structure with a ramp. Nevertheless, if the *Dragonfly* is side tied to the *Chattahoochee Princess,* there may still be some room for another boat to tie up at the wharf downstream from these two boats. But good attachment points (i.e., dock cleats, bollards, or eyes) are lacking at the lower end on the wharf.

In 1833, the striking Dillingham Street Arch Bridge, near the Old Steamboat Wharf, was one of the first bridges connecting Alabama to Georgia. On April 16, 1865, the first wooden covered bridge was burned down during one of the last land battles of the Civil War.

Columbus Civic Center on the Chattahoochee River

Chattahoochee Princess at Rotary Park ramp, Columbus, Georgia

Amphitheater in Phenix City, Alabama

One week after General Lee surrendered to General Grant at Appomattox, Virginia, 11,000 Union cavalry troops stormed into Columbus.

The convention center, the visitor's center, the Hilton Hotel, and much more are only about a block away from the Old Steamboat Wharf, right in the heart of the 26-block Historic District. When Union troops attacked Columbus in 1865, they spared the local food-producing industries, including the large gristmill located across the street from Iron Works. In 1887, that mill (then called Empire Mills) was the largest flour, bran, grits, and cornmeal mill in the entire South. Today it's the Hilton Hotel. The impressive Columbus Convention and Trade Center building used to be the old Columbus Iron Works. The Iron Works began operations in 1853, but not long afterward, the factory was producing wartime munitions and much machinery for the small Confederate navy. During the Civil War, by 1862, the major Confederate shipyards at Norfolk, Virginia; Pensacola, Florida; and New Orleans, Louisiana, were rendered non-operational by the Union blockade of the South. This inland port of Columbus, along with the Port of Selma on the Alabama River, had to pick up the slack. The Iron Works became one of the largest plants casting cannons and assembling boilers. Chattahoochee River boatyards were constructing steamboats as late as 1904.

Elsewhere in the Historic District, the Springer Opera House, when it opened in 1871, soon had one of the best reputations between Washington and New Orleans. In 1999 it was restored. The formula for Coca-Cola was first concocted at a local apothecary near Broadway and Seventh streets. The nearby Coca-Cola Space Science Center is quite popular, especially for youngsters, because it has many hands-on exhibits. This science center has a space-shuttle simulator, a mock-up command module of *Apollo 11,* a planetarium, and an observatory remotely connected to other *real* observatories. Columbus hosts a Riverfest Weekend each April.

Broadway is a wide median boulevard running north-south through the heart of the Historic District. There are several restaurants along Broadway north of the Historic District and in between Tenth and Thirteenth streets. The downtown post office is nearby on Twelfth Street. Cannon and Fieldcrest have textile mills along the river north of Thirteenth Street.

After the Civil War, both Columbus and Phenix City prospered again as mill towns. Across the river from Columbus, not that long ago, Phenix City, Alabama, used to be a near lawless free-for-all full of honky-tonks, gambling, prostitution, and gangsters. I can even recollect some old army buddies talking about it. That has changed, and now Phenix City is one of Alabama's most progressive cities. The modern Phenix City Amphitheater sits in opposition, across the Chattahoochee River, from the heart of Columbus. Troy State University is also in Phenix City, Alabama.

Columbus, with a population of around 200,000, is the second-largest city in Georgia. Besides being home to Fort Benning and several major corporations, including AFLAC insurance, Columbus is also home to Columbus State University. Up and down the Chattahoochee River, I've heard talk of building a full-service marina in Columbus—with a view capitalizing on that not-so-distant Atlanta market. I'm not sure how serious, or how feasible, this idea is. As a boater, I like the idea, but to see it to practical fruition, well, that's another story. Columbus does takes much pride in being called Rivertown. This well-deserved moniker prevails everywhere in Columbus, Georgia.

Large boat tied up on the Suwannee River

CHAPTER 17

The Suwannee River, from Suwannee to Little River Springs

The Suwannee River originates 120 feet above sea level in southeastern Georgia's Okefenokee Swamp or the Okie. Early settlers called the Okefenokee Swamp the "land of trembling earth" because of the large mats of floating and quaking vegetation. The Suwannee River basin drains an area of nearly 10,000 square miles. More than 70 crystal-clear natural springs (and some springs are very large) pour millions of gallons of water into the Suwannee River on a daily basis. The river meanders for about 280 miles before reaching the Gulf of Mexico near the town of Suwannee, Florida. Not far from the Suwannee River's origin, and also in the Okefenokee Swamp, the St. Marys River originates. The St. Marys flows to the Atlantic Ocean. During the Franklin Roosevelt administration, there was talk of connecting these two rivers and making a Gulf of Mexico-to-the-Atlantic waterway. Today, this trip could probably be accomplished with a long canoe portage.

"God has created a river lovely as a song," wrote noted statesman Jonathan Daniels on describing a journey down the Suwannee River. The name Suwannee is likely to have come either from the Creek Indian word *swani*, meaning "echo," or from a corruption of the Spanish name San Juan-ee.

Like the Apalachicola River—a historic boundary between west and east Florida—the Suwannee River is often considered the divid-ing line between north Florida and subtropical Florida.

In 1836, not long after steamboats were first built, they arrived on the Suwannee River. In the nineteenth century, shipyards in Rowland's Bluff (later to be renamed Branford) built some of these paddlewheel steamboats. Throughout much of the nineteenth century, the Suwannee was a major steamboat river and a transportation artery in north-central Florida. The cargo heading down the river to major ports and markets was often cotton, lumber, and naval stores. In the other direction, most steamboats could make it up the river as far as Ellaville—126 miles from the Gulf of Mexico. The 120-foot *Madison* was one of the most famous steamboats to ply the Suwannee River. The *Madison* made weekly trips up from Cedar Key, sailing past Branford and Troy Springs and then, depending on the fluctuating water level, ended this weekly trip somewhere between 85 and 126 miles from the Gulf of Mexico. One lucky time, with favorably high water levels, the *Madison* made it all the way up to White Springs, 169 miles from the Gulf of Mexico! Traveling upriver, the *Madison* carried general merchandise that was exchanged for hogs, chickens, eggs, venison hams, animal hides and skins, honey, and currency. During the Civil War, the captain and crew of the *Madison* went off to Virginia to fight the Union. To keep the *Madison* from falling into enemy hands, the captain had the *Madison* scuttled in Troy Springs—where she lies to this day.

After the Civil War, steamboat commerce once again returned to the Suwannee. One of the most famous post-Civil War steamboats was the 156-foot *City of Hawkinsville*. The *City of Hawkinsville* was primarily employed in the timber industry. This grand vessel was sunk in 1922, about 100 yards south of the railroad bridge in Old Town, Florida. And she lies there to this day. Near the dawn of the twentieth century, railroads stymied and eventually killed steamboat commerce on the Suwannee River, as well as on other rivers in the entire country. By the early twentieth cen-tury, commercial waterway traffic had ceased on the Suwannee River.

The Gulf of Mexico sturgeon can be found in many of the rivers and bays in the Big Bend. Its Gulf Coastal range is loosely from Louisiana to Tampa Bay. But the sightings and the lore of this threatened fish are greatest on the Suwannee River. The rather ugly sturgeon has been around since the age of the dinosaurs—and with its bony plates, it looks like something from a prehistoric age. Each spring, sturgeon swim up the Suwannee, often going as far as Georgia, to spawn on the rocky bottom. And each fall, they return to the Gulf of Mexico to spend the winter. The sturgeon

Houseboat beneath bridge, Suwannee River (Note the 10+-foot nontidal water level fluctuation on the pilings.)

can grow to be nine feet long and weigh 300 pounds. If you are startled by a large splash in the summer, it just might be a leaping sturgeon. In 1995, a five-foot sturgeon, weighing a mere 75 pounds, leaped into the air and landed on a 24-foot Suwannee River pontoon boat. After some serious thrashing aboard the vessel, there were more than a few folks aboard who wish they never saw this creature. The boat's windshield was cracked and two of the three people aboard suffered minor lacerations. A similar incident occurred on the Suwannee River in the late summer of 2002. Largemouth bass are the sturgeon's biggest enemy, feeding on juvenile sturgeon.

The NOAA-stated controlling depth of the Suwannee River, all the way to Ellaville (i.e., 109 miles up), is stated to be only three and a half feet. We found this to be ludicrously shallow for the lowest 80-mile portion. But we were warned not to try the last 30 miles to Ellaville. The lowest 80 miles of the river is generally much deeper, and we navigated at a time of very low water. Another good public source indicated that, for the lowest 76 miles (i.e., below Branford), the Suwannee River depths ranged between seven and 55 feet in depth, taking care to avoid certain sand bars). In our opinion, these stated depths seem much more accurate. But we would not recommend taking a large vessel past Troy Springs (i.e., six miles beyond Branford), or possibly even past

Home in the cypress trees along the Suwannee River

Branford, because the possibility of encountering a submerged rock starts to increase significantly.

The best information on overhead bridge clearances indicates that the first bridge, the U.S. Route 98 near Fanning Springs and 34 miles up, has about 34 feet of overhead clearance (more during low water, possibly less clearance during periods of high water). HAZARD *The U.S. Coast Pilot indicates that this bridge has 15 feet of clearance at high water and 30 feet at low water.* The lowest bridge we encountered is the old Seaboard Coastline Railroad Bridge (the swing is now nonoperational) only another three and half miles upriver from the U.S. Route 98 highway bridge. This bridge now supports a hiking and bicycle trail—the Nature Coast Greenway. The overhead clearance, depending on the Suwannee River water level, might be as low as ten feet. When we passed beneath this bridge, there was at least 12 to 15 feet of overhead clearance. And if you can make it under this bridge, at mile 37.5, it's clear sailing to and past Branford. You will encounter a few more bridges (e.g., at Rock Bluff, U.S. Route 27 at Branford, and U.S. Route 129 over the Santa Fe River) and a handful of

Lower Suwannee River

power lines, but their overhead clearances are significantly greater than this controlling bridge height at the Nature Coast Greenway. Forty-four-foot houseboats from Miller's Marina are usually able to make it beneath the limiting clearance of Nature Coast Greenway Bridge.

The Suwannee River is tidal for about 25 miles until about Manatee Springs. Upriver from Manatee Springs, the current only flows one way—downhill to the Gulf of Mexico. In the nontidal parts of the Suwannee, we experienced a downhill current of between one and two knots. When rains swell the rivers to the north, the current would increase significantly. Furthermore, the water level can fluctuate considerably. In late October 2001 when we made our trip, many locals touted the river as having real low water. So our depth observations are likely to be on the safe side. On the other hand, overhead-clearance observations may be slightly generous.

Going Upriver

After the town of Suwannee, heading upriver (see chapter 10 for the mouth of the river and the town of Suwannee), your first decision will be to determine which fork should be taken near river mile four. The main river channel is on the RDB side. But the LDB side is fine, too, with five- to six-foot water depths at MLW in Magnesia Pass. You can pass that large island on either side. Less than a mile after Magnesia Pass rejoins the Suwannee River, there is another serious fork. This time the LDB shore leads to East Pass. Deep East Pass leads back out to Suwannee Sound. Negotiating East Pass is easy, but the same cannot be said after you arrive in Suwannee Sound (review the "Derrick Key Gap" section in chapter 10). The larger fork on the RDB side is the Suwannee River and the direction most of us wish to head.

The lower Suwannee River is, by far, the widest river (e.g., often more than 150 yards wide) on Florida's Big Bend. The banks of the lower Suwannee are lined with large cypress and live oak trees. Turkey Island is near mile 13.5, and Little Turkey Island is near mile 14.5. Both should be passed on your starboard side and treated like LDB. Fowler Bluff, near mile 16 and on the LDB, is the first settlement to which you'll come. It stretches out for about a mile on this LDB side. Treasure Camp, with about a 40-foot dock, is close to the middle of Fowler Bluff. Treasure Camp is a spirited place and often has live music on Saturdays. When we arrived, a wedding ceremony was about to start on the grounds. Several boats were anchored out.

Treasure Camp (352) 493-2950

Accepts transients—yes
Fixed wooden dock—yes
Gasoline—yes
Boat ramp—nearby
Variety store—yes
Restaurant—light meals

The following table presents features, and some interesting sites, that we observed on the lowest 83 statute miles of the Suwannee River. There is no officially posted information on Suwannee River bridge clearance heights. We can only offer you our best guess (or a few times, someone else's better guess). And, please, be mindful that we made our trip at a time of low water and the bridge clearance heights would be less if the river has been swollen by recent rains.

FEATURE	MILEAGE	SIDE	COMMENTS
Mouth	0.0	center	Mouth of Suwannee River on the Gulf of Mexico
Town	4.2	RDB	Town of Suwannee with five boating facilities
Town	16.5	LDB ramp	Town of Fowler Bluff, Treasure Camp, and a boat
Obstacle	20.5-21.0	LDB LDB	Jacks Sand Bar extends past middle of river from
Dock/Ramp	23.8	RDB	Yellow Jacket Campground—dock, boat ramp, and cabins
Boat Ramp	24.8	LDB	Old Clay Landing, no dock
Park/Spring	25.1	LDB	Manatee Springs State Park, dock, spring, other facilities
Boat Ramp	28.0	LDB	New Clay Landing, with 25-foot dock
Boat Ramp	29.0	RDB	Pine Landing, no dock
Boat Ramp	32.0	RDB	Hinton Landing, 30-foot dock, covered pavilions, park area
Facilities	33.8	RDB	In very shallow canals, two small boating facilities
Town/Park	34.1	LDB	Fanning Springs, dock, spring, town, swimming area
Bridge	34.3	center	34-foot stated clearance beneath U.S. Routes 19, 27, and 98
Dock	35.7	RDB	Suwannee River Inn with docks
Dock	35.8	RDB	Suwannee Gables Motel and Marina with 250-foot dock
Site	37.5	RDB	Sunken steamship, *City of Hawkinsville*
Bridge	37.6	center	10-foot stated clearance beneath old SCL Railroad Bridge
Dock/Gas	39.8	RDB	KOA campground, dock, gas, trailer park, laundry
Ramp	40.3	LDB	Otter Springs near a ramp, no dock
Ramp	41.0	RDB	Purvis Landing with a 40-foot dock
Obstacle	42.1-42.6	LDB LDB	Sand bar in middle of river, extending from upriver
Facility	42.4	LDB	Hart Springs Subdivision II, private boating facility
Ramp	55.0	RDB	Guaranto Springs, 40-foot dock, springs, and park facilities
Bridge	56.5	center	Estimated 20- to 30-foot clearance beneath State Route 340
Junction	66.9	LDB	Enchanting Santa Fe River enters from the northeast
Restaurant	73.5	LDB	Suwannee River Cove Restaurant, campground, small dock
Town/Park	76.0	LDB	Ivey Memorial Park, Branford Springs, welcoming town of Branford
Bridge	76.1	center	Estimated 20- to 30-foot clearance beneath U.S. Route 27
Spring/Site	80.2	LDB	Little River Springs and a popular dive site
Spring/Site	82.8	RDB	Troy Springs and site of the scuttled *Madison*

Jacks Sand Bar

HAZARD *Beyond Suwannee River mile 20, notorious Jacks Sand Bar blocks much of the Suwannee River.* This wide sand bar is about a half-mile long and extends more than halfway into the Suwannee River from the LDB. If you closely hug the RDB shore between latitude 29.26.350N and latitude 29.26.800N, you'll never know there was such a thing as Jacks Sand Bar. I know you might want to experience it; nevertheless, we recommend that you hug the RDB side for this half-mile. If you don't like GPS latitudes, northbound Jacks Sand Bar starts near the lily pads on the LDB and ends near the large near-beached houseboat on the LDB (if it is still there).

Yellow Jacket Campground is on the RDB at mile 23.8. This facility has a 60-foot-long floating dock, RV park, cabins, and rental boats. The owners have big plans that include a heated pool and a Jacuzzi. The Camp Azalea boat ramp, with no dock, is across the river from Yellow Jacket Campground, on the LDB. Upriver from Yellow Jacket, there is another boat ramp on the LDB shore near Old Clay Landing.

Yellow Jacket Campground (352) 542-8365
www.yellowjacketcampground.com

Dockside depth—5-8 feet
Accepts transients—yes, if staying in cabins
Floating wooden docks—yes
Showers—yes
Laundromat—yes
Boat ramp—yes
Cabins—yes

Manatee Springs

Manatee Springs State Park has about 100 feet of floating steel dock on the LDB. Manatee Spring is situated in a 2,000-acre state park with a campground, picnic pavilions, and toilet facilities. Manatee Springs is one of Florida's 27 first-magnitude springs. A first-magnitude spring discharges more than 100 cubic feet of water per second! The state of Florida has more first-magnitude springs than any other state in the country. Another first-magnitude spring can be found on the lower Suwannee River at Fanning Springs. There are no less than 70 other large springs and many smaller springs and tributaries that feed the Suwannee River. If you are certified for such, you can make a cave dive in Manatee Springs. All the springs on the Suwannee River maintain a 72-degree water temperature year around. Throughout history, Manatee Springs has been a popular gathering place for Native Americans, Spaniards, settlers, and present-day tourists. Groups of canoeists and divers regularly congregate here. Manatee Springs State Parks also hosts a river party music festival each April.

Back on the Suwannee River, there is another boat ramp on the LDB at mile 28.0 at New Clay Landing. This double-wide concrete ramp has about a 25-foot-long pier between the two ramps. At mile 29.0, on the opposite (RDB) shore, there is another ramp with no dock in the Pine Landing area. There are also a few nice homes and private docks in this area. The nice Hinton Landing ramp is at mile 32.0 on the RDB. The boat ramp is tucked in that narrow canal on the RDB. The Hinton Landing dock on the Suwannee River is a floating aluminum dock that is about 30 feet long. Hinton Landing has one large picnic pavilion, five smaller covered pavilions, many picnic tables, a latrine, and trash receptacles. Hinton Landing is in a well-maintained park.

LOWER
SUWANNEE
RIVER

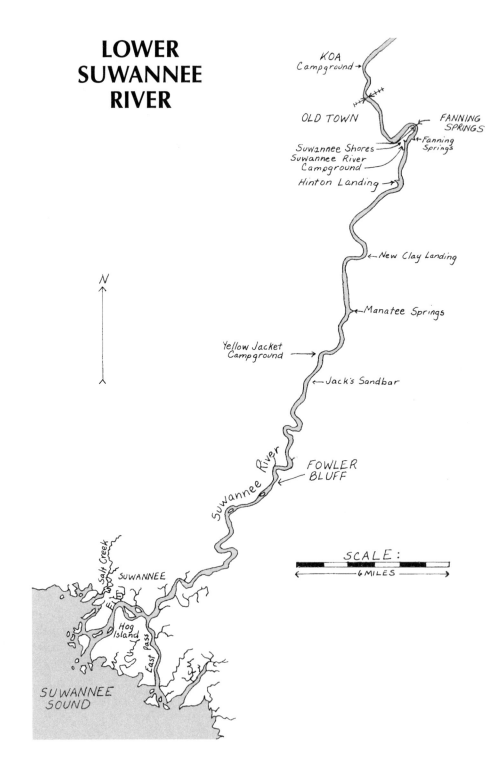

KOA
Campground →

OLD TOWN

FANNING
SPRINGS

Suwannee Shores
Suwannee River
Campground
Hinton Landing →

← Fanning
Springs

← New Clay Landing

← Manatee Springs

Yellow Jacket
Campground →

← Jack's Sandbar

Suwannee River

FOWLER
BLUFF

N

SCALE:

← 6 MILES →

Salt Creek

SUWANNEE

Hog
Island

East Pass

SUWANNEE
SOUND

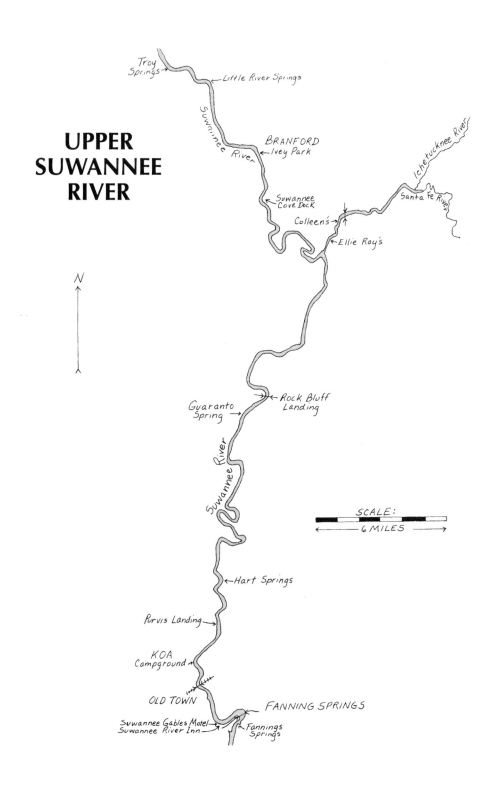

UPPER SUWANNEE RIVER

Troy Springs

Little River Springs

Suwannee River

BRANFORD
Ivey Park

Suwannee
Cove Dock

Colleen's

Ellie Ray's

Ichetucknee River

Santa Fe River

N

Rock Bluff
Landing

Guaranto
Spring

Suwannee River

SCALE:

6 MILES

Hart Springs

Purvis Landing

KOA
Campground

OLD TOWN

FANNING SPRINGS

Suwannee Gables Motel
Suwannee River Inn

Fannings
Springs

When you tie up to any dock out in the Suwannee River, even for a short period of time, use fenders. Many small local boats have a tendency to neglect paying attention to their own wake. One of these wakes could easily rap, scuff, or damage another boat that is side tied to a steel or concrete dock if fenders are not tucked in between the boat and the dock. Likewise, if your boat is creating a wake, it is proper etiquette to slow down for other moving boats, as well as for any boat tied to a public or private dock.

There is a very narrow and very shallow canal on the RDB near mile 33.8. Two marginal boating facilities are located in this canal. We'd be hard-pressed to call either of them anything resembling a marina. These canals are no place for a trawler or sailboat. *Beware, we had a most difficult time getting my less-than-two-foot-draft vessel in this canal—but it was also a time of low water on the Suwannee.* A spur canal heads off to the left, on the RDB side. HAZARD *If the thin water depth permits, you still must negotiate beneath a 25- to 30-foot overhead power line in this spur canal.* The two facilities are near the head of this spur canal. Suwannee River Campground is on the canal's LDB and Suwannee Shores Marina is at the head of the canal. Suwannee River Campground does have a small 20-foot-long floating dock with access to the campground. Suwannee Shores Marina is nothing more than a boat ramp into the canal.

Suwannee River Campground (352) 542-7680

Approach depth—very shallow
Accepts transients—yes, but only if staying on campground
Floating wooden dock—yes
Showers—yes

Laundromat—yes

Suwannee Shores Marina (352) 542-7482

Approach depth—very shallow
Mechanical repairs—yes
Boat ramp—yes

Fanning Springs and Old Town

In 1838, Fort Fanning was strategically built on the high bluffs on the east side of the Suwannee River during the second Seminole war. Fanning Springs is the second-largest spring found on the lower Suwannee River and another one of Florida's first-magnitude springs. Small boats can take the channel off the Suwannee's LDB and tie up to the floating concrete dock just outside of the enchanting Fanning Springs swimming hole. Larger boats need to stay in the Suwannee River and tie up to another steel floating dock, about 45 feet long, on the LDB to access gorgeous Fanning Springs State Park. There is a wide but closed-down boat ramp across the river (on the RDB) from this steel dock. Fanning Springs State Park has a boat ramp, picnic pavilions, telephones, soda machines, and toilet facilities but no showers. Heck, who needs a shower when there are all of these fabulous crystal-clear springs to take a dip in? And hungry alligators usually don't hang out in these springs. Or do they? The nearby town of Fanning Springs has a few motels, a convenience store, a gas station, and a great restaurant. The Lighthouse Restaurant has excellent food at reasonable prices and is about a third of a mile from the river. Fanning Springs hosts a Christmas Boat Parade every December and a Naturefest each April.

Near Old Town on the RDB, Suwannee River

Fanning Springs swimming hole

Inn has a nice dock housing a fleet of small pontoon rental boats. Suwannee Gables Motel and Marina is next door, about one and a half miles past the 34-foot-clearance highway bridge, on the RDB. Suwannee Gables has about 250 feet of docking on an exceptionally beautiful portion of the river near Old Town. Suwannee Gables Restaurant, a BP gas station, and a liquor store are just across the highway. About 150 years ago, Old Town just may have been the largest Native American settlement in Florida.

Suwannee River Inn Bed and Breakfast
(352) 542-0613

Approach depth—8-9 feet

Accepts transients—yes, limited to dock space
Floating wooden docks—yes
Dockside power connections—limited 15 amp
Restaurants—across the street
Bed and breakfast—yes

Suwannee Gables Motel and Marina (352) 542-7752

Approach depth—7-8 feet
Accepts transients—yes, if staying in cabins or motel
Floating wooden docks—yes
Laundry—yes
Boat ramp—yes
Restaurants—across the street
Pool—yes
Motel and cabins—yes

Dock at Suwannee Gables Motel and Marina

The *City of Hawkinsville,* an underwater archaeological preserve, is submerged about 100 yards south of the railroad bridge, in the RDB side of the river. This underwater dive site is also marked by two white buoys. HAZARD *The lowest overhead obstruction in the next 100 miles of Suwannee River is at mile 37.6.* This is the old Seaboard Coastline Railroad Bridge, now converted to the Nature Coast Greenway bridge and trail. We visited this trail a few times, and we never noted any pedestrians or bicycles on this paved hiking/biking trail. If you can make it beneath this bridge, you can go much farther up the river. When we went under, we estimated the overhead clearance to be at least 12 to 15 feet. Large houseboats from Miller Marina usu-ally can negotiate beneath this bridge.

The Suwannee River KOA has about a 40-foot floating dock with some questionable cleats on the RDB at mile 39.8. But their gas pump is some distance from this dock. You'd have to beach your boat to reach their gas-pump hoses. The KOA campground has a small variety store, a phone, and a Laundromat.

Suwannee River KOA (352) 542-7636

Approach depth—5 feet
Accepts transients—no
Floating wooden docks—yes
Laundromat—yes
Gasoline—yes

Boat ramp—yes

Variety store—yes

There are about a dozen boat ramps located on the next 25-mile section of the Suwannee River. We'll mention only those public ramps with docking facilities. The Purvis Landing ramp, on the RDB near mile 41.0, has about a 40-foot floating aluminum dock. A rather unkempt private boating facility with about 150 feet of dockage can be found on the LDB after mile 42. HAZARD *There is also a large sand bar in the middle of the river.* The only approach to this facility is from about 250 yards downriver (i.e., the south), hugging close to the LDB. The facility is called Hart Springs Subdivision II and basically doesn't wish to cater to any transient river traffic. After this facility and sand bar, the Suwannee shallows some and narrows considerably—to about 70 yards wide—and logs and stumps become more common in the river. Therefore, you need to notch up your navigational attentiveness. The nature of the Suwannee shoreline is also changing. The tall wild cypress trees are giving way to sycamore trees, more manicured residential development, and many small docks.

Hart Springs Subdivision II

Approach depth—5 feet, avoiding sand bar in middle of river

Accepts transients—no

Floating wooden docks—yes

Dockside power connections—15 amp

There is a small dock at Hart Springs Landing, near mile 43.3 on the LDB. But don't even try to get in here. I ran my relatively shallow-draft vessel aground trying to reach this dock. Guaranto Springs (colloquialized to Gornto Springs), at mile 55.0 on the RDB, is quite accessible. The park area has a boat ramp, a floating aluminum dock about 40 feet long, covered picnic pavilions, a swimmable spring, and trash receptacles. There are also rest-room facilities near the Guaranto Springs dock and ramp. We found about seven feet of water off the dock.

A relatively high bridge crosses the river near mile 56.5 at Rock Bluff Landing. At Rock Bluff Landing, on the LDB, there is a general store selling groceries, gas, and sandwiches. However, the store was inaccessible, even to our boat. The long narrow steep boat ramp on the LDB had no dock, nor was there any other place nearby to dock a vessel. The Santa Fe River flows into the Suwannee from the LDB at Suwannee mile 66.9. Heading upriver, this junction is almost like a *T* in the river. The Santa Fe goes to the right, and the continuation of the Suwannee goes to your left, toward the RDB side.

At about mile 71 on the RDB of the Suwannee River, you'll notice a new and wide concrete ramp but no dock. The Suwannee is about 80 yards wide, and the river is regaining some of the aesthetic appeal that was partially lost immediately north of Hart Springs. We found river depths toward Branford beginning to shallow slightly and become somewhat more erratic—ranging between five and 12 feet but with many deeper holes. The Suwannee River Cove Restaurant is at mile 73.5 on the LDB. This restaurant has about a 50-foot-long floating dock, but it was closed, and possibly out of business, both times that we visited. Nor were we able to contact them on the telephone. Captain Don's Bait and Tackle Shop is on the RDB, slightly upriver from Suwannee Cove Restaurant, at mile 74.

Suwannee River Cove Restaurant and Family Campground

Dockside depth—3-4 feet
Floating wooden docks—yes
Showers—in nearby campground
Restaurant—yes, but likely out of business
Campground and pool—yes

Mediterranean Mooring

It's a bit tricky landing a boat in Branford. Unlike in yesteryear, today there is no steamboat dock around Branford. Most think of a Mediterranean Mooring as a system to make a boat fast to a dock when dock space is limited (e.g., like in Keaton Beach), but we'll describe a hybrid system for landing a boat onto a beach. There is an acceptable beach on the LDB near the Branford boat ramp. Slightly downriver from the boat ramp, we slowly approached a clear spot on the beach (i.e., we aimed for a spot devoid of branches and small stones). And we headed toward the shore at about a 45-degree downstream angle. When our boat was between two and four boat lengths from the beach, we dropped our stern anchor. Make sure this stern anchor line is hitched to a cleat somewhere on the stern of your boat. After the stern anchor hits bottom, someone needs to either quickly pay out that stern line or already have plenty of slack built into the stern anchor rode. Gently run the bow of the boat onto that clear spot on the beach. After the bow has been beached, jump off the boat and run a long bow line or your anchor line to a secure attachment somewhere on the beach. You could tie a long bow

line to one of the larger trees or set your anchor and anchor line behind a large rock. Try to tie this bow- or anchor line slightly upriver from where the bow rests on the beach. In the meantime, I hope your stern anchor has set in several feet of water, because if that stern anchor didn't set, you should backup and redo this drill. Put some tension in your stern anchor line, and you'll soon know if that stern anchor has set properly. If it has set, apply more tension in that stern anchor line and pull the stern of your boat well back into the river and away from the shore. Only the tip of your bow should be making contact with the shore. Normally, the stern line would be tensioned so that the entire boat is perpendicular to the shoreline. But in this steady river current, I preferred the stern of the boat to be angled slightly downstream. If you've done this—even after your fourth try—congratulations! You've just done a Mediterranean Mooring—and in a river with a current, to boot!

Departing is easier. The last person aboard should detach the bow or anchor line from the shore attachment stump, rock, or ledge. The stern anchor is now the only thing holding the boat. From the stern, pull the boat backward toward that stern anchor and out in the river. When you're comfortable with the water depth beneath the propeller, you can assist with the engine. Now up-anchor your stern line and stern anchor just like you'd up-anchor any anchor line off the bow.

Branford, Florida

You are now Mediterranean Moored off Ivey Memorial Park. Besides a good boat ramp, the neat park has covered picnic pavilions, water spigots, trash receptacles, and a few 120-volt

Kent and Mediterranean Mooring in Branford

outlets. (We utilized these outlets to recharge our cell phone.) Branford Springs are also in the park, nearer the highway bridge. The knowledgeable personnel at the Dive Shack, (386) 935-0246, also in Ivey Memorial Park, can tell you all that you want to know about the many local spring-diving sites. They can also rent you diving equipment. In addition to spring diving, cave diving is also popular. Most of the cave-diving sites are north of Branford.

The heart of the town of Branford is about a fifth of a mile from Ivey Memorial Park. In town, within about a three-block radius, you'll find three gasoline stations, two great sit-down local restaurants, two fast-food restaurants, a grocery mart, a Laundromat, a post office, a hardware store, an auto-parts store, a barber shop, a motel, and an interesting bike/hiking trail called the Suwannee River Greenway. If you walk about five or six blocks farther north on the main road, you'll find Tony's pizza restaurant, a library, and the larger Scaff's grocery store. But you won't find a tavern or a liquor store in Branford. Suwannee County, Florida, is a dry county. There is also a significant Latin-American population in Branford. Most come from the

Welcome to Branford

Captain Rick in Branford

BRANFORD

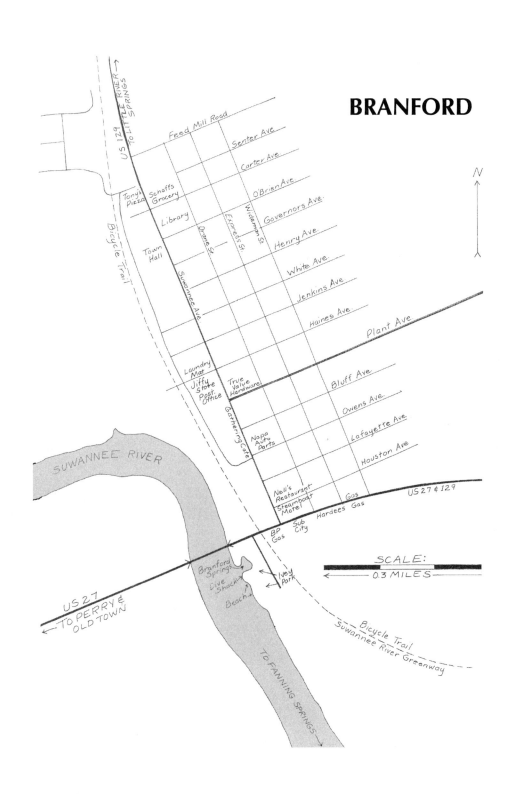

To Little River Springs →

US 129

To Little River Springs

Bicycle Trail

Feed Mill Road

Senter Ave.

Carter Ave.

O'Brien Ave.

Governors Ave.

Henry Ave.

White Ave.

Jenkins Ave.

Haines Ave.

Plant Ave.

Tony's Pizza

Schaffs Grocery

Library

Town Hall

Orane St.

Express St.

Wideman St.

Suwannee Ave.

Laundry Mat

Jiffy Store

Post Office

True Value Hardware

Gathering Cafe

Napa Auto Parts

Bluff Ave.

Owens Ave.

Lafayette Ave.

Houston Ave.

US 27 & 129

Nell's Restaurant

Steamboat Motel

Gas

Hardees Gas

BP Gas

Sub City

N

SUWANNEE RIVER

US 27

TO PERRY & OLD TOWN

Branford Springs

Dive Shack

Beach

Ivey Park

SCALE:

0.3 MILES

Bicycle Trail

Suwannee River Greenway

To Fanning Springs

same part of the state of Oaxaca in southern Mexico to work primarily at harvesting pine straw at the nearby longleaf pine plantations.

If the Suwannee River isn't real low, you may be able to travel another six miles up the river past Branford to Troy Springs. We generally observed water depths between five and 17 feet, with a few holes as deep as 30 feet. Our shallow-draft boat made it beyond Branford with no problems at a time of low water. HAZARD *Be cautioned, there are more and more rocks as you go farther and farther up this river.* Thankfully, we never encountered any, but we could have just missed them. Little River Springs is about four miles upriver from Branford on the LDB. This spring supposedly has four miles of caves for diving.

If you make it all the way to Troy Springs on the RDB, about two miles beyond Little River Springs, you can dive on the remains of the pre-Civil War steamship *Madison*.

Oh yeah, I almost forgot to mention that there was some famous song written about the Suwannee River—something about an "old folks home"? The song was written in 1851 near Pittsburgh, Pennsylvania, by Steven Collins Foster, a person who never even visited Florida. He was just looking for a "two-syllable" name of a river down South that fit his latest melody. Mississippi's Yazoo River and South Carolina's Pee Dee River lost out to Florida's Suwannee River. And, anyway, according to Webster's dictionary, isn't Su-wan-nee three syllables? And get this. In the

Little River Springs diving hole, Suwannee River

1930s, the Suwannee River song "Old Folks at Home" became the state song of Florida. Talk about a stroke of being politically correct without doing the field research. Foster was a prolific writer of beautiful songs and lead a short and tragic life.

The Santa Fe River

The Santa Fe River enters the Suwannee just before Suwannee River mile 67 on the LDB. The Santa Fe River is narrower than the Suwannee, at about 40 yards wide. The water depths on the Santa Fe between the Suwannee and Ichetucknee rivers (in a seven-mile stretch) range between eight and 12 feet, with 11 feet of water being common in most places. The river is too narrow for comfortable anchoring, but there are a few docks if you want to stop. Without a doubt, the prettiest, the largest, the most haunting and unusual, and the greatest number of cypress trees per mile, on any river in the entire Big Bend area, are along the banks of the Santa Fe River. We also observed a high-water line on the cypress trees that was about six feet higher than the present water level.

Cypress trees along the Santa Fe River

FEATURE	MILEAGE	SIDE	COMMENTS
Junction	0.0	LDB	Santa Fe River flows into Suwannee River
RV Resort	1.0	LDB	Ellie Ray's River Landing, RV Resort, and spring
Restaurant	2.0	RDB	Colleen's Restaurant has a few small docks
Bridge	2.3	center	U.S. Route 129 Bridge has about 20-25 feet of clearance
Boat Ramp	2.3	RDB	Beneath the bridge
Junction	7.0	RDB	The Ichetucknee River flows into the Santa Fe

There are also a few nice beaches in this area. Oftentimes, many big turtles can be seen sunning themselves on large branches protruding from the water. Ellie Ray's River Landing is one mile up the Santa Fe on the LDB. Ellie Ray's has about 200 feet of floating wooden dock and a small swimming area in another enchanting spring. Colleen's Restaurant is about a mile upstream from Ellie Ray's, on the opposite bank (RDB). Colleen's has a small floating dock and several beached pontoon boats. Colleen's has the nicer eating establishment, but the restaurant is only open Thursday through Sunday. Both Colleen's and Ellie Ray's have an RV park.

Ellie Ray's River Landing and RV Resort
(386) 935-9518

Approach depth—2-6 feet
Accepts transients—very limited
Floating wooden docks—yes
Showers—yes
Laundromat—yes
Boat ramp—yes
Camp store—yes
Tavern—serving defrosted pizzas

Colleen's Restaurant (386) 935-3824

Dockside depth—3-6 feet
Accepts transients—yes, if the boat can be beached

Floating steel dock—yes
Showers—yes
Gasoline—yes
Boat ramp—yes
Restaurant—on site, Thursday-Sunday
Motel and campground—yes

The U.S. Route 129 highway bridge crosses the Santa Fe upstream from Colleen's. When we went beneath it, we estimated that the overhead clearance was between 20 and 25 feet. The William Guy Lemmon Memorial Park public boat ramp sits beneath this bridge on the RDB. This park has ample boat trailer parking and a picnic pavilion. Besides those magnificent cypress trees, and a few white-sand beaches, there are many limestone rocky outcroppings along the Santa Fe shoreline. Some scattered residential development also tastefully dots the RDB of the Santa Fe River. The Ichetucknee River meets the Santa Fe at mile seven in ten feet of water. Beyond the mouth of the clear and sparkling Ichetucknee River, we could see small rapids and decided against exploring the Ichetucknee River. Past the junction with the Ichetucknee, the Santa Fe shallows somewhat to between five and ten feet. The Santa Fe River meanders upstream for about another 70 miles. Like the St. Marks River, the Santa Fe disappears into sinkholes and then reemerges on the other side of O'Leno State Park, about 20 miles upstream. Ginnie Springs Resort, (904) 454-2202, renown for its cave diving, is about 12 miles up the Santa Fe River, past the junction with the Ichetucknee. We'd likely agree with anything nice that has previously been stated about this enchanting Santa Fe River! And now we come to our journey's end on the major rivers of Florida's Big Bend.

Acknowledgments and Dedication

One person needs help from many to produce a book like this. It is intrusive visiting and cold calling on many marinas, then prying the tenders away from their paying customers to try to obtain a few good kernels of local knowledge. Naturally, some folks were more helpful than others. I'd like to recognize those marinas and boating interests that especially helped us out—at least those whom I can remember. In Columbus, Georgia, Wes Bain and my friends at Action Marine always helped whenever they could. Farther down on the Chattahoochee River, Ranger Keith Fleming at Florence Marina State Park, the ladies at the Historical Chattahoochee Commission in Eufaula, Alabama, and the staff at Lakepoint Marina were very helpful. On Lake Seminole, both Jack Wingate and Monte Anderson added some useful insights. All the lock tenders, especially those at Jim Woodruff Lock, answered whatever questions we had. I thank Derrick of Bristol, Florida, for pulling my car out of a ditch one night. Dr. John Davis of Dothan, Alabama, volunteered his insights and his heart. Both were appreciated. On the Suwannee River, Shirley Clark, at the Branford Public Library, and Miller Marina added some substantial information. In Apalachicola, the Apalachicola Chamber of Commerce and Scipio Creek Marina enhanced our knowledge. There were many friendly marina folks along the Gulf Coast who took time to go out of their way. These include Brian at Panacea Harbor Marina, the folks at Keaton Beach Marina and Horseshoe Beach Marina, Thomas Gaughan of the Steinhatchee River

Realty Company, Brett Shields in St. Marks, Pete Stair in Hernando Beach, Bob Morse in Hudson, Carl and Barbara Hanover on the Withlacoochee River, Capt. Bill Roberts in Cedar Key, the Cedar Key Historical Society Museum, the Chamber of Commerce in Crystal River, and PO Nicholas Ostrander at the U.S. Coast Guard Station in Yankeetown.

Aboard, I received help from Cecile Sangiamo and Kent Wiley. Cecile took some great notes and helped our team endure some rougher-than-expected seas between Apalachicola and Steinhatchee. Captain Kent was aboard providing insight and helping with the research on the Suwannee River. Lewis Lederer deserves special recognition. Twice Lewis made long trips, driving from Clearwater, Florida, to the Big Bend—first, to get us started, and later, to make a logistical resupply. Lewis also offered, and I accepted, his GPS unit and a comprehensive Florida street-map book. I also thank Claiborne Young for sharing his invaluable insights and providing some excellent advice on this, and my previous, guide.

After the research was completed, several folks helped me improve this book. Ray Beth Durham, Lewis Lederer, and my father helped me narrow the selection of candidate photographs. As usual, artist Pat Champagne came through and produced those outstanding street maps, as well as the river, lake, and canal sketches for your benefit. Several other folks reviewed and critiqued this book. The suggestions and comments of Janis and Ralph Fischer, Lewis Lederer, Kent Wiley, William Wilson,

Louis Kouvaris, Hank Ulrich, Barbara and Karl Edler, and my father are woven into and improved this guide. Over the years, Louis Kouvaris also put out several fires relating to long-distance distribution challenges associated with my Potomac River cruising guide. In his review, Hank Ulrich made some great organizational suggestions and caught many things that only a resourceful sailor could catch. Barbara and Karl Edler's review prompted me to better clarify several nuances. My father also read and considerably improved this book, as well as managed the day-to-day affairs of my nascent cruising-guide business while I was out in my boat "having fun."

The always-dependable Durham family distributed and filled Internet orders for my cruising guides and were fundamental in keeping my titles alive while I was in Ecuador with the Peace Corps. Mark Durham and I go back 30 years to our college days at West Virginia University. Mark grew up without a father on the tough streets of northeast Baltimore. He vowed that it would be different for his children. And it was. When Mark sets his heart on any job, he always gives it a 110 percent effort. After a distinguished and dedicated 22-year navy career as a submariner, Mark continues to excel as a supervisor for Rockwell. His wife, Ray Beth, is one of the dearest ladies I know. So this book is dedicated to Mark and Ray Beth Durham and their three children—Rachel, Eric, and Brittany.

List of U.S. Government Chart Books, Corps of Engineers Aerial Photograph Book, and Independent Charts and Maps

U.S. Government, NOAA Charts

Chart #	Coverage	Scale
11400:	"Tampa Bay to Cape San Blas"	1:456,394
11401:	"Apalachicola Bay to Cape San Blas"	1:80,000
11402:	"Intracoastal Waterway, Apalachicola Bay to Lake Wimico"	1:40,000
11404:	"Intracoastal Waterway—Carrabelle to Apalachicola"	1:40,000
11404:	"Inset—Carrabelle River"	1:20,000
11405:	"Apalachee Bay"	1:80,000
11406:	"St. Marks River Approaches"	1:15,000
11407:	"Horseshoe Point to Rock Islands"	1:80,000
11407:	"Inset—Horseshoe Beach"	1:20,000
11408:	"Crystal River to Horseshoe Point"	1:80,000
11408:	"Inset—Cedar Key"	1:40,000
11408:	"Inset—Suwannee River Entrance"	1:20,000
11409:	"Anclote Key to Crystal River"	1:80,000

U.S. Army Corps of Engineers Aerial Photograph Book: "Apalachicola, Chattahoochee and Flint Rivers," Mobile District, February 1994 (contains government information on locks and dams, bridge type, and bridge clearances)—with 25 black-and-white aerial photos of the Apalachicola River; 9 black-and-white aerial photos of the Flint River and Lake Seminole; 42 black-and-white aerial photos of the Chattahoochee River, Lake George, and Lake Seminole

Independent Chart/Map Publications: "Boating and Angling Guide to Apalachicola Bay," McShane Communications, Inc., the Florida Marine Institute, Apalachicola National Estuarine Research Reserve, and the Florida Department of Environmental Protection—best resource for depicting the channels leading to and in Ochlockonee Bay

"Coastal Charts for Cruising Guide to Western Florida," Pelican Publishing Company, Gretna, LA

"Lake Eufaula Walter George Lock, Dam—Recreation and Fishing Guide," Atlantic Mapping Company, Marietta, GA

"Lake Seminole—Recreation and Fishing Guide," Atlantic Mapping Company, Marietta, GA

"Lower Suwannee and Santa Fe Rivers—Boating, Canoeing and Recreation Guide," Fanning Springs Greater Chamber of Commerce, Trenton, FL

"Upper Suwannee and Withlacoochee Rivers—Boating, Canoeing and Recreation Guide," Suwannee Canoe Outpost, Live Oak, FL

"Suwannee River," Grif's Explorers Map

GPS Location Indices on the Gulf of Mexico

FEATURE	WAY POINTS NORTH LAT.	WEST LON.
Near sea buoys outside Government Cut, near Apalachicola	29.36.075N/	84.57.184W
Eastpoint Channel, in St. George Sound	29.44.090N/	84.52.262W
Dog Island Area:		
Off unlighted aid "C7," East Pass Channel, southwest of Dog Island	29.46.005N/	84.40.028W
Tyson Harbor Cove anchorage channel	29.49.352N/	84.35.495W
Alligator Harbor, off aid "R2"	29.55.270N/	84.27.141W
Ochlockonee Bay Channel:		
Off green channel daymark "OB"	29.56.091N/	84.17.987W
Off intermediate daymarks "G1and R2"	29.57.144N/	84.18.545W
Panacea Channel, outside Dickerson Bay, off aid "R2"	30.00.362N/	84.18.653W
Shell Point Area:		
Spring Creek Channel, off outside structure	30.02.341N/	84.17.623W
Shell Point Channel, off outside structure	30.02.825N/	84.17.070W
St. Marks River Channel	30.01.480N/	84.10.530W
Aucilla River Channel	30.04.070N/	84.00.254W
Econfina River, off quadrapod "T12," about 3 miles out	29.58.546N/	83.55.972W
Keaton Beach Channel, off aid "G1"	29.48.811N/	83.37.850W
Steinhatchee River Channel in Deadman Bay	29.39.353N/	83.27.452W
Horseshoe Beach Channel:		
Off navigation aid "R2"	29.23.260N/	83.20.426W
Off navigation aids "G11 and R10"	29.24.930N/	83.18.375W
Suwannee River Channels:		
McGriff Pass Channel	29.18.570N/	83.12.060W
Alligator Pass Channel	29.14.577N/	83.11.802W
Derrick Key Gap-Suwannee Sound Area:		
Outside, off aid "R2"	29.09.265N/	83.06.255W
Near aid "R10"	29.12.030N/	83.05.585W
East Pass, leaving Suwannee Sound	29.16.030N/	83.08.000W
Suwannee River:		
Jacks Sand Bar:		
South end	29.26.350N	off LDB
North end	29.26.800N/	off LDB
Little River Springs, 80 miles up the Suwannee River	29.59.752N/	82.58.025W

FEATURE	WAY POINTS	
	NORTH LAT.	WEST LON.
Cedar Key Area:		
Northwest Channel:		
Off aid "R2"	29.08.500N/	83.07.900W
Off aid "G3"	29.08.471N/	83.06.261W
Main Ship Channel, off aid "G1"	29.03.988N/	83.04.577W
South Bar Channel, off aid "R2"	29.07.210N/	82.58.826W
Waccasassa River Channel, off aid "R2"	29.06.438N/	82.51.235W
Withlacoochee River Channel, off aid "G1"	28.58.127N/	82.49.727W
North-south gap in Crystal River power plant		
Channel and near navigation aids "G39 and R40"	28.56.222N/	82.48.100W
Crystal River Channel, off aids "G1 and R2"	28.54.703N/	82.44.920W
Inside route between Crystal River Channel and		
Homosassa River Channel, off quadrapod	28.49.987N/	82.46.018W
Homosassa River Channel, off aid "R4"	28.43.588N/	82.45.925W
Chassahowitzka Bay Channel of aid "CW"	28.39.440N/	82.44.225W
Weeki Wachee River Channel, off Beacon Rocks		
and aids "G1" and "R2"	28.32.765N/	82.42.244W
Hernando Beach Area:		
Turn light, off aid "HB"	28.30.880N/	82.44.091W
Near Bill Watts Rack, off aids "G1 and R2"	28.31.088N/	82.42.359W
Aripeka Area:		
Turn light, off aid "AR"	28.27.401N/	82.44.634W
Beginning of channel, off aids "G1 and R2"	28.27.401N/	82.44.490W
Hudson Area:		
Sea Pines Channel	28.23.177N/	82.44.890W
Main Hudson Channel	28.21.798N/	82.45.023W
Leisure Beach Channel	28.20.890N/	82.43.800W
Pithlachascotee River Channel	28.17.129N/	82.46.297W
Gulf Harbors Area:		
North Channel, off aids "G1 and R2"	28.14.690N/	82.47.176W
South Channel, off aid "G1"	28.14.179N/	82.47.274W
Off Anclote Key:		
North end, off aid "R6"	28.12.611N/	82.49.219W
South end, off aids "G9 and R10"	28.09.601N/	82.50.033W

GPS and Other Location Indices on Lake Eufaula

Way points for Lake Eufaula (Chapter 16)

Feature	Way point	Mile	Side	More Specifics
Highland Park Rec. Area	31.37.88N/ 85.05.84W	76.0	AL	The way point is in 18 feet of water and is 60 yards from the dock.
Hardridge Creek Access	31.38.30N/ 85.05.84W	76.5	AL	The way point is in 6 to 7 feet of water.
Sandy Creek	31.39.80N/ 85.05.24W	78.0	GA	Two campgrounds and one marina are in this creek.
Sandy Branch	31.41.01N/ 85.05.73W	79.0	GA	The way point is in 12 to 14 feet of water and on a heading of 70 degrees into the creek.
Thomas Mill Creek	31.42.14N/ 85.07.77W	81.5	AL	The way point is in 32 to 38 feet of water.
Pataula Creek (near channel)	31.44.02N/ 85.07.06W	83.0	GA	The way point is off the red side of Chattahoochee River Channel on the lake.
Pataula Creek (near creek)	31.43.69N/ 85.05.50W	—	GA	The way point is in 20 feet of water and near the physical mouth of winding creek.
White Oak Creek	31.46.16N/ 85.08.04W	86.0	AL	Way point in 25 feet of water and one-third of a mile off the Main Chattahoochee River Channel
Cheneyhatchee Creek	31.49.57N/ 85.08.96W	89.5	AL	The way point is in 35- to 40-foot water depths.
Barbour Creek	31.50.40N/ 85.08.80W	90.5	AL	The way point is in 14-foot depths near the creek.
Water tower	31.51.20N/ 85.09.00W		AL	A great landmark from many places, especially to the south on Lake Eufaula
Cool Branch	31.50.60N/ 85.07.90W	91.5	GA	Leading to a protected cove with a ramp, dock, and picnic area
Chewalla Creek	31.53.60N/ 85.07.90W	95.0	AL	Marina, small yacht club, motel, campground and best access to Eufaula are from the creek.
River Bluff Park	31.53.67N/ 85.06.70W	96.0	GA	Way point is in very deep water off channel. Best access to Georgetown, GA from park
Old Creek	31.54.89N/ 85.06.81W	97.5	AL	The way point is 100 yards away from green side of the channel.
Cowikee Creek	31.57.61N/ 85.05.18W	101.7	AL	This channel heads toward Lakepoint Marina and Resort.
Head of Lake Eufaula	31.58.95N/ 85.04.19W	104.0	AL-GA	Where the floating buoys give way to standing daymarks
Rood Creek	32.01.36N/ 85.02.82W	107.2	GA	Leads to a charming creek with ramp and park

List of NOAA and USGS Chart Extracts and Other Sketches

Illustration:	Chapter:	Form:
"Florida's Big Bend and Inland Rivers"	Introduction	Map Drawing
"Eight-Day Sample Itinerary"	Introduction	Table
"Tarpon Springs to Suwannee River"	3	NOAA Extract
"Suwannee River to St. Marks Light"	3	NOAA Extract
"St. Marks Light to Apalachicola Bay"	3	NOAA Extract
"Example of Hypothetical Tides on Big Bend"	3	Graph
"Wind Roses on the Northeastern Gulf of Mexico"	3	Sketch
"Sine Curve—Magnetic Deviation for MV Free State"	3	Graph
"Apalachicola"	5	Town Map Sketch
"Apalachicola Bay"	5	NOAA Extract
"St. George Sound"	5	NOAA Extract
"Carrabelle"	6	Town Map Sketch
"Carrabelle Area"	6	NOAA Extract
"Ochlockonee Bay and Alligator Harbor"	7	NOAA Extract
"Western Apalachee Bay"	7	NOAA Extract
"Northwestern Apalachee Bay"	7	NOAA Extract
"Channels near Shell Point"	7	Bay Sketch
"St. Marks Channel"	8	NOAA Extract
"Lower St. Marks River"	8	NOAA Extract
"Upper St. Marks River"	8	NOAA Extract
"St. Marks"	8	Town Map Sketch
"Northeastern Apalachee Bay"	8	NOAA Extract
"Fenholloway River Area"	8	NOAA Extract
"Keaton Beach Area"	9	NOAA Extract
"Steinhatchee"	9	Town Map Sketch
"Steinhatchee and Deadman Bay"	9	NOAA Extract
"Horseshoe Beach Area"	9	NOAA Extract

Bibliography

Brown, Fred; Sherri M. L. Smith; Vicki L. Rice. *The Riverkeeper's Guide to the Chattahoochee River.* Atlanta: CI Publishing, 1994.

Burnett, Gene M. *Florida's Past Volume 1: People and Events That Shaped the State.* Sarasota, FL: Pineapple Press, 1986.

Burnett, Gene M. *Florida's Past Volume 2: People and Events That Shaped the State.* Sarasota, FL: Pineapple Press, 1988

Cabbage, Henry. *Tales of Historic Tallahassee.* Tallahassee, FL: Artemis Associates, 1999.

Carter, W. Horace. *Florida Nature Coast Tales and Truths.* Tabor City, NC: Atlantic Publishing Company, 1993.

Coker, William S., and Jerrell H. Shofner. *Florida: From the Beginning to 1992: A Columbus Jubilee Commemorative.* Houston, TX: Pioneer Publications, 1991.

Cox, Merlin G., and J. E. Dovell. *Florida: From Secession to Space Age.* St. Petersburg, FL: Great Outdoors Publishing Company, 1974.

Garrison, Webb. *A Treasury of Florida Tales.* Nashville, TN: Rutledge Hill Press, 1989.

Jahoda, Gloria. *Florida: A History.* New York: W.W. Norton and Company, 1976.

Kirby, Jan. *The Florida Gulf Coast.* Santa Fe, NM: John Muir Publications, 1997.

Lenfestey, Tom. *A Gunkholer's Cruising Guide to Florida's West Coast.* St. Petersburg, FL: Great Outdoors Publishing Company, 2000.

Lovel, Leo. *Spring Creek Chronicles.* Tallahassee, FL: Leo V. Lovel, 2001.

Maloney, Elberrt S. *Chapman Piloting, Seamanship and Boat Handling.* 63rd ed. New York: Hearst Marine Books, 1999.

Marth, Del, and Marty Marth. *The Rivers of Florida.* Sarasota, FL: Pineapple Press, 1990.

McReynolds, Edwin C. *The Seminoles.* Norman, OK: University of Oklahoma Press, 1957.

Milanich, Jerald T. *Florida's Indians from Ancient Times to the Present.* Gainesville, FL: University of Florida Press, 1998.

Milanich, Jerald T., and Charles Hudson. *Hernando de Soto and the Indians of Florida.* Gainesville, FL: University Press of Florida, 1993.

Schueler, Donald G. *Adventuring along the Gulf of Mexico.* San Francisco, CA: Sierra Club Books, 1986.

Spencer, H. Nelson. *Quimby's 2002 Cruising Guide.* St. Louis, MO: Waterway Journal, 2002.

U.S. Department of Commerce, National Oceanic and Atmospheric Administration. *U.S. Coast Pilot,* vol. 5, *Gulf of Mexico,* 29th ed. Washington, D.C.: National Ocean Service, 2002.

Young, Claiborne S. *Cruising Guide to the Northern Gulf Coast: Florida, Alabama, Mississippi, Louisiana.* 3rd ed. Gretna, LA: Pelican Publishing Company, 1998.

Young, Claiborne S. *Cruising Guide to Western Florida.* 5th ed. Gretna, LA: Pelican Publishing Company, 2000.

Index

A

Action Marine, 307, 309
Adams, John Quincy, 19
aids to navigation, 53
airboats, 141, 166, 194
Alabama State Docks, 280, 307
Alligator Harbor, 85
Alligator Pass Channel, 141
alligators, 23
American Marina, 220
anchoring, 32, 59, 237, 259, 279, 287
Anclote Key, 197, 228
Andrews, George W., 279
angel of mercy, 228
Angler's Resort Marina and RV Park, 149
Apalachee, 17
Apalachee Bay, 15, 98, 103
Apalachee Bay Yacht Club, 100
Apalachee Indians, 15
Apalachicola, 61, 231
Apalachicola Bay, 23, 65
Apalachicola-Chattahoochee-Flint River System, 53,
    231, 236
Apalachicola Municipal Marina, 65
Apalachicola National Estuarine Research Reserve, 63, 231
Apalachicola National Forest, 89, 93
Apalachicola National Wildlife Forest, 29
Apalachicola River, 17, 23, 67, 231, 233-34, 237, 239, 248
Apalachicola River Delta, 245
Apalachicola River Inn, 67
aquarium, 85, 231
archaeological sites, 179
Aripeka, 197, 209
Army Corps of Engineer, 203, 235-36, 247, 250, 264, 275
Army Infantry School, 309
Atlanta, 234, 264, 275, 303, 315
Atlanta Rhythm Section, 275
Atsena Otie Key, 155, 159
Aucilla River, 17

B

Bainbridge, Georgia, 17, 269, 273

bald eagles, 23, 231
Barbour Creek, 293
barge windows, 233, 284
bass fishing, 255, 284
Battery Park Marina, 65
Battle of Natural Bridge, 112
Bay City Lodge, 239
Bayport, 198
Beacon Rock, 198
bicycle trail, 113
Big Oaks Campground, 177
Bill's Fish Camp and Motel, 149
Bill Watts Rack, 204
Billy Bowlegs, 21
Bird Island, 83
black bears, 23
blockade-running, 150, 153, 198
Blountstown, 250
Bluff Creek, 305
Boathouse Restaurant and Lounge, 135
boating catastrophes, 60
Boat/U.S, 79
Boat/U.S. towboat, 186, 208
Bob Sikes Pass, 63
Branford, 319, 331
Branford Springs, 331
Breakaway Marina and Motel, 239
BRENC, 56, 235, 236
brick-making, 309
bridge clearances, 56
Bridge Marina, 81
Bristol, 251
British, 19, 153
Brothers River, 245
B's Marina and Campground, 175
Bulkhead Shoal, 72
Bum's Marina, 149
Butler-Douglas Memorial Park, 139
Buzzard Islan, 184

C

Calusa, 15
Calusa Indians, 15
camino, 273
Camp Gordon Johnston, 83

CRUISING GUIDES AND COASTAL CHARTS
From Pelican

Pelican's comprehensive cruising guides present firsthand up-to-date information about marinas, restaurants, fueling stations, and depth soundings. Each area's shoreside attractions, history, and folklore are also included. The coastal charts are cross-referenced to the cruise guides and feature large-format color maps based on the National Oceanic and Atmospheric Administration charts. Both are indispensable tools for all cruising boaters.

CRUISING GUIDE TO EASTERN FLORIDA
 Fourth Edition
By Claiborne S. Young
544 pp. 8 x 9¼ 127 b/w photos 71 maps Index
ISBN: 1-56554-736-5 pb

Claiborne Young's guides have become the gold standard of cruising guides. The author and his navigator wife, Karen, are avid, experienced boaters who have logged countless hours onboard and ashore to ensure the accuracy of their descriptions and recommendations.

CRUISING GUIDE TO WESTERN FLORIDA
 Fifth Edition
By Claiborne S. Young
512 pp. 8 x 9¼
74 b/w photos 56 maps Biblio. Index
ISBN: 1-56554-737-3 pb

COASTAL CHARTS FOR CRUISING GUIDE
 TO WESTERN FLORIDA
By Claiborne S. Young
96 pp. 12 x 17 14 color charts
ISBN: 1-56554-154-5 sp

CRUISING GUIDE TO THE NORTHERN
 GULF COAST: Florida, Alabama, Mississippi,

 Louisiana, Fourth Edition
By Claiborne S. Young
"A fine, new guidebook, a bona fide keeper."
—Sailing
464 pp. 8 x 9¼ B/w photos Maps Index
ISBN: 1-58980-093-1 pb

COASTAL CHARTS FOR CRUISING GUIDE
 TO THE NORTHERN GULF COAST
By Claiborne S. Young
112 pp. 12 x 17 14 color charts
ISBN: 1-58980-085-0 sp

COASTAL CHARTS FOR CRUISING GUIDE
   TO COASTAL NORTH CAROLINA
By Claiborne S. Young
104 pp. 12 x 17 14 color charts
ISBN: 1-56554-738-1 sp

CRUISING THE FLORIDA KEYS
By Claiborne S. Young and Morgan Stinemetz
576 pp. 8 x 9¼
169 b/w photos 76 maps Index
ISBN: 1-56554-026-3 pb

COASTAL CHARTS FOR CRUISING THE
   FLORIDA KEYS
By Claiborne S. Young
64 pp. 12 x 17 12 color charts
ISBN: 1-58980-029-X sp

CRUISING GUIDE TO NEW YORK WATER
   WAYS AND LAKE CHAMPLAIN
By Chris W. Brown III
Edited by Claiborne S. Young
480 pp. 8 x 9¼
B/W photos Maps Appendixes Biblio. Index
ISBN: 1-56554-250-9 pb

CRUISING GUIDE FROM LAKE MICHIGAN
   TO KENTUCKY LAKE: The Heartland
   Rivers Route
By Captain Rick Rhodes
208 pp. 8 x 9¼ 70 b/w photos 26 maps
Index Appendixes Biblio.
ISBN: 1-56554-995-3 pb

CRUISING GUIDE TO FLORIDA'S BIG
   BEND
By Captain Rick Rhodes
304 pp. 8 x 9¼ 45 b/w photos 13 illus.
37 maps Appendixes Biblio. Index
ISBN: 1-58980-072-9 pb

POWER CRUISING
   The Complete Guide to Selecting,
   Outfitting, and Maintaining Your Power
   Boat, Second Edition
By Claiborne S. Young
240 pp. 6 x 9 Illus. b/w photos Glossary
Index
ISBN: 1-56554-635-0 pb

Future Publications:

COASTAL CHARTS FOR CRUISING GUIDE
   TO EASTERN FLORIDA
By Claiborne S. Young

COASTAL CHARTS FOR CRUISING GUIDE
   TO COASTAL SOUTH CAROLINA AND
   GEORGIA
By Claiborne S. Young

Available at better bookstores,
1-800-843-1724, or www.pelicanpub.com